STUDY GUIDE
VOLUME 1: CHAPTERS 1–14

INTERMEDIATE ACCOUNTING
IFRS Edition

Barbara J. Muller, C.P.A, C.F.E.
Senior Lecturer, School of Accountancy
W.P. Carey School of Business
Arizona State University

Douglas W. Kieso, Ph.D., C.P.A.
Aurora University
Aurora, Illinois

Donald E. Kieso, Ph.D., C.P.A.
KPMG Peat Marwick Emeritus Professor of Accounting
Northern Illinois University
DeKalb, Illinois

Jerry J. Weygandt, Ph.D., C.P.A.
Arthur Andersen Alumni Professor of Accounting
University of Wisconsin
Madison, Wisconsin

Terry D. Warfield, Ph.D.
Associate Professor
Director, Anderson Center for Financial Reporting and Control
University of Wisconsin
Madison, Wisconsin

WILEY
JOHN WILEY & SONS, INC.

COVER PHOTO: Stone/Getty Images, Inc.

ISBN-13   978-0-470-61330-6

Printed in the United States of America

10 9 8 7 6 5 4 3 2 1

Printed and bound by Bind-Rite/Robbinsville

Contents

NOTE TO STUDENTS

This Study Guide is provided as an aid to your study of *Intermediate Accounting: IFRS Edition, Volume I* by Donald E. Kieso and Jerry J. Weygandt, and Terry Warfield. If used wisely, it can supplement and reinforce your understanding of the concepts and techniques presented in the textbook. **Never rely on the Study Guide as a substitute for a thorough reading of the textbook material.** This Study Guide merely highlights the in-depth presentation in the textbook.

An approach that combines use of the Study Guide and textbook material is suggested below.

1. Read the textbook presentation of the chapter.

2. Read the chapter review paragraphs in the Study Guide.

3. Answer the questions and review exercises appearing at the end of the chapter review paragraphs and compare your answers with those found at the end of each chapter. The extent of your success in answering these questions and exercises will indicate your understanding of the chapter. If you were unsuccessful in answering a large percentage of these questions correctly, you should read the textbook again.

4. Work the problems assigned from the textbook.

Solutions to the Study Guide review questions and exercises are found at the end of each chapter. In addition to identifying the correct answer to each true-false and multiple choice question, an explanation is provided indicating why the answer is false and why a particular alternative (for multiple choice questions) is correct. This approach is designed to aid you in gaining a complete understanding of the material in each chapter.

When preparing for examinations, the Study Guide material may be used to determine your recall of the information presented in specific chapters. Once you have identified those subject areas in need of further review, return to the textbook material for a complete discussion of the subject matter involved. Remember, the Study Guide merely highlights the textbook material; it cannot be relied upon as a comprehensive treatment of a subject area.

In the study of accounting, there is no substitute for hard work and a desire to learn. A proper attitude and a willingness to work will go a long way toward ensuring your success in intermediate accounting.

ACKNOWLEDGEMENTS

The authors wish to acknowledge James Emig, Villanova University; Maureen Mascha, Marquette University; LuAnn Bean, Florida Institute of Technology; and Rex Schildhouse, San Diego Community College District – Miramar for his assistance in reviewing and accuracy checking this manuscript.

Barbara Muller
Douglas W. Kieso

1

Financial Reporting and Accounting Standards

CHAPTER LEARNING OBJECTIVES

1. Identify the major financial statements and other means of financial reporting.
2. Explain how accounting assists in the efficient use of scarce resources.
3. Explain the need for high-quality standards.
4. Identify the objective of financial reporting.
5. Identify the major policy-setting bodies and their role in the standards-setting process.
6. Explain the meaning of IFRS.
7. Describe the challenges facing financial reporting.

CHAPTER REVIEW

1. Chapter 1 describes the environment that has influenced the widespread adoption of International Financial Reporting Standards (IFRS). There are many challenges facing the process of developing IFRS such as a sound conceptual framework, fair value measurements, and off-balance-sheet financing. The many benefits derived from sound financial reporting are also discussed. Finally, the groups that play a part in the standard-setting process are introduced and discussed.

Nature of Financial Accounting

2. (L.O. 1) **Financial accounting** is the process that culminates in the preparation of financial reports on the enterprise for use by both internal and external parties.

3. **Financial statements** are the principal means through which a company communicates its financial information to those outside it. The financial statements most frequently provided are (1) the statement of financial position, (2) the income statement or statement of comprehensive income, (3) the statement of cash flows, and (4) the statement of changes in equity. Note discloses are an integral part of each financial statement. Other means of communicating information that might not be included in the financial statements include the president's letter or supplementary schedules in the corporate annual report, prospectuses, and reports filed with government agencies.

4. (L.O. 2) Accounting is important for markets, free enterprise, and competition because it assists in providing information that leads to efficient capital allocation. Higher-quality information promotes an effective process of capital allocation which ultimately leads to a healthier economy.

5.   (L.O. 3) In order to ensure efficient capital allocation across borders, investors need a relevant and faithful representation of information. A single, widely-accepted set of accounting standards enables users to assess potential investments anywhere in the world. Some elements of a single set of high-quality standards includes:

      a.   Consistency in application and interpretation.
      b.   Common disclosures.
      c.   Common high-quality auditing standards.
      d.   Education and training of market participants.
      e.   Common delivery systems (XBRL).

6.   (L.O. 4) The objective of financial reporting is to provide financial information that is useful to present and potential investors and creditors and other users in making rational investment, credit, and similar decisions. Investors, as the providers of capital for organizations, are the primary users of financial statements. An entity perspective is used in general-purpose financial reporting which means companies are viewed as being distinct from their owners. Finally, financial reporting needs to provide investors information that is useful in assessing the amount, timing and uncertainty of the entity's cash flows, this is best done by using accrual accounting techniques.

Standard-Setting Organizations

7.   (L.O. 5) There are currently two major standard-setting organizations in the world, the International Accounting Standards Board (IASB) and the Financial Accounting Standards Board (FASB). The IASB issues International Financial Reporting Standards (IFRS) used by over 115 countries throughout the world. The FASB issues accounting standards used by companies based in the United States. The International Organization of Securities Commissions (IOSCO) does not set accounting standards, but is dedicated to ensuring that the global markets operate efficiently and effectively.

8.   Under the IASB umbrella there are four separate organizations, each charged with a specific aspect of international standard setting:

      a.   The International Accounting Standards Committee Foundation, which selects members of the IASB, and funds and oversees its activities.
      b.   The International Accounting Standards Board (IASB) is the major operating unit of standard setting, charged with developing high-quality IFRS.
      c.   The Standards Advisory Council consults with the IASB on major policy and technical issues.
      d.   The International Financial Reporting Interpretations Committee (IFRIC) develops implementation guidance for the IASB.

9.   The IASB has a due process for establishing financial accounting standards including an independent standard-setting board, a thorough, systematic process for developing standards, communication with financial statement users throughout the process, and collaboration with standard setters throughout the world.

10. The IASB issues 3 major types of pronouncements:

   a. International Financial Reporting Standards (IFRS), financial reporting standards covering a wide variety of subjects.

   b. Framework for financial reporting, sets forth the fundamental objectives and concepts used by the IASB in standard setting.

   c. International Financial Reporting Interpretations (IFRIC), cover newly identified issues or issues where there is unsatisfactory or conflicting guidance; considered authoritative.

11. (S.O. 6) The IASB does not have enforcement authority, therefore it relies on other regulators to enforce the use of its standards.

   a. The hierarchy used to determine what recognition, valuation and disclosure requirements should be used is as follows:
      1. International Financial Reporting Standards.
      2. International Accounting Standards (established by IASB predecessor).
      3. Interpretations of the IFRIC (or their predecessor).

   b. If there is no standard or interpretation, these sources are used in the following order:
      1. The requirements and guidance in standards and interpretations dealing with similar or related issues.
      2. The framework for financial reporting.
      3. Most recent pronouncements of other similar standard-setting bodies.

12. (S.O. 7) Challenges facing financial reporting include:

   a. IFRS are established in a political environment where the parties most affected by IFRS attempt to influence the standard setting process.

   b. The expectations gap between what accountants do and what others think they do.

   c. Some significant financial reporting needs remain unresolved including
      1. Nonfinancial measures in financial reports.
      2. Forward-looking information.
      3. How to report soft assets (know-how or brand image).
      4. Timeliness of financial reporting.

   d. Ethical dilemmas continue to present challenges. Some of these ethical dilemmas can be easily resolved while others require difficult choices. Often, doing the right thing isn't immediately obvious because pressure is applied to "be a team player" or "bend the rules just this once." Our text will bring up some common ethical situations you may encounter in your career; this allows you the opportunity to consider the challenges and form ideas in a low-pressure environment.

   e. International convergence to one high-quality set of standards requires cooperation among different standard setting bodies and changes to regulations for various world securities exchanges.

Appendix: The U.S. Standard-Setting Environment

13.   (L.O. 8)The SEC is a federal agency and administers the Securities Exchange Acts of 1933 and 1934, the Sarbanes-Oxley Act of 2002, and several other acts. Most companies that issue securities to the public or are listed on a stock exchange are required to file audited financial statements with the SEC. In addition, the SEC has broad powers to prescribe the accounting practices and standards to be employed by companies that fall within its jurisdiction.

      a.   The SEC has encouraged a public/private partnership for accounting standard setting and has affirmed its support for the FASB by indicating that financial statements conforming to standards set by the FASB will be presumed to have substantial authoritative support.

      b.   The SEC provides oversight of standard setting and generally relies on the Financial Accounting Standards Board (FASB) to develop accounting standards.

      c.   The SEC enforces accounting standards; for example if the SEC believes that an accounting or disclosure irregularity exists regarding a company's financial statements, the SEC sends a deficiency letter to the company. If the company's response to the deficiency letter proves unsatisfactory, the SEC has the power to issue a "stop order," which prevents the registrant from issuing securities or trading securities on the exchanges. Criminal charges may also be brought by the Department of Justice.

The FASB

14.   The mission of the FASB is to establish and improve standards of financial accounting and reporting for the guidance and education of the public, which includes issuers, auditors, and users of financial information. The FASB differs from its predecessor Accounting Principles Board (APB) in the following ways:

      a.   Smaller membership (5 versus 18 on the APB).

      b.   Full-time remunerated membership (APB members were unpaid and part-time).

      c.   Greater autonomy (APB was a senior committee of the AICPA).

      d.   Increased independence (FASB members must sever all ties with firms, companies, or institutions).

      e.   Broader representation (it is not necessary to be a CPA to be a member of the FASB).

Two basic premises of the FASB are that in establishing financial accounting standards: (a) it should be responsive to the needs and viewpoints of the entire economic community, not just the public accounting profession, and (b) it should operate in full view of the public through a "due process" system that gives interested persons ample opportunity to make their views known.

15.   The FASB issues three major types of pronouncements:

      a.   Standards, Interpretations, and Staff Positions, are considered GAAP and must be followed, Interpretations modify or extend an existing standard, and Staff Positions provide interpretive guidance.

      b.   Financial Accounting Concepts represent an attempt to move away from the problem-by-problem approach to standard setting that has been characteristic of the accounting profession. The Concept Statements are intended to form a cohesive set of interrelated concepts, a conceptual framework, that will serve as tools for solving existing and emerging problems in a consistent manner. Unlike FASB statements, the Concept Statements do not establish GAAP.

      c.   Emerging Issues Task Force Statements address how to account for new and unusual financial transactions that have the potential for creating differing financial reporting practices.

16.   U.S. GAAP is comprised of over 2,000 documents that have been developed over the past 60 years. Recently the FASB developed the Accounting Standards Codification. The Codification provides in one place, all the authoritative literature related to a particular topic. Accounting Standards Updates are made periodically whenever the FASB develops a new standard or staff position. For ease of accessibility, the Codification Research System provides online, real time access to a database of the Codification.

17.   The SEC appears committed to move to IFRS in order to achieve international accounting convergence. The conditions for the adoption of IFRS are described in a document referred to as the "Roadmap." Currently, foreign companies issuing securities in U.S. markets may use IFRS. The FASB and the IASB are working together to develop one set of world-class international standards. In 2011 the SEC will decide whether to mandate use of IFRS.

18.   The SEC has developed a "Work Plan" designed to provide:

a.   Sufficient development and application of IFRS by developing an infrastructure to ensure that IFRS are consistently interpreted and applied.

b.   Independent standard-setting for the benefit of investors by directing SEC staff will work to ensure that the IASB is independent and that the IFRS Foundation is stable and independent.

c.   Investor understanding and education by identifying the need for investor education.

d.   Assistance with the transitional requirements of the regulatory environment. The SEC must determine whether to appoint the IASB as the designated standard setter, or to retain the FASB and have the FASB incorporate all IFRS.

e.   Consideration of the impact of IFRS on large and small financial statement preparers. SEC staff will consider the cost and effort required to implement IFRS.

f.   Consideration of the readiness of most accountants in the U.S. to move to IFRS. SEC staff will examine the readiness of all parties involved in the financial reporting process, such as education, training, and auditor capacity.

GLOSSARY

American Institute of Certified Public Accountants (AICPA).	The national professional organization of practicing Certified Public Accountants in the U.S.
The Codification.	Created by the FASB and provides in one place all the authoritative literature to a particular topic of GAAP.
Emerging Issues Task Force (EITF).	Created by the FASB with the purpose of having members reach a consensus on how to account for new and unusual financial transactions that have the potential for creating differing financial reporting practices.
Financial Accounting Concepts.	A series of pronouncements issued by the FASB with the purpose of setting forth fundamental objectives and concepts that the FASB will use in developing future standards of financial accounting and reporting.
Financial Accounting Interpretations.	Pronouncements issued by the FASB which represent modifications or extensions of existing standards.
Financial Accounting Standards.	Pronouncements issued by the FASB which are considered generally accepted accounting principles.
Financial Accounting Standards Board (FASB).	A seven member board created in 1973 which currently establishes and improves standards of financial accounting and reporting for the guidance and education of the public.
Framework for Financial Reporting (Framework).	Sets forth fundamental objectives and concepts used in development of standards of financial reporting. Issued by the predecessor to the IASB.
Generally accepted accounting principles (GAAP).	A common set of standards and procedures adopted by the accounting profession.

International Accounting Standards Board (IASB).	Based in London, it produces International Financial Reporting Standards (IFRS).
International Accounting Standards Committee Foundation (IASCF).	Trustees of IASCF select members of the IASB and the Standards Advisory Council and oversee and fund their activities.
International Financial Reporting Standards (IFRS).	Financial accounting standards issued by the IASB; there are nine to date covering a variety of issues.
International Financial Reporting Interpretations (IFRIC).	Authoritative interpretations of IFRS; may also cover new issues or issues where current guidance is unsatisfactory or lacking.
International Organization Of Securities Commissions (IOSCO).	An organization dedicated to ensuring that the global markets operate effectively and efficiently.
Securities and Exchange Commission (SEC).	An agency of the federal government that administers the Securities Exchange Act of 1934.
Standards Advisory Council (SAC).	Consults with the IASB on major policy and technical issues.

CHAPTER OUTLINE

Fill in the outline presented below.

(L.O. 1) Financial Statements and Financial Reporting

(L.O. 2) Accounting and Capital Allocation

(L.O. 3) The Need for High-Quality Standards

(L.O. 4) Objective of Financial Reporting

(L.O. 5) Major Parties Involved and Their Role in Standard Setting

(L.O. 6) Meaning of IFRS

(L.O. 7) Challenges Facing Financial Reporting

(L.O. 8) The U.S. Standard Setting Environment

REVIEW QUESTIONS

TRUE-FALSE

Indicate whether each of the following is true (T) or false (F) in the space provided.

_____ 1. (L.O. 1) The essential characteristics of accounting include identification and measurement.

_____ 2. (L.O. 1) Financial accounting is the process that culminates in the preparation of financial reports on an enterprise and that are used by both internal and external parties.

_____ 3. (L.O. 2) An effective process of capital allocation is **not** important to a healthy economy.

_____ 4. (L.O. 4) General-purpose financial reporting adopts a proprietary perspective.

_____ 5. (L.O. 4) The objective of financial reporting is to provide information that is useful to present and potential equity investors, lenders, and other creditors in making decisions as capital providers.

_____ 6. (L.O. 5) International Financial Reporting Standards are considered rules-based and tax-oriented.

_____ 7. (L.O. 5) The International Organization of Securities Commissions (IOSCO) sets accounting standards for its members.

_____ 8. (L.O. 5) The International Accounting Standards Committee Foundation (IASCF) sets accounting standards for companies throughout the world.

_____ 9. (L.O. 5) The IASB's due process includes discussion papers and exposure drafts to ensure that public response is part of the standard-setting process.

_____ 10. (L.O. 5) The IASB's "Framework for the Preparation and Presentation of Financial Statements" is considered authoritative and its guidance overrides specific international accounting standards.

_____ 11. (L.O. 5) Interpretations issued by the International Financial Reporting Interpretations Committee (IFRIC) are considered authoritative and must be followed.

_____ 12. (L.O. 5) The International Accounting Standards Board (IASB) consists of 6 volunteer members who represent their company and country in the financial reporting standard setting process.

_____ 13. (L.O. 6) The overriding requirement of IFRS is that financial statements provide a true and fair view of the company.

_____ 14. (L.O. 5) The Standards Advisory Council (SAC) is responsible for ensuring that global markets can operate efficiently and effectively.

_____ 15. (L.O. 7) The expectations gap, the difference between what the public thinks accountants do and what accountants think they do, will be closed once IFRS is adopted worldwide.

_____ 16. (L.O. 7) IFRS requires companies to include nonfinancial measures, such as customer satisfaction indexes, and forward-looking financial information as part of their annual financial reports.

_____ 17. (L.O. 8) The "Roadmap" is a document that spells out the conditions required for the SEC to adopt IFRS.

_____ 18. (L.O. 8) Generally accepted accounting principles (GAAP) are defined, in part, as those principles that have substantial authoritative support.

_____ 19. (L.O. 8) The Codification provides in one place all the authoritative literature related to a particular topic of GAAP.

_____ 20. (L.O. 8) Financial accounting standards, interpretations and staff positions issued by the FASB are all considered generally accepted accounting principles.

SOLUTIONS TO REVIEW QUESTIONS

TRUE-FALSE

1. (T)

2. (T)

3. (F)   An effective process of capital allocation is critical to a healthy economy.

4. (F)   Under the proprietary perspective, financial reporting is focused only on the needs of shareholders, which is not considered appropriate. Currently financial reporting has an entity perspective in which companies are viewed as separate and distinct from their owners (shareholders).

5. (T)

6. (F)   Standards developed by the IASB (IFRS) are considered more conceptual and more principles-based.

7. (F)   The International Organization of Securities Commissions (IOSCO) does not set accounting standards. Instead, this organization is dedicated to ensuring that the global markets can operate in an efficient and effective basis.

8. (F)   The International Accounting Standards Committee Foundation (IASCF) selects the members of the IASB, funds their activities, and generally oversees the IASB's activities.

9. (T)

10. (F)   The IASB's "Framework for the Preparation and Presentation of Financial Statements" is a set of fundamental objectives and concepts used in developing future standards of financial reporting; nothing in the Framework overrides specific international accounting standards.

11. (T)

12. (F)   The IASB consists of 14 members (2 part-time) who are well-paid and who are not selected to represent a company or country. IASB members must sever all ties to the former employers.

13. (T)

14. (F)   The SAC consults with the IASB on major policy and technical issues and also helps select task force members.

15. (F)   The expectations gap is difficult to close and the profession must continue to strive to meet the needs of society. However, accountants cannot be responsible for every financial catastrophe.

16. (F)   Significant financial issues that still need to be addressed include how to include non-financial measures, forward-looking information, and the value of soft assets in more timely financial reporting.

17. (T)

18. (T)

19. (T)

20. (T)

2

Conceptual Framework
for Financial Reporting

CHAPTER LEARNING OBJECTIVES

1. Describe the usefulness of a conceptual framework.

2. Describe efforts to construct a conceptual framework.

3. Understand the objective of financial reporting.

4. Identify the qualitative characteristics of accounting information.

5. Define the basic elements of financial statements.

6. Describe the basic assumptions of accounting.

7. Explain the application of the basic principles of accounting.

8. Describe the impact that constraints have on reporting accounting information.

CHAPTER REVIEW

1. Chapter 2 outlines the development of a conceptual framework for financial reporting. The conceptual framework is composed of a basic objective, fundamental concepts, and recognition, measurement, and disclosure concepts. Each of these topics is discussed in Chapter 2 and should enhance your understanding of the topics covered in intermediate accounting.

Conceptual Framework

2. (L.O. 1) A **conceptual framework** in accounting is important because rule-making should be built on and relate to an established body of concepts. The benefits of a soundly developed conceptual framework are as follows: (a) it should be easier to promulgate a coherent set of standards and rules; and (b) practical problems should be more quickly solved.

3. (L.O. 2) The IASB's conceptual framework is described in a single documents ("Framework for Preparation and Presentation of Financial Statements") while the FASB's conceptual framework is developed in a series of concept statements (collectively the Conceptual Framework). Further, the IASB and the FASB are working together to develop an improved common conceptual framework that will be used as the foundation for developing future standards. The Framework has the following 3 levels:

   a. First level: The objective of financial reporting, the "why" or purpose of accounting.
   b. Second level: The qualitative characteristics and the elements, which form a bridge between the 1st and 3rd levels.
   c. Third level: Recognition, measurement, and disclosure concepts, the "how" or implementation.

First Level: Basic Objective

4.   (L.O. 3) The basic objective of financial reporting is the foundation of the Framework and requires that general-purpose financial reporting provide information about the reporting entity that is useful to present and potential equity investors, lenders, and other creditors in making their decisions as capital providers. In order to understand general-purpose financial reporting, users need reasonable knowledge of business and financial matters..

Second Level: Fundamental Concepts

5.   (S.O. 4) Companies must decide what type of information to disclose and how to disclose it. These choices are determined by which method or alternative provides the most decision-useful information. The qualitative characteristics of accounting information distinguish better and more useful information from inferior and less useful information.

Fundamental qualities:

6.   The fundamental qualities of accounting information are:

    a.   Relevance – information that is capable of making a difference in a decision. Comprised of
        1.   Predictive value meaning the information can help users form expectations about the future.
        2.   Confirmatory value meaning the information validates or refutes expectations based on previous evaluations.
    b.   Faithful representation – numbers and descriptions match what really happened or existed. Comprised of
        1.   Completeness meaning all necessary information is provided.
        2.   Neutrality meaning the information is unbiased.
        3.   Free from error meaning the information is accurate.

Enhancing qualities:

7.   Enhancing qualities complement the fundamental qualities and include:

    a.   Comparability – companies record and report information in a similar manner. Consistency is another type of comparability and means the company uses the same accounting methods from period to period.
    b.   Verifiability – independent people using the same methods arrive at similar conclusions.
    c.   Timeliness – information is available before it loses its relevance.
    d.   Understandability – reasonably informed users should be able to comprehend the information that is clearly classified and presented.

Basic Elements

8.   (S.O. 5) An important aspect of developing an accounting theoretical structure is the body of basic elements or definitions. Five basic elements that are most directly related to measuring the performance and financial status of an enterprise are put into two groups and formally defined by the IASB:

Elements related to the measurement of financial position:

Assets. A resource controlled by the entity as a result of past events and from which future economic benefits are expected to flow to the entity.

Liabilities. A present obligation of the entity arising from past events, the settlement of which is expected to result in an outflow from the entity of resources embodying economic benefits.

Equity. The residual interest in the assets of an entity that remains after deducting its liabilities.

Elements related to the measurement of financial position:

Income (revenue). Increases in economic benefits during the accounting period in the form of inflows or enhancements of assets or decreases of liabilities that result in increases in equity, other than those relating to contributions from equity participants.

Expenses. Decreases in economic benefits during the accounting period in the form of outflows or depletions of assets or incurrences of liabilities that result in decreases in equity, other than those relating to distributions to equity participants.

Third Level: Recognition, Measurement, and Disclosure Concepts

9.   (S.O. 6) In the practice of financial accounting, certain basic assumptions are important to an understanding of the manner in which data are presented. The following five basic assumptions underlie the financial accounting structure:

Economic Entity Assumption. The economic activities of an entity can be accumulated and reported in a manner that assumes the entity is separate and distinct from its owners or other business units.

Going Concern Assumption. In the absence of contrary information, a business entity is assumed to have a long life. The current relevance of the cost principle and the justification for depreciation and amortization are dependent on the going-concern assumption.

Monetary Unit Assumption. Money is the common denominator of economic activity and provides an appropriate basis for accounting measurement and analysis. The monetary unit is assumed to remain relatively stable over the years in terms of purchasing power. In essence, this assumption disregards any inflation or deflation in the economy in which the entity operates.

Periodicity Assumption. The life of an economic entity can be divided into artificial time periods for the purpose of providing periodic reports on the economic activities of the entity.

Accrual Basis of Accounting. Transactions that impact a company are recorded in the period they occur rather than in the period when cash is paid or received.

Basic Principles

10.   (S.O. 7) Certain **basic principles** are followed by accountants in recording the transactions of a business entity. Three basic principles are:

Measurement Principles : Currently there is a "mixed-attribute" system in which either the cost principle or the fair value principle is used to measure a transaction.

  a. The cost principle requires that companies account for and report many assets and liabilities on the basis of acquisition price. Cost is thought to be a faithful representation and a verifiable benchmark.
  b. The fair value principle is a market-based measurement. Elements are measured at "the amount for which an asset could be exchanged, a liability settled, or an equity instrument granted could be exchanged, between knowledgeable, willing parties in an arm's length transaction." While it is more subjective than the cost principle, it is also thought to be more relevant.

Revenue Recognition Principle. Revenue is recognized when it is probable that future economic benefits will flow to the company and reliable measurement of the amount of revenue is possible. Generally revenue is recognized at the point of sale, but there are exceptions:

a. During production – such as with certain long-term construction contracts, revenue is recognized based on the percentage of completion of the work.

b. At the end of production – such as with certain minerals and agricultural products when revenue is recognized because there's a ready market with a quoted price.

c. Upon receipt of cash – installment sales with high risk of uncollectibility that cannot be estimated.

Expense Recognition Principle. Using the matching principle accountants attempt to match expenses incurred while earning revenues with the related revenues; "let the expenses follow the revenues." Costs are classified into two groups:

a. Product costs which have a direct relationship between cost and revenue and are recognized in the same period as the revenue.

b. Period costs which lack a direct relationship between cost and revenue and are expensed as incurred.

Full Disclosure Principle. In the preparation of financial statements, the accountant should include sufficient information to permit the knowledgeable reader to make an informed judgment about the financial condition of the enterprise in question. There's a trade-off between sufficient detail and sufficient condensation, with an eye to the costs of preparing and using the information. Information can be disclosed:

a. Within the body of the financial statements.

b. In the notes to the financial statements.

c. As supplementary information.

Constraints

11.   (S.O. 8) Although accounting theory is based upon certain assumptions and the application of basic principles, there are some exceptions to these assumptions. These exceptions, often called constraints, sometimes justify departures from basic accounting theory:

Cost. This constraint relates to the notion that the benefits to be derived from providing certain accounting information should exceed the costs of providing that information. The difficulty in cost-benefit analysis is that the costs and especially the benefits are not always evident or measurable.

Materiality. An item is material if its inclusion or omission would influence or change the judgment of a reasonable person. In deciding what is material, both quantitative and qualitative aspects of the information must be considered. Deciding when an amount is material in relation to other amounts is a matter of judgment and professional expertise.

GLOSSARY

Asset.	A resource controlled by the entity as a result of past events and from which future economic benefits are expected to flow to the entity.
Comparability.	Ability to compare accounting information of different companies because they measure and report information in a similar manner.
Conceptual framework.	A coherent system of interrelated objectives and fundamentals that can lead to consistent standards.
Confirmatory value.	Information that confirms or corrects prior expectations.
Completeness.	All information necessary for faithful representation is provided.
Consistency.	An entity applies the same accounting treatment to similar events from period to period.
Cost principle.	An IFRS requirement that companies account for and report many assets and liabilities on the basis of acquisition price.
Cost constraint.	The constraint that states that information should be provided only if the benefits of providing such information outweigh the costs of providing it.
Economic entity assumption.	An assumption that states economic activity can be identified with a particular unit of accountability.
Expenses.	Decreases in economic benefits during the accounting period in the form of outflows or depletions of assets or incurrences of liabilities that result in decreases in equity, other than those relating to distributions to equity participants.
Expense Recognition Principle	The recognition of expenses is related to revenues; "Let the expense follow the revenues."
Equity.	Residual interest in the assets of an entity that remains after deducting its liabilities.
Faithful representation.	Numbers and descriptions match what really existed or happened.
Fair value principle.	Defined as "the amount for which an asset could be exchanged, a liability settled, or an equity instrument granted could be exchanged, between knowledgeable, willing parties in an arm's length transaction." Used increasingly in IFRS.

Full disclosure principle.	The principle that information should be provided if it is of sufficient importance to influence the judgment and decisions of an informed user.
Going concern assumption.	An assumption that states an enterprise will continue in operation long enough to carry out its existing objectives and commitments.
Cost principle.	An accounting principle that states that assets and liabilities should be recorded at their acquisition price.
Income.	Increases in economic benefits during the accounting period in the form of inflows or enhancements of assets or decreases of liabilities that result in increases in equity, other than those relating to contributions from equity participants.
Liability.	A present obligation of the entity arising from past events, the settlement of which is expected to result in an outflow from the entity of resources embodying economic benefits.
Losses.	Decreases in equity (net assets) from peripheral or incidental transactions of an entity and from all other transactions and other events and circumstances affecting the entity during a period except those that result from expenses or distributions to owners.
Materiality.	The constraint of determining if an item is important enough to likely influence the decision of a reasonably prudent investor or creditor.
Measurement Principles.	A "mixed attribute" system that permits the use of various measurement bases.
Monetary unit assumption.	An assumption stating that money is the common denominator of economic activity and provides an appropriate basis for accounting measurement and analysis.
Neutrality.	Information is unbiased and cannot be selected to favor one set of parties over another.
Objective of financial reporting	Provide financial information about the reporting entity that is useful to present and potential equity investors, lenders, and other creditors in making decisions in their capacity as capital providers.
Periodicity assumption.	An assumption stating that the economic activities of an enterprise can be divided into artificial time periods.
Qualitative characteristics.	Characteristics that make accounting information useful.
Relevance.	Information capable of making a difference in a decision.

Revenue recognition principle.	The principle that revenue be recognized when it is probable that future economic benefits will flow to the company and reliable measurement of the amount of revenue is possible.
Revenues.	Inflows or other enhancements of assets of an entity or settlement of its liabilities (or a combination of both) during a period from delivering or producing goods, rendering services, or other activities that constitute the entity's ongoing major or central operations.
Understandability.	Informed users perceive the significance of information.
Verifiability.	The ability to have information confirmed by independent persons.

CHAPTER OUTLINE

Fill in the outline presented below.

(S.O. 1) Need for Conceptual Framework

(S.O. 2) Development of Conceptual Framework

(S.O. 3) First Level: Basic Objective

Second Level: Fundamental Concepts

(S.O. 4) Qualitative Characteristics

Fundamental Qualities

Enhancing Qualities

(S.O. 5) Basic Elements

(S.O. 6) Basic Assumptions

Third Level: Recognition and Measurement Concepts

(S.O. 7) Basic Principles of Accounting

(S.O. 8) Constraints

REVIEW QUESTIONS

TRUE-FALSE

Indicate whether each of the following is true (T) or false (F) in the space provided.

_____   1. (S.O. 1) A conceptual framework is a coherent system of interrelated objectives and fundamentals that can lead to consistent standards and that prescribes the nature, function, and limits of financial accounting and financial statements.

_____   2. (S.O. 1) A conceptual framework underlying financial accounting is necessary because future accounting practice problems can be solved by reference to the conceptual framework and a formal standard-setting body will not be necessary.

_____   3. (S.O. 1) Use of a sound conceptual framework in the development of accounting principles will make financial statements of all entities comparable because alternative accounting methods for similar transactions will be eliminated.

_____   4. (S.O. 2) Accounting theory is developed without consideration of the environment within which it exists.

_____   5. (S.O. 2) Relevance and faithful representation are the two fundamental qualities that make accounting information useful for decision making.

_____   6. (S.O 2) To be relevant, accounting information must be capable of making a difference in a decision.

_____   7. (S.O. 4) Information that has been measured and reported in a similar manner for different enterprises is considered comparable.

_____   8. (S.O. 4) Adherence to the concept of consistency requires that the same accounting principles be applied to similar transactions for a minimum of five years before any change in principle is adopted.

_____   9. (S.O. 5) The IASB Framework defines the ten interrelated elements that most directly relate to measuring the performance and financial status of a business enterprise.

_____   10. (S.O. 5) The three elements—assets, liabilities, and equity—describe transactions, events, and circumstances that affect an enterprise during a period of time.

_____   11. (S.O. 6) The economic entity assumption is useful only when the entity referred to is a profit-seeking business enterprise.

_____   12. (S.O. 6) The going-concern assumption is generally applicable in most business situations unless liquidation appears imminent.

_____   13. (S.O. 6) The monetary unit assumption means that money is the common denominator of economic activity and provides an appropriate basis for accounting measurement and analysis.

_____   14. (S.O. 6) The periodicity assumption is a result of the demands of various financial statement user groups for timely reporting of financial information.

_____   15. (S.O. 7) If Company A wishes to acquire an asset owned by Company B, the cost principle would require Company A to record the asset at the original cost to Company B.

_____   16. (S.O. 7) Generally, confirmation of a sale to independent interests is used to indicate the point at which revenue is recognized.

_____   17. (S.O. 7) Recognition of revenue when cash is collected is appropriate only when it is impossible to establish the revenue figure at the time of sale because of the uncertainty of collection.

_____ 18. (S.O. 7) Under the expense recognition principle, it is possible to have an expense reported on the income statement in one period and the cash payment for that expense reported in another period.

_____ 19. (S.O. 7) Period costs such as officer salaries and administrative expenses attach to the product and are carried into future periods if the revenue from the product is recognized in subsequent periods.

_____ 20. (S.O. 7) The full disclosure principle states that information should be provided when it is of sufficient importance to influence the judgment and decisions of an informed user.

_____ 21. (S.O. 7) The notes to financial statements generally summarize the items presented in the main body of the statements.

_____ 22. (S.O. 8) The difficulty in applying the cost constraint is that the costs and especially the benefits are not always evident or measurable.

_____ 23. (S.O. 8) When an amount is determined by the accountant to be immaterial in relation to other amounts reported in the financial statements, that amount may be deleted from the financial statements.

_____ 24. (S.O. 8) The basis for determining whether an item is material is based on both quantitative and qualitative factors.

_____ 25. (S.O. 8) The conservatism convention allows for the reporting of financial information in any manner the accountant desires when there is doubt surrounding a particular issue.

MULTIPLE CHOICE

_____ 1. (S.O. 1) Which of the following is **not** a benefit associated with the IASB's and FASB's joint project to develop a common conceptual framework?

      A.   A conceptual framework should increase financial statement users' understanding of and confidence in financial reporting.

      B.   Practical problems should be more quickly solvable by reference to an existing conceptual framework.

      C.   A coherent set of accounting standards and rules should result.

      D.   Business entities will need far less assistance from accountants because the financial reporting process will be quite easy to apply.

_____ 2. (S.O. 4) Which of the following violates the concept of faithful representation?

      A.   The management report refers to new discoveries and inventions made, but the financial statements do not report the results.

      B.   Financial statements included buildings with a carrying amount estimated by management.

      C.   Financial statements were issued one year late.

      D.   All of the choices violate faithful representation.

_____ 3. (S.O. 4) Which of the following is a characteristic describing the fundamental quality of relevance?

      A.   Materiality.
      B.   Predictive value.
      C.   Verifiability.
      D.   Understandability.

_____ 4. (S.O. 4) Ingredients of fundamental qualities include

	Completeness	Timeliness
A.	Yes	Yes
B.	Yes	No
C.	No	No
D.	No	Yes

_____ 5. (S.O. 4) If accounting information is complete, free from error, and neutral, it can be considered:

      A.   relevant
      B.   timely.
      C.   comparable.
      D.   a faithful representation.

_____ 6. (S.O. 4) The major objective of the quality of comparability is to:

      A.   provide timely financial information for statement users.
      B.   promote comparability between financial statements of different accounting periods.
      C.   enable users to identify the real similarities and differences in economic events between companies.
      D.   be sure the same information is disclosed in each accounting period.

_____ 7. (S.O. 5) Income as defined by the IASB is

      A.   all sales revenues less all expenses.
      B.   inflows that result from investments by owners.
      C.   sales to a particular entity where ultimate payment by the entity is doubtful.
      D.   increases in economic benefits that result in an increase in equity, other than those relating to contributions from equity participants.

_____ 8. (S.O. 5) According to the IASB conceptual framework, which of the following elements describes transactions or events that affect a company during a period of time?

      A.   asset.
      B.   expense.
      C.   equity.
      D.   liability.

_____ 9. (S.O. 5) According to the IASB Conceptual Framework, the elements—assets, liabilities, and equity—describe amounts of resources and claims to resources at/during a

	Moment in Time	Period of Time
A.	Yes	No
B.	Yes	Yes
C.	No	Yes
D.	No	No

_____ 10. (S.O. 6) The economic entity assumption in accounting is best reflected by which of the following statements?

A.   When a parent and subsidiary company are merged for accounting and reporting purposes the economic entity assumption is violated.
B.   The best way to truly measure the results of enterprise activity is to measure them at the time the enterprise is liquidated.
C.   The activity of a business enterprise can be kept separate and distinct from its owners and any other business unit.
D.   A business enterprise is in business to enhance the economic well being of its owners.

_____ 11. (S.O. 6) Continuation of an accounting entity in the absence of evidence to the contrary is an example of the basic concept of

	Consistency	**Going Concern**
A.	No	No
B.	Yes	No
C.	No	Yes
D.	Yes	Yes

_____ 12. (S.O. 6) In accounting an economic entity may be defined as:

A.   a business enterprise.
B.   an individual.
C.   a division within a business enterprise.
D.   all of the above.

_____ 13. (S.O. 6) Which of the following basic accounting assumptions is threatened by the existence of severe inflation in the economy?

A.   Monetary unit assumption.
B.   Periodicity assumption.
C.   Going-concern assumption.
D.   Economic entity assumption.

_____ 14. (S.O. 6) During the lifetime of an entity accountants produce financial statements at artificial points in time in accordance with the concept of:

	Objectivity	**Periodicity**
A.	No	No
B.	Yes	No
C.	No	Yes
D.	Yes	Yes

_____ 15. (S.O. 7) Although many objections have been raised about the "cost" principle, it is still widely supported for financial reporting because it

A.   is an objectively determinable amount.
B.   is a good measure of current value.
C.   facilitates comparisons between years.
D.   takes into account price-level adjusted information.

_____ 16. (S.O. 7) Under the revenue recognition principle, revenue is generally recognized when:

A.   the sale takes place.
B.   the merchandise has been ordered.
C.   all expenses have been identified.
D.   all of the choices are correct.

_____ 17. (S.O. 7) Which of the following is a correct statement regarding the expense recognition principle?

     A.   Expenses are recognized when they make a contribution to revenue.

     B.   Costs can be charged to the current period as an expense simply because no connection with revenue can be determined.

     C.   In recognizing expenses, accountants attempt to follow the approach of let the expense follow the revenue.

     D.   All of the choices are correct.

_____ 18. (S.O. 7) The revenue recognition principle allows for revenue to be recognized at all of the following points in time except

     A.   When the customer recognizes the related expense on its income statement.

     B.   At the point of sale.

     C.   During the production process.

     D.   At the end of production but before the sale takes place.

_____ 19. (S.O. 7) In complying with the full disclosure principle, an accountant must determine the amount of disclosure necessary. How much disclosure is enough?

     A.   Information sufficient for a person without any knowledge of accounting to understand the statements.

     B.   All information that might be of interest to an owner of a business enterprise.

     C.   Information that is of sufficient importance to influence the judgment and decisions of an informed user.

     D.   Information sufficient to permit most persons coming in contact with the statements to reach an accurate decision about the financial condition of the enterprise.

_____ 20. (S.O. 8) What is the constraint that supports considering that the benefits of the information outweigh the sacrifices to provide the information?

     A.   Cost.

     B.   Prudence.

     C.   Consistency.

     D.   Conservatism.

SOLUTIONS TO REVIEW QUESTIONS

TRUE-FALSE

1. (T)

2. (F)   Development of a conceptual framework will not provide a solution to all future accounting problems, nor will it eliminate the need for a formal standard-setting body. However, a soundly developed conceptual framework should enable the IASB to issue more useful and consistent standards resulting in easier solutions to emerging practical problems.

3. (F)   Use of a sound conceptual framework will not eliminate alternative accounting methods for similar transactions. However, a sound conceptual framework should allow practitioners to dismiss certain alternatives quickly and focus on a logical and acceptable treatment.

4. (F)   The environment within which any discipline exists plays an integral role in shaping the theory of that discipline. The purpose of accounting is to serve the business environment through the issuance of timely and relevant financial information. To present such information, accounting theory must be developed with consideration being given to the business environment.

5. (T)

6. (T)

7. (T)

8.   (F)   Consistency means that a company applies the same methods to similar accounting transactions from period to period. It does not mean that companies cannot switch from one method to another. Companies can change to a new method that is considered preferable to the old method as long as financial statement users are made aware of the change.

9.   (F)   The IASB Framework defines the five interrelated elements that most directly relate to measuring the performance and financial status of a business enterprise.

10.   (F)   The three elements—assets, liabilities, and equity—describe amounts of resources and claims to resources at a moment of time.

11.   (F)   The economic entity assumption holds that the activity of a business entity can be kept separate and distinct from its owners and any other business unit. This assumption has nothing to do with the nature of the business organization.

12.   (T)

13.   (T)

14.   (T)

15.   (F)   The cost principle requires that assets be accounted for on the basis of acquisition cost. Whatever it costs a particular entity to acquire an asset is that entity's acquisition cost.

16.   (T)

17.   (T)

18.   (T)

19.   (F)   Product costs such as material, labor, and overhead attach to the product and are carried into future periods if the revenue from the product is recognized in subsequent periods. Period costs such as officers' salaries and other administrative expenses are charged off immediately because no direct relationship between cost and revenue can be determined.

20.   (T)

21.   (F)   The notes to financial statements generally amplify or explain the items presented in the main body of the statements.

22.   (T)

23.   (F)   Because an item is deemed to be immaterial does not justify its deletion from financial statements. If an amount is so small that it is quite unimportant when compared with other items, application of a particular standard may be considered of less importance. However, companies must consider both quantitative and qualitative factors in determining whether an item is material.

24.   (T)

25.   (F)   Prudence or conservatism means when in doubt, choose the solution that will be least likely to overstate assets or income and/or understate liabilities or expenses. The Framework indicates that prudence or conservatism generally is in conflict with the quality of neutrality, and accordingly, the Framework does not include prudence or conservatism as desirable qualities of financial reporting information.

MULTIPLE CHOICE

1. (D) The financial reporting process will always require the expertise of a person trained in accounting. The development of a conceptual framework will aid the accountant because new and emerging practical problems should be more quickly solvable by reference to an existing framework. Alternatives A, B, and C are benefits of the joint effort to develop a common conceptual framework.

2. (B) Accounting information is a faithful representation to the extent that it is complete, neutral, and is reasonably free of error and bias. An estimate of the carrying amount of buildings is deemed unreliable, the buildings should be recorded at their cost at the date of purchase and subsequently depreciated.

3. (B) For information to be relevant, it should have predictive or confirmatory value. Answer (A), materiality is a constraint which relates to the magnitude of an omission or misstatement that in light of the circumstances, may change or influence the decision of a person relying on the information. Answer (C) is incorrect because verifiability is an enhancing quality. Answer (D) is incorrect because understandability is an enhancing quality.

4. (B) Ingredients of the fundamental qualities include predictive and confirmatory value, completeness, neutrality, and free from error. Timeliness is an enhancing quality.

5. (D) To be a faithful representation, accounting information must possess three key characteristics: completeness, freedom from error, and neutrality.

6. (C) Comparability between financial statements of different companies ensures that users can identify real similarities and differences in economic events between companies.

7. (D) The IASB defines income as increases in economic benefits during the accounting period in the form of inflows or enhancements of assets or decreases of liabilities that result in increases in equity, other than those relating to contributions from equity participants.

8. (B) Transactions or events that affect a company during a period of time include income and expenses; resources and claims to resources at a point in time are assets, liabilities, and equity.

9. (A) The IASB classifies the elements of financial statements into two distinct groups. The first group of three elements—assets, liabilities, and equity—describes amounts of resources and claims to resources at a moment in time. The other two financial statement elements describe transactions, events, and circumstances that affect an enterprise during a period of time, income and expenses.

10. (C) The economic entity assumption holds that economic activity can be identified with a particular unit of accountability. Alternative A represents the essence of the economic entity assumption not a violation. Alternative B is related to the periodicity assumption and alternative D is not a basic accounting assumption.

11. (C) The going concern assumption in accounting implies that unless there is evidence to the contrary, an entity will continue to exist in order to carry out its objectives and fulfill its commitments. Consistency describes when an entity applies the same accounting treatment to similar events from period to period.

12. (D) All of the alternatives (A, B, and C) are economic entities for accounting purposes.

13. (A) The monetary unit assumption holds that the unit of measure remains reasonably stable. Severe inflation would cause this assumption to lose its relevance.

14. (C) The concept of periodicity implies that economic activity can be divided into artificial time periods—months, quarters, and years for example.

15. (A) Cost is still widely supported for financial reporting because it is an objectively determinable amount. Answer (B) is incorrect because historical cost and current value are generally not the same amount subsequent to the date of acquisition. Answers (C) and (D) are incorrect because it does not facilitate comparisons between years, nor does it take into account price-level adjusted information.

16. (A) Revenue is generally recognized when an objective test such as a sale indicates that it is probable that future economic benefits will flow to the company and reliable measurement of the amount of revenue is possible.

17. (D) The expense recognition principle allows for letting the expense follow the revenue (expense is recognized when it makes a contribution to income); however, immediate expensing is appropriate when there's no apparent association between an expense and a revenue.

18. (A) Revenue may be recognized at the point of sale, during production, at the completion of production or during the cash collection process. Revenue recognition is unrelated to when the customer recognizes the related expense on its income statement.

19. (C) In deciding what information to report, accountants follow the general practice of providing information that is of sufficient importance to influence the judgment and decisions of an informed user. Alternatives A and D are wrong because they do not assume an informed user. Alternative B would result in disclosing a significant amount of extraneous information.

20. (A) The cost constraint requires weighing the costs of providing the information with the benefits derived from using it. Conservatism or prudence reflects a general tendency toward early recognition of unfavorable events. The IASB believes this detracts from neutrality. Consistency relates to using the same accounting principles over time.

3

The Accounting Information System

CHAPTER LEARNING OBJECTIVES

1. Understand basic accounting terminology.
2. Explain double-entry rules.
3. Identify steps in the accounting cycle.
4. Record transactions in journals, post to ledger accounts, and prepare a trial balance.
5. Explain the reasons for preparing adjusting entries.
6. Prepare financial statements from the adjusted trial balance.
7. Prepare closing entries.
*8. Differentiate the cash basis of accounting from the accrual basis of accounting.
*9. Identify adjusting entries that may be reversed.
*10. Prepare a 10-column worksheet.

CHAPTER REVIEW

1. Chapter 3 presents a concise yet thorough review of the accounting process. The basic elements of the accounting process are identified and explained, and the way in which these elements are combined in completing the accounting cycle is described.

Accounting Information System and the Double-Entry Recording Process

2. (L.O. 1) **The accounting information system** collects and processes transaction data and then disseminates the financial information to interested parties. To understand the accounting process, one must be aware of the basic terminology employed in the process. The basic terminology includes: **events, transactions, accounts, real accounts, nominal accounts, ledger, journal, posting, trial balance, adjusting entries, financial statements,** and **closing entries.** These terms refer to the various activities that make up the **accounting cycle.** As we review the steps in the accounting cycle, the individual terms will be defined.

3. (L.O. 2) **Double-entry accounting** refers to the process used in recording transactions. As used in the accounting process, the term **debit means left** and the term **credit means right. Double-entry accounting requires that when recording transactions, debits must equal credits. In an account, when the debit side is larger than the credit side, the account is said to have a debit balance; the opposite is true if the credit side of the account is larger.** Assets and expenses are increased by debits and decreased by credits. Liabilities, owners' equity, and revenues are increased by credits and decreased by debits.

* *Note: All asterisked (*) items relate to material contained in the Appendices to the chapter.*

The Accounting Cycle

4.   The basic equation in accounting is: Assets = Liabilities + Stockholders' Equity. The accounts that make up Stockholders' Equity include Revenues, Expenses, and Dividends, among other accounts.

5.   (L.O. 3) The first step in the accounting cycle is **analysis of transactions and selected other events.** The purpose of this analysis is to determine which events represent transactions that should be recorded.

6.   Events can be classified as **external** or **internal**.   External events are those between the enterprise and its environment, whereas internal events relate to transactions totally within the enterprise.

Journalizing

7.   (L.O. 4) In order to have a complete record of each transaction or event in one place, each transaction is initially recorded in a **journal,** sometimes referred to as **the book of original entry.** The **general journal** is merely a chronological listing of transactions expressed in terms of debits and credits to particular accounts.   In addition to a general journal, **specialized journals** are used to accumulate transactions possessing common characteristics.

Posting

8.   The next step in the accounting cycle involves transferring amounts entered in the journal to the **general ledger**. The ledger contains all the asset, liability, and equity accounts. Transferring amounts from a journal to the ledger is called **posting**. Transactions recorded in a general journal must be posted individually, whereas entries made in specialized journals are generally posted by columnar total.

Trial Balance

9.   The next step in the accounting cycle is the preparation of a **trial balance.** A trial balance is a list of all open accounts in the general ledger and their balances. An entity may prepare a trial balance at any time in the accounting cycle. A trial balance prepared after posting has been completed serves to check the mechanical accuracy of the posting process and provides a listing of accounts to be used in preparing financial statements. A trial balance does not ensure that there have been no errors in the posting process or that all transactions have been posted.

Adjusting Entries

10.   (L. O. 5) Preparation of **adjusting journal entries** is the next step in the accounting cycle. Adjusting entries are entries made at the end of accounting period to bring all accounts up to date on an accrual accounting basis so that correct financial statements can be prepared. Adjusting entries allow a company to properly report its statement of financial position with all assets, liabilities, and equities accurately stated. Adjusting entries also allow a company to properly report its income statement with the appropriate revenues and expenses for the period. One common characteristic of adjusting entries is that they affect at least **one real account** (asset, liability, or equity account) and **one nominal account** (revenue or expense account). Adjusting entries can be classified as: **(1) The deferrals (prepaid expenses, unearned revenues), or (2) accruals (accrued revenues, and accrued expenses).**

11.   The deferrals, prepaid expenses and unearned revenues, refer to situations where cash has been paid or received but the corresponding expense or revenue will not be recognized until a future period. Accrued revenues and accrued expenses are revenues and expenses recognized in the current period; however, the cash payment or receipt will occur in a future period. Estimated items are expenses such as bad debts and depreciation whose amounts are a function of unknown future events or developments.

Adjusted Trial Balance

12.   After adjusting entries are recorded and posted, an **adjusted trial balance** is prepared. It shows the balance of all accounts at the end of the accounting period.

Financial Statements

13.   (L.O. 6) From the adjusted trial balance a company can directly prepare its financial statements.

Closing-Basic Process

14.   (L.O. 7) After financial statements have been prepared, nominal (revenues and expenses) accounts should be reduced to zero in preparation for recording the transactions of the next period. This **closing process** requires recording and posting of closing entries. All nominal accounts are reduced to zero by closing them through the **Income Summary** account. The net balance in the Income Summary account is equal to net income or net loss for the period. The net income or net loss for the period is transferred to owners' equity by closing the Income Summary account to Retained Earnings.

Post-Closing Trial Balance

15.   A third trial balance may be prepared after the closing entries are recorded and posted. This **post-closing trial balance** shows that debits are equal to credits after the closing entries have been properly posted to the Income Summary account.

Reversing Entries

16.   After closing the books, a company may reverse some of the adjusting entries before recording the regular transactions of the next period.

17.   In summary, the steps in the accounting cycle performed every fiscal period are as follows:

    a.   Enter the transactions of the period in appropriate journals.
    b.   Post from the journals to the ledger (or ledgers).
    c.   Prepare an unadjusted trial balance.
    d.   Prepare adjusting journal entries and post them to the ledger(s).
    e.   Prepare a trial balance after adjusting (adjusted balance).
    f.   Prepare the financial statements from the adjusted trial balance.
    g.   Prepare closing journal entries and post them to the ledger(s).
    h.   Prepare a trial balance after closing (post-closing trial balance).
    i.   Prepare reversing entries (optional) and post them to the ledger(s).

Cash Versus Accrual Basis Accounting

*18.   (L.O. 8) **Cash Basis Accounting Versus Accrual Basis Accounting,** is presented in Appendix A of Chapter 3 for the purpose of demonstrating the difference between cash basis and accrual basis accounting. Under the strict cash basis of accounting, revenue is recognized only when cash is received, and expenses are recorded only when cash is paid. The accrual basis of accounting recognizes revenue when it is earned and expenses when incurred without regard to the time of receipt or payment of cash.

*Reversing Entries

*19.   (L.O. 9) Appendix B covers preparation and posting of **reversing entries,** the final step in the accounting cycle. A reversing entry is made at the beginning of the next accounting period and is the exact opposite of the adjusting entry made in the previous period. The recording of reversing entries is an optional step in the accounting cycle that may be performed at the beginning of the next accounting period. The entries most frequently reversed are the adjusting entries for accrued revenues and accrued expenses recorded at the close of the previous accounting period.

WorkSheet

20.   (L.O. 10) Appendix C covers the use of a 10-column **worksheet,** which serves as an aid to the accountant in adjusting the account balances and preparing the financial statements. The worksheet provides an orderly format for the accumulation of information necessary for preparation of financial statements. Use of a worksheet does not replace any financial statements, nor does it alter any of the steps in the accounting cycle.

GLOSSARY

Account.	A systematic arrangement that shows the effect of transactions and other events on a specific asset, liability or equity.
Accrued expenses.	Expenses incurred but not yet paid.
Accrued revenue.	Revenues earned but not yet received.
Adjusted trial balance.	A trial balance prepared immediately after all adjustments have been posted.
Adjusting entries.	Entries made at the end of an accounting period to bring all accounts up to date on an accrual accounting basis.
Closing entries.	The formal process by which all nominal accounts are reduced to zero and the net income or net loss is determined and transferred to the owners' equity account.
Credit.	The right side of an account.
Debit.	The left side of an account.
Double-entry system.	A system that records the dual effect of each transaction in its appropriate account.
Event.	A happening of consequence.
External event.	A transaction between an entity and its environment.
Financial statements.	Statements that reflect the collection, tabulation, and final summarization of the accounting data.
General ledger.	A collection of all the asset, liability, owners' equity, revenue, and expense accounts.
Income statement.	The financial statement which measures the results of operations during the period.
Internal event.	A transaction that occurs within an entity.
Journal.	The book of original entry where transactions and selected other events are initially recorded.
Ledger.	The book (or computer printouts) containing the accounts.
Nominal accounts.	Nominal (temporary) accounts are revenue, expense and dividend accounts; except for dividends, they appear on the income statement.
Post-closing trial balance.	A trial balance prepared immediately after closing entries have been posted.

Posting.	The process of transferring the essential facts and figures from the book of original entry (journal) to the ledger accounts.
Prepaid expense.	An item paid and recorded in advance of its use or consumption, part of it properly represents expense of the current period and part represents an asset on hand at the end of the period.
Real accounts.	Real (permanent) accounts are asset, liability, and equity accounts and they appear on the statement of financial position.
***Reversing entries.**	Entries at the beginning of the next accounting period that are the exact opposite of the adjusting entries made in the previous period.
Statement of cash flows.	The financial statement which measures the cash provided and used by operating, investing, and financing activities during the period.
Statement of financial position.	The financial statement that shows the financial condition of the enterprise at the end of the period.
Statement of retained earnings.	The financial statement which reconciles the balance of the retained earnings account from the beginning to the end of the period.
Subsidiary ledger.	Contains the details related to a given general ledger account.
Transaction.	An external event involving a transfer or exchange between two or more entities.
Trial balance.	A list of all open accounts in the ledger and their balances.
Unearned revenue.	Cash received and recorded as a liability because it has not yet been earned by providing goods or services to customers.
***Worksheet.**	An electronic spreadsheet (or columnar sheet of paper) used to adjust the account balances and prepare the financial statements.

CHAPTER OUTLINE

Fill in the outline presented below.

(L.O. 1) Basic Terminology

(L.O. 2) Double-Entry Recording Process

(L.O. 3) Identifying Steps in the Accounting Cycle

(L.O. 4) Journalizing

Posting to the Ledger

Trial Balance

(L.O. 5) Adjustments

Prepaid Expense

Chapter Outline (continued)

Unearned Revenue

Accrued Liabilities or Expenses

Accrued Assets or Revenues

(L.O. 6) Prepare the Financial Statements

(L.O. 7) Closing Entries

Post-Closing Trial Balance

*(L.O. 8) Accrual versus Cash Basis

*(L.O. 9) Reversing Entries

*(L.O. 10) Using a WorkSheet

REVIEW QUESTIONS AND EXERCISES

TRUE-FALSE

Indicate whether each of the following is true (T) or false (F) in the space provided.

_____ 1. (L.O. 1) Real (permanent) accounts are revenue and expense accounts and are periodically closed.

_____ 2. (L.O. 2) In general, debits refer to increases in account balances, and credits refer to decreases.

_____ 3. (L.O. 2) An example of an internal event would be a flood that destroyed a portion of an entity's inventory.

_____ 4. (L.O. 2) Double-entry accounting is the process that leads to the basic equality in accounting expressed by the formula: assets = liabilities + owners' equity.

_____ 5. (L.O. 4) A general journal may be used by any entity in recording its transactions, whereas special journals may be used only by entities whose transactions meet certain requirements.

_____ 6. (L.O. 4) If an entity fails to post one of its journal entries to its general ledger, the trial balance will not show an equal amount of debit and credit balance accounts.

_____ 7. (L.O. 4) One purpose of a trial balance is to prove that debits and credits of an equal amount are in the general ledger.

_____ 8. (L.O. 5) Adjusting entries are an optional step in the accounting process.

_____ 9. (L.O. 5) Adjusting entries are used to correct errors that occur during the posting process.

_____ 10. (L.O. 5) Adjusting entries result from compliance with the accrual system of accounting.

_____ 11. (L.O. 5) An adjustment for wages expense, earned but unpaid at year end, is an example of an accrued liability.

_____ 12. (L.O. 5) Proper matching of revenues and expenses requires that bad debts be recorded as an expense of the period in which the sale was made.

_____ 13. (L.O. 7) The Income Summary account used during the closing process is shown in the owners' equity section of the statement of financial position.

_____ 14. (L.O. 7) It is not necessary to post the closing entries to the ledger accounts because new revenue and expense accounts will be opened in the subsequent accounting period.

_____ 15. (L.O. 7) The account "interest expense" is credited during the closing process.

_____ 16. (L.O. 7) The post-closing trial balance consists of asset, liability, owners' equity, revenue and expense accounts.

_____ *17. (L.O. 9) Because each accrued item involves either a later receipt of cash for income or a later disbursement of cash for expense, a reversing entry may be made to offset part of the credit to income or part of the debit to expense.

_____ *18. (L.O. 9) Reversing entries are made at the end of the accounting cycle to correct errors in the original recording of transactions.

_____ *19. (L.O. 9) In general, all adjusting entries for prepaid items for which the original amount was entered in a revenue or expense account and for all accrued items should be reversed.

_____ *20. (L.O. 10) A worksheet completed through the adjusted trial balance column provides the information needed for preparation of the financial statements without reference to the ledger or other records.

_____ *21. (L.O. 10) The use of a worksheet at the end of each month or quarter permits the preparation of interim financial statements even though the books are closed only at the end of each year.

_____ *22. (L.O. 10) An adjusted trial balance that shows equal debit and credit columnar totals proves the accuracy of the adjusting entries.

MULTIPLE CHOICE

Select the best answer for each of the following items and enter the corresponding letter in the space provided.

_____ 1. (L.O. 2) The accounting equation (A = L + OE) must remain in balance:

      A.   throughout each step in the accounting cycle.
      B.   only when journal entries are recorded.
      C.   only at the time the trial balance is prepared.
      D.   only when formal financial statements are prepared.

_____ 2. (L.O. 2) The difference between the accounting process and the accounting cycle is:

      A.   the accounting process results in the preparation of financial statements, whereas the accounting cycle is concerned with recording business transactions.
      B.   the accounting cycle represents the steps taken to accomplish the accounting process.
      C.   the accounting process represents the steps taken to accomplish the accounting cycle.
      D.   merely semantic, because both concepts refer to the same thing.

_____ 3. (L.O. 2) A trial balance prepared at year end showed Puccineli Co.'s debit total exceeding the credit total by $6,300. This discrepancy could have been caused by:

      A.   the balance of $47,000 in accounts receivable being entered in the trial balance as $40,700.
      B.   an error in adding the Sales Journal.
      C.   the balance of $700 in the Office Equipment account being entered as a debit of $7,000.
      D.   a net loss of $6,300.

_____ 4. (L.O. 4) Which of the following is not a principal purpose of an unadjusted trial balance?

      A.   It proves that debits and credits of equal amounts are in the ledger.
      B.   It is the basis for any adjustments to the account balances.
      C.   It supplies a listing of open accounts and their balances.
      D.   It proves that debits and credits were properly entered in the ledger accounts.

_____ 5. (L.O. 5) Which of the following journal entries is appropriate when a company receives payment in advance for goods or services?

      A.   Debit cash and credit an expense account.
      B.   Credit cash and debit a revenue account.
      C.   Debit cash and credit a liability account or a revenue account.
      D.   Credit cash and debit a liability or revenue account.

_____ 6. (L.O. 5) During the first year of Wisnewski Co.'s operations, all purchases were recorded as assets. Store supplies in the amount of $6,540 were purchased. Actual year-end store supplies inventory amounted to $2,150. The adjusting entry for store supplies will:

    A.   increase net income $4,390.
    B.   increase expenses by $4,390.
    C.   decrease store supplies by $6,540.
    D.   debit accounts payable for $2,150.

_____ 7. (L.O. 5) An adjusting entry should never include:

    A.   a debit to expense and a credit to a liability.
    B.   a debit to expense and a credit to revenue.
    C.   a debit to a liability and a credit to revenue.
    D.   a debit to revenue and a credit to a liability.

_____ 8. (L.O. 5) Which of the following is an example of an accrued liability?

    A.   Office supplies purchased at the beginning of the year and debited to an expense account.
    B.   Property taxes incurred during the year, to be paid in the first quarter of the subsequent year.
    C.   Depreciation expense.
    D.   Rent earned during the period, to be received at the end of the year.

_____ 9. (L.O. 5) A prepaid expense can best be described as an amount:

    A.   Paid and currently reported with earnings.
    B.   Paid and **not** currently reported with earnings.
    C.   **Not** paid and **not** currently reported with earnings.
    D.   **Not** paid and currently reported with earnings.

_____ 10. (L.O. 5) Rent collected in advance by a landlord is a (an):

    A.   Accrued liability.
    B.   Deferred asset.
    C.   Accrued revenue.
    D.   Unearned revenue.

_____ 11. (L.O. 5) An accrued expense can best be described as an amount:

    A.   Paid and **not** currently reported with earnings.
    B.   **Not** paid and currently reported with earnings.
    C.   **Not** paid and **not** currently reported with earnings.
    D.   Paid and currently reported with earnings.

_____ 12. (L.O. 5) The Murphy Company sublet a portion of its warehouse for five years at an annual rental of $24,000, beginning on May 1, 2012. The tenant, Sheri Charter, paid one year's rent in advance, which Murphy recorded as a credit to unearned rental income. Murphy reports on a calendar-year basis. The adjustment on December 31, 2012 for Murphy should be:

		Dr.	Cr.
A.	No entry		
B.	Unearned rental income	8,000	
	Rental income		8,000
C.	Rental income	8,000	
	Unearned rental income		8,000
D.	Unearned rental income	16,000	
	Rental income		16,000

_____ 13. (L.O. 7) Which of the following statements best describes the purpose of closing entries?

     A.   To facilitate posting and preparing a trial balance.
     B.   To determine the amount of net income or net loss for the period.
     C.   To reduce the balances of revenue and expense accounts to zero so that they may be used to accumulate the revenues and expenses of the next period.
     D.   To complete the record of various transactions that were started in a prior period.

_____ 14. (L.O. 7) If expenses are greater than revenues, the Income Summary account will be closed by a debit to:

     A.   Income Summary and a credit to Cash.
     B.   Income Summary and a credit to Retained Earnings.
     C.   Cash and a credit to Income Summary.
     D.   Retained Earnings and a credit to Income Summary.

_____ 15. Which of the following statements is **not** true as it pertains to the accounting process?

     A.   The established system for recording transactions and other events as they occur is referred to as double entry accounting.
     B.   Events are of two types: (1) external and (2) internal. Accountants record events that affect the financial position of the enterprise.
     C.   Adjustments are necessary to achieve a proper recording of revenues and expenses to determine net income for the current period and to achieve an accurate statement of the assets and equities existing at the end of the period.
     D.   Posting is the initial recording of all transactions in chronological order.

_____ *16. (L.O. 9) A reversing entry should never be made for an adjusting entry that:

     A.   accrues unrecorded revenue.
     B.   adjusts expired costs from an asset account to an expense account.
     C.   accrues unrecorded expenses.
     D.   adjusts unexpired costs from an expense account to an asset account.

_____ *17. (L.O. 9) If the following journal entry was made for the purchase of a three-year insurance policy in February of the first year, would an adjusting entry and/or a reversing entry be appropriate at the end of the first year?

     Unexpired Insurance   3,000
        Cash   3,000

	Adjusting Entry	**Reversing Entry**
A.	Yes	No
B.	No	Yes
C.	Yes	Yes
D.	No	No

_____ *18. (L.O. 10) The worksheet for Sharko Co. shows net income of $14,400 in the Income Statement columns. The company will also enter the net income

     A.   in the Statement of Financial Position debit column.
     B.   in the Statement of Financial Position credit column.
     C.   in the Income Statement credit column.
     D.   in both the Income Statement credit column and the Statement of Financial Position debit column.

REVIEW EXERCISES

1.   (L.O.4) The accounts listed below have been taken from Davies Co.'s general ledger as of December 31, 2012. The accounts all have normal balances. This is the end of Davies Co.'s first year of operations.

Cash	$ 34,000
Buildings (net)	210,000
Note Payable	72,000
Salary Expense	19,000
Inventory	36,000
Accounts Payable	60,000
Share Capital	185,000
Accounts Receivable	48,000
Sales	
Notes Receivable	22,000
Bonds Payable	75,000
Rent Expense	15,000
Land	125,000
Cost of Goods Sold	165,000
Tax Expense	20,000
Tax Payable	31,000

Determine sales for the year and prepare the following items for Davies Co. as of the year ended December 31, 2012:

    a.   trial balance,
    b.   income statement, and
    c.   statement of financial position.

a.

b.

c.

_____

_____

_____

_____

_____

_____

_____

_____

_____

2.   (L.O.4) The following changes occurred in the account balances of Cihla's Corporation during 2012.

Accounts Increasing	Amount
Cash	$50,000
Inventory	30,000
Building	25,000
Share Capital – Ordinary	30,000
Share Premium – Ordinary	10,000

Accounts Decreasing	Amount
Accounts Receivable	$10,000
Accounts Payable	20,000

The accounts shown above represent all the statement of financial position accounts for Cihla's Corporation with the exception of Retained Earnings. No dividends were declared during 2012.

Instructions
From the changes above, determine the amount of net income or net loss for 2012.

_____

_____

_____

_____

_____

_____

_____

_____

_____

_____

_____

_____

_____

_____

3.   (L.O.5) The following data relate to the accounts of Scacco Company (all amounts in 1,000s).

a.   A three-year insurance policy was purchased on March 1, 2012. The $360 insurance premium was fully paid on that date and a debit to Prepaid Insurance was recorded.

b.   Unpaid salaries at year end amount to $650.

c.   Service Revenue was credited for $816 on May 1, 2012. The amount represents a one-year advance payment for services to be performed by Scacco Company through April 30, 2013.

d.   The Office Supplies account shows a balance of $1,250 on December 31, 2012. A physical count of the supplies on hand at this date reveals a total of $480 available.

e.   Scacco Company holds bonds of another corporation that pay interest at a rate of $900 per year. These bonds were purchased on August 1, 2012, and the first interest payment will be received on August 1, 2013.

Instructions
Prepare the necessary adjusting journal entries indicated by each item for the year ended December 31, 2012.

General Journal			
			J1
Date	**Account Title**	**Debit**	**Credit**

4. (L.O.2, 4, 5, 6, 7 and *11) The post-closing trial balance of the Pat Callahan Company at December 31, 2011 is shown below.

Account

No.	Account	Debit	Credit
101	Cash	$46,000	
102	Investment in Bonds	50,000	
103	Accounts Receivable	28,000	
104	Allowance for Doubtful Accounts		900
105	Interest Receivable		
106	Inventory (perpetual)	*24,000	
107	Building (15-year life)	45,000	
108	Accumulated Depreciation-Building		12,000
109	Delivery Truck (5-year life, $3,000 salvage)	18,000	
110	Accumulated Depreciation-Trucks		6,000
200	Accounts Payable		18,000
201	Notes Payable		29,000
202	Wages Payable		
203	Income Taxes Payable		5,000
300	Share Capital – ordinary, par value $1.00		85,000
301	Retained Earnings		55,100
400	Sales		
401	Interest Revenue		
500	Operating Expenses		
501	Wages Expense		
502	Depreciation Expense-Building		
503	Depreciation Expense-Trucks		
504	Bad Debt Expense		
505	Cost of Goods Sold		
506	Income Tax Expense		
		$211,000	$211,000

Ending Inventory (12/31/12) $26,000.

The following transactions took place during 2012.

1. Collected: Accounts Receivable, $25,000; Interest on Bonds $5,000; Cash Sales, $80,000 (Cost of Goods Sold $14,000).
2. Paid: Accounts Payable, $15,000; Notes Payable, $21,000; Income Taxes Payable, $5,000; Operating Expenses, $37,000.
3. Purchased inventory, $32,000, of which $16,000 was purchased on account. (Assume perpetual inventory.)
4. Made sales on account, $85,000 (Cost of Goods Sold $16,000).
5. On June 30, 2012, purchased a second delivery truck for $15,000, paying cash. The truck has useful life of 10 years and a salvage value of $3,000.

Instructions

a. Journalize each of the transactions above of the Pat Callahan Company. Some items require more than one journal entry.

b. Post the entries to appropriate accounts. (You should set up a T-account for each account noted on the trial balance.)

c. Prepare a trial balance after posting the journal entries and enter the amounts on a 10-column worksheet like the one shown in the text. Enter all the accounts shown on the original trial balance.

d. Enter the following adjustments on the worksheet: (a) Accrued wages at year end total $700; (b) Bad debt expense is estimated at 1% of credit sales; (c) Record straight-line depreciation on the building and trucks; (d) Accrued interest on the investments in bonds is $1,500; (e) Income tax expense for 2012 is $21,065. The tax is not due until 2013.

e. Complete the income statement and statement of financial position columns of the worksheet.

f. Prepare closing journal entries.

a.

	General Journal		
			J1
Date	**Account Title**	**Debit**	**Credit**

b.

Cash	Investment in Bonds	Accounts Receivable

Allowance for Doubtful Accounts	Interest Receivable	Inventory

Building	Accumulation Depreciation—Bldg	Delivery Truck

Accumulated Depreciation—Trucks	Accounts Payable	Notes Payable

Wages Payable

Income Taxes
Payable

Share Capital – Ordinary

b.

Retained Earnings

Sales

Interest Revenue

Operating Expenses

Wages Expense

Depreciation
Expense—Bldg

Depreciation
Expense—Trucks

Bad Debts
Expense

Cost of Goods Sold

Income
Tax Expense

c. d. e.

Pat Callahan Company
Ten-Column WorkSheet
December 31, 2012

No.	Account	Trial Balance Dr.	Trial Balance Cr.	Adjustments Dr.	Adjustments Cr.	Adjusted Trial Balance Dr.	Adjusted Trial Balance Cr.	Income Statement Dr.	Income Statement Cr.	Statement of financial position Dr.	Statement of financial position Cr.
101	Cash										
102	Investment in Bonds										
103	Accounts Receivable										
104	Allowance for Doubtful Accounts										
105	Interest Receivable										
106	Inventory										
107	Building										
108	Accumulated Depreciation—Bldg										
109	Delivery Trucks										
110	Accumulated Depreciation—Trucks										
200	Accounts Payable										
201	Notes Payable										
202	Wages Payable										
203	Income Taxes Payable										
300	Share Capital—Ordinary										
301	Retained Earnings										
400	Sales										
401	Interest Revenue										
500	Operating Expense										
501	Wages Expense										
502	Depreciation Expense—Bldg										
503	Depreciation Expense—Trucks										
504	Bad Debts Expense										
505	Cost of Goods Sold										
506	Income Tax Expense										
	Net Income										

(f)

SOLUTIONS TO REVIEW QUESTIONS AND EXERCISES

TRUE-FALSE

1. (F) Real (permanent) accounts are asset, liability, and owners' equity accounts. Nominal (temporary) accounts are revenue and expense accounts. Nominal accounts are periodically closed; real accounts are not.

2. (F) Debits are recorded on the left side of an account and can be increases or decreases in account balances, depending on the account involved. Debits increase asset and expense accounts; they decrease liability, owner equity, and revenue accounts. Credits result in the opposite effect on account balances.

3. (F) This statement characterizes an external event rather than an internal event. Internal events occur within an entity, whereas external events involve interaction between an entity and its environment.

4. (T)

5. (F) Special journals can be used by any entity for any groups of transactions possessing common characteristics.

6. (F) Failure to post one journal entry to the general ledger will misstate the debit and credit side of a trial balance by the same amount. Thus, the trial balance will show an equal amount of debits and credits.

7. (T)

8. (F) Adjusting entries are necessary for a company to properly report its statement of financial position with all assets, liabilities, and equities accurately stated. Adjusting entries are also necessary for a company to properly report its income statement with the appropriate revenues and expenses for the period.

9. (F) Adjusting entries are necessary for a company to properly report its statement of financial position with all assets, liabilities, and equities accurately stated. Adjusting entries are also necessary for a company to properly report its income statement with the appropriate revenues and expenses for the period. If errors are made in the posting process, they are corrected by means of correcting entries, not adjusting entries.

10. (T)

11. (T)

12. (T)

13. (F) The income summary account is a clearing account through which all revenue and expense accounts are closed at the end of an accounting period. Once the revenue and expense accounts have been closed, any balance existing in the income summary account is closed to retained earnings. Thus, the income summary account never appears on a financial statement.

14. (F) Failure to post closing entries to the general ledger will leave a balance in revenue and expense accounts from a previous period and the retained earnings account will be misstated.

15. (T)

16. (F) The post-closing trial balance consists only of asset, liability, and owners' equity (the real) accounts.

*17. (T)

*18. (F) Reversing entries are made to simplify the recording of a subsequent transaction related to an adjusting entry. When an entry is reversed, the related subsequent transaction can be recorded as if the adjusting entry had never been recorded. Reversing entries have nothing to do with the correction of errors.

*19. (T)

*20. (T)

*21. (T)

*22. (F) An adjusted trial balance that shows equal debit and credit columnar totals proves nothing more than the fact that each adjusting entry contained an equal amount of debits and credits. Adjusting entries could have included the wrong total dollar amount or an inappropriate account could have been debited or credited. Mistakes such as these would still produce an adjusted trial balance that shows equal debit and credit columnar totals.

MULTIPLE CHOICE

1. (A) If the accounting equation is out of balance at any time during the accounting cycle, then an error has been made.

2. (C) The basic procedures normally used to ensure that the effects of transactions and selected other events are recorded correctly and transmitted to the user are often called the steps in the accounting cycle. The accounting process encompasses all the steps in the accounting cycle.

3. (C)
Recorded debit amount	$7,000
Actual debit balance...	700
Excess debit total	$6,300

4. (D) The trial balance accomplishes the things listed in the first three alternatives. However, the purpose of the trail balance is not to prove that the debits and credits were properly entered in the ledger accounts. The fact that the trial balance is in balance proves that an equal amount of debits and credits were made, but there is no assurance that the postings were made to the correct accounts.

5. (C) An advance payment for goods or services requires a debit to cash, but the corresponding credit can be made to a liability or a revenue account. When the goods or services are delivered to the customer, consideration of the account credited in the original entry will dictate the manner in which this event is reflected in the accounts.

6. (B)
Purchased..	$6,540
Year-end inventory	2,150
Used during year..	$4,390

Adjusting entry: Supplies Expense   4,390
                           Store Supplies   4,390

7. (B) All adjusting entries include one statement of financial position account (asset or liability) and one income statement account (revenue or expense). Thus, all alternatives other than alternative B represent possible adjusting entry descriptions.

8. (B) An accrued liability is an item of expense that has been incurred during the period, but has not been recorded or paid. The property taxes fits this definition, as they are an expense of the period in which they were incurred and represent a liability until they are paid in the subsequent period. The office supplies are a prepaid expense, depreciation is an estimated item, and the rent earned is an accrued revenue item.

9. (B) A prepaid expense can best be described as an amount paid and not currently reported with earnings. The journal entry to record a prepaid expense involves debiting an asset account and crediting cash. The asset is deferred to and expensed in future years. Answer (A) is incorrect because it is not reported with earnings until it is expensed in future years. Answers (C) and (D) are incorrect because a prepaid expense is one that has been paid.

10. (D)   Rent collected in advance by a landlord is an unearned revenue. Cash received in advance should not be recognized as revenue until it has been earned as evidenced by providing a product, service, or facility. Answer (A) is incorrect because an accrued liability is the result of an expense which has been incurred but not yet paid. Answer (B) is incorrect because a deferred asset is a cost which has been incurred but the benefits will be received in the future. Answer (C) is incorrect because an accrued revenue is revenue that has been earned but not yet received.

11. (B)   An accrued expense can best be described as an amount not paid and currently reported with earnings. The journal entry to record an accrued expense involves debiting an expense account which is deducted from revenues in determining income and crediting a liability account. Accrued expenses are generally incurred as a result of passage of time (e.g., interest, rent, salaries, etc.). Answers (A) and (D) are incorrect because by definition an accrued expense is one that has been incurred but **not** yet paid. Answer (C) is incorrect because the purpose of accruing an expense is to report it currently with earnings.

12. (D)   Murphy Company should make an adjusting entry to recognize that two-thirds (8 months) of an annual rental of $24,000 has been earned and should be recognized as rental income in 2012. The journal entry that should be made is:

Unearned rental income   16,000
    Rental income ($24,000 × 2/3)   16,000

13. (C)   Closing entries represent the formal process by which all nominal accounts (revenue and expense) are reduced to zero and the net income or net loss is determined and transferred to owners' equity. Even though the amount of net income or net loss is determined through the closing process (alternative B), this is not the primary purpose of closing entries.

14. (D)   If expenses are greater than revenues, then the Income Summary account will have a debit balance after closing entries have been made. Thus, to close the Income Summary account the journal entry would include a debit to Retained Earnings and a credit to Income Summary.

15. (D)   Alternatives A, B, and C are statements of fact as they relate to the accounting process. Alternative "D" describes journalization, not the posting process.

*16 (B)   The adjusting entry shown in the solution to multiple-choice question 6 above is an example of an adjusting entry that adjusts expired costs from an asset to an expense account. To reverse such an entry would increase the Store Supplies account. This is obviously inappropriate because the only way to increase Store Supplies is to purchase additional supplies. The other three alternatives represent appropriate candidates for reversing entries.

*17 (A)   An adjusting entry is necessary because a portion of the insurance has expired as of the end of the first year. However, because this prepaid item was originally entered in an asset account a reversing entry would be inappropriate.

*18 (B)   When a company reports net income in the worksheet, it will debit net income in the income statement columns and credit net income in the statement of financial position columns to report the increase in retained earnings.

REVIEW EXERCISES

1. a.

Davies Co.
Trial Balance
December 31, 2012

Cash	$34,000	
Accounts Receivable	48,000	
Notes Receivable	22,000	
Inventory	36,000	
Building, net	210,000	
Land	125,000	
Accounts Payable		$60,000
Notes Payable		72,000
Tax Payable		31,000
Bonds Payable		75,000
Share Capital		185,000
Sales		**271,000**
Cost of Goods Sold	165,000	
Rent Expense	15,000	
Salary Expense	19,000	
Tax Expense	20,000	
	$694,000	$694,000

b.

Davies Co.
Income Statement
Year Ended December 31, 2012

Sales		$271,000
Cost of Goods Sold		165,000
Gross Profit on Sales		$106,000
Expenses:		
Rent Expense	$ 15,000	
Salary Expense	19,000	
Tax Expense	20,000	
Total Expenses		54,000
Net Income		$52,000

c.

Davies Co.
Statement of Financial Position
As of December 31, 2012

Assets

Fixed Assets:

Buildings (net)	$210,000	
Land	125,000	
Total Fixed Assets		$335,000

Current Assets:

Inventory	36,000	
Notes Receivable...	22,000	
Accounts Receivable..	48,000	
Cash...	34,000	
Total Current Assets		140,000
Total Assets		$475,000

Equity and Liabilities

Equity:

Share capital...	$185,000	
Retained Earnings	52,000	$237,000

Long-term Liabilities:

Bonds Payable...	75,000	75,000

Current Liabilities:

Accounts Payable...	60,000	
Note Payable	72,000	
Tax Payable..	31,000	
Total Current Liabilities		163,000
Total Equity and Liabilities		$475,000

2. **Net change in assets:**

Cash...	$50,000	
Accounts Receivable..	(10,000)	
Inventory	30,000	
Building..	25,000	
Net Change		$ 95,000
Less net change in equity and liabilities:		
Accounts Payable...	($20,000)	
Share Capital – Ordinary..................................	30,000	
Share Premium – Ordinary	10,000	
Net Change		20,000
Net Income for 2012 (Change in Retained Earnings)		$ 75,000

3.	a.	Insurance Expense		100	
		Prepaid Insurance			100
	b.	Salaries Expense		650	
		Salaries Payable			650
	c.	Service Revenue		272	
		Unearned Service Revenue			272
	d.	Supplies Expense		770	
		Office Supplies			770
	e.	Interest Receivable		375	
		Interest Income			375

4.	a.	Item 1:	Cash	25,000	
			Accounts Receivable		25,000
			Cash	5,000	
			Interest Revenue		5,000
			Cash	80,000	
			Sales		80,000
			Cost of Goods Sold	14,000	
			Inventory		14,000
		Item 2:	Accounts Payable	15,000	
			Cash		15,000
			Notes Payable	21,000	
			Cash		21,000
			Income Taxes Payable	5,000	
			Cash		5,000
			Operating Expenses	37,000	
			Cash		37,000
		Item 3:	Inventory	32,000	
			Cash		16,000
			Accounts Payable		16,000
		Item 4:	Accounts Receivable	85,000	
			Sales		85,000
			Cost of Goods Sold	16,000	
			Inventory		16,000
		Item 5:	Delivery Truck	15,000	
			Cash		15,000

b.

	Cash		
	46,000	15,000	(2)
(1)	25,000	21,000	(2)
(1)	5,000	5,000	(2)
(1)	80,000	37,000	(2)
		16,000	(3)
		15,000	(5)
	47,000		

Investment in Bonds	
50,000	

	Accounts Receivable		
	28,000	25,000	(1)
(4)	85,000		
	88,000		

Allowance for Doubtful Accounts	
	900

Interest Receivable	

	Inventory		
	24,000	14,000	(1)
(3)	32,000	16,000	(4)
	26,000		

Building	
45,000	

Accumulated Depreciation—Bldg	
	12,000

	Delivery Truck	
	18,000	
(5)	15,000	
	33,000	

Accumulated Depreciation—Trucks	
	6,000

	Accounts Payable		
(2)	15,000	18,000	
		16,000	(4)
		19,000	

	Notes Payable		
(2)	21,000	29,000	
		8,000	

b. (continued)

Wages Payable		Income Taxes Payable		Share Capital – Ordinary	
		(2) 5,000	5,000		85,000
		0	0		

Retained Earnings		Sales		Interest Revenue	
	55,100		80,000 (1)		5,000 (1)
			85,000 (3)		
			165,000		

Operating Expenses		Wages Expense		Depreciation Expense—Bldg	
(2) 37,000					

Depreciation Expense—Trucks		Bad Debts Expense		Cost of Goods Sold	
				(1) 14,000	
				(4) 16,000	
				30,000	

Income Tax Expense	

c. d. e.

Pat Callahan Company
Ten-Column WorkSheet
December 31, 2012

No.	Account	Trial Balance Dr.	Trial Balance Cr.	Adjustments Dr.	Adjustments Cr.	Adjusted Trial Balance Dr.	Adjusted Trial Balance Cr.	Income Statement Dr.	Income Statement Cr.	Statement of financial position Dr.	Statement of financial position Cr.
101	Cash	47,000				47,000				47,000	
102	Investment in Bonds	50,000				50,000				50,000	
103	Accounts Receivable	88,000				88,000				88,000	
104	Allowance for Doubtful Accounts		900		(b) 850		1,750				1,750
105	Interest Receivable			(d) 1,500		1,500				1,500	
106	Inventory	26,000				26,000				26,000	
107	Building	45,000				45,000				45,000	
108	Accum. Deprec.—Bldg		12,000		(c) 3,000		15,000				15,000
109	Delivery Trucks	33,000				33,000				33,000	
110	Accum. Deprec.—Trucks		6,000		(c) 3,600		9,600				9,600
200	Accounts Payable		19,000				19,000				19,000
201	Notes Payable		8,000				8,000				8,000
202	Wages Payable				(a) 700		700				700
203	Income Taxes Payable				(e) 21,065		21,065				21,065
300	Share Capital – ordinary		85,000				85,000				85,000
301	Retained Earnings		55,100				55,100				55,100
400	Sales		165,000				165,000		165,000		
401	Interest Revenue		5,000		(d) 1,500		6,500		6,500		
500	Operating Expense	37,000				37,000		37,000			
501	Wages Expense			(a) 700		700		700			
502	Depreciation Expense—Bldg			(c) 3,000		3,000		3,000			
503	Depreciation Expense—Trucks			(c) 3,600		3,600		3,600			
504	Bad Debts Expense			(b) 850		850		850			
505	Cost of Goods Sold	30,000				30,000		30,000			
506	Income Tax Expense			(e) 21,065		21,065		21,065			
	Totals	$356,000	$356,000	$ 30,715	$ 30,715	$386,715	$386,715	96,215	171,500	215,215	
	Net Income							75,285			75,285
								$171,500	$171,500	$290,500	$290,500

a.	Wages expense	700	
	Wages payable		700

b.	Bad debts expense	850	
	Allowance for doubtful accounts		850

c.	Depreciation expense – Trucks	3,600*	
	Accumulated depreciation		3,600
	Depreciation expense – Bldg.	3,000	
	Accumulated depreciation		3,000

*($15,000 – 3,000)/10 × 6/12 = $600 + ($18,000 - $3,000)/5 = $3,000

d.	Interest receivable	1,500	
	Interest revenue		1,500

e.	Income tax expense	21,065	
	Income tax payable		21,065

f.	Interest Revenue	6,500	
	Sales	165,000	
	Cost of Goods Sold		30,000
	Operating Expenses		37,000
	Wages Expense		700
	Depreciation Expense—Bldg.		3,000
	Depreciation Expense—Trucks		3,600
	Bad Debts Expense		850
	Income Tax Expense		21,065
	Income Summary		75,285

(To close revenues and expenses to income summary)

Income Summary	75,285	
Retained Earnings		75,285

(To close income summary to retained earnings)

4

Income Statement
and Related Information

CHAPTER LEARNING OBJECTIVES

1. Understand the uses and limitations of an income statement.
2. Understand the content and format of the income statement.
3. Prepare an income statement.
4. Explain how to report items in the income statement.
5. Identify where to report earnings per share information.
6. Explain intraperiod tax allocation.
7. Understand the reporting of accounting changes and errors.
8. Prepare a retained earnings statement.
9. Explain how to report other comprehensive income.

CHAPTER REVIEW

1. Chapter 4 presents a detailed discussion of the concepts and techniques that underlie the preparation of the Income Statement and Statement of Retained Earnings and the reporting of other comprehensive income. The requirements for adequate presentation of reported net income are described and illustrated throughout the chapter.

2. (L.O. 1) The income statement helps users of financial statements (1) evaluate the past performance of the enterprise, (2) provide a basis for predicting future performance, and (3) help assess the risk or uncertainty of achieving future cash flows. The limitations of the income statement include (1) items that cannot be measured reliably are not reported in the income statement, (2) income numbers are affected by the accounting methods employed, and (3) income measurement involves judgment.

3. Quality of earnings is important because markets are based on trust and it is imperative that investors have faith in the numbers reported. If that trust is damaged, capital markets will be damaged.

Elements of the Income Statement

4. The major elements of net income are: **income and expenses.** The definition of income includes both revenues and gains, and the definition of expenses includes both expenses and losses. When inflows or enhancements of assets result from typical business activities (generally the activities the entity is in business to perform), revenues result. Likewise, outflows or the using up of assets resulting from typical business activities will generate expenses. Nontypical business activities resulting in inflows or outflows of assets will normally generate transactions classified as gains or losses.

Content and Format of the Income Statement

5.   (L.O. 2) While IFRS does not specify a particular set of components that must be used on an income statement, the statement needs to provide enough information for users to understand the entity's current performance and to provide a basis for predicting future performance. At a minimum, the following items are required to be presented on the income statement: (a) revenue, (b) tax expense, (c) interest expense, (d) amount of profit or loss resulting from application of the equity method, (e) the total gain or loss resulting from discontinued operations (including both operations and disposal), and (f) net income or loss. IFRS also requires additional line items, headings or subtotals when their presentation is relevant.

6.   Common totals or sections shown within an income statement include:
   A.   **Sales or revenue section** reports sales less discounts, allowances, returns and other information to arrive at net sales.
   B.   **Cost of goods sold section.**
   C.   **Gross profit.**
   D.   **Selling expenses.**
   E.   **Administrative or general expenses.**
   F.   **Other income and expense,** including gains and losses from asset sales, impairment and restructuring charges, and dividend and interest revenue.
   G.   **Income from operations.**
   H.   **Financing costs** or interest expense is shown as a separate item.
   I.   **Income from continuing operations** is reported only if a company has discontinued operations.
   J.   **Discontinued operations**.
   K.   **Net income.**
   L.   **Non-controlling interest** is an allocation of net income to primary and non-controlling shareholders.
   M.   **Earnings per share.**

7.   (L.O. 3) Page 149 of the text shows a sample income statement. Sometimes, a company reports a very condensed income statement that is supported by supplementary schedules. These schedules provide detail for the totals found in the income statement and should be studied by users of financial statements.

Reporting Within the Income Statement

8.   (L.O. 4) Items or totals reported within the income statement include:.

   A.   **Gross profit** is computed as sales minus cost of goods sold.
   B.   **Income from operations** highlights items affecting regular business activities.
   C.   **Expense classification** by either nature or function. Classifying by function is viewed as more relevant; however, it requires allocations that may be arbitrary.
   D.   **Gains and losses** include such items as restructuring charges, losses on write-downs of inventory or other assets, and gains or losses from dispositions.
   E.   **Allocation to non-controlling interest** occurs when the parent/reporting company owns more than 50% of the ordinary shares of an investee /subsidiary company. If the subsidiary is not wholly owned, the parent company must allocate net income to the non-controlling shareholders.

Earnings per Share

9. (L.O. 5) In general, **earnings per share** represents the ratio of net income minus preference dividends (income available to ordinary shareholders) divided by the weighted average number of ordinary shares outstanding. It is considered by many financial statement users to be the most significant statistic presented in the financial statements, and **must be disclosed on the face of the income statement.**

10. The IASB defines a **discontinued operation** as a component of an entity that either has been disposed of or is classified as held-for-sale. When an entity decides to dispose of a component of its business, certain classification and disclosure requirements must be met. A separate income statement category for gain or loss from disposal of a component of a business must be provided. In addition, the results of operations of a component that has been or will be disposed of are also reported—separately from continuing operations. Effects of discontinued operations are shown net of tax, after continuing operations.

Intraperiod Tax Allocation

11. (L.O. 6) **Intraperiod tax allocation** is the process of relating the income tax effect of an unusual item to that item when it appears on the income statement. Companies use intraperiod tax allocation for (a) income from continuing operations, and (2) discontinued operations.

Other Reporting Issues

Changes in Accounting Principles

12. (L.O. 7) A **change in accounting principle** results when an entity adopts a new accounting principle that is different from the one previously used (including changes in method of inventory pricing and changes in accounting for long-term construction contracts). A company recognizes a change in accounting principle by making a **retrospective adjustment** to the financial statements. Such an adjustment recasts the prior years' statements on a basis consistent with the newly adopted principle. The company records the cumulative effect of the change for prior periods as an adjustment to beginning retained earnings of the earliest year presented.

Changes in Estimates

13. Accountants make extensive use of estimates in preparing financial statements. Adjustments that grow out of the use of estimates in accounting are used in the determination of income for the current period and future periods and are not charged or credited directly to Retained Earnings. It should be noted that **changes in estimates** are not considered errors (prior period adjustments).

Corrections of Errors

14. Companies must correct errors by making proper entries in the accounts and reporting corrections in the financial statements. Corrections of errors are treated as prior period adjustments, similar to changes in accounting principles. Companies record an error in the year in which it is discovered. They report the effect of the error as an adjustment to the beginning balance of retained earnings. If a company prepares comparative financial statements, it should restate the prior statements for the effects of the error.

Retained Earnings

15.   (L.O. 8) The **statement of retained earnings** serves to reconcile the balance of the retained earnings account from the beginning to the end of the year. The important information communicated by the statement of retained earnings includes: (a) prior period adjustments (income or loss related to corrections of errors in the financial statements of a prior period net of tax), (b) changes in accounting principle, (c) the relationship of dividend distributions to net income for the period, and (d) any transfers to and from retained earnings.

Comprehensive Income

16.   (L.O. 9)   Items that bypass the income statement are included under the concept of comprehensive income. **Comprehensive income** includes all changes in equity during a period except those resulting from investments by owners and distributions to owners. The IASB requires companies to display the components of other comprehensive income as either (1) a second separate income statement, or (2) a combined statement of comprehensive income.

Statement of Changes in Equity

17.   In addition to a statement of comprehensive income, companies must present a statement of changes in equity. This statement reports the change in each equity account and in total equity for the period.

GLOSSARY

Appropriated retained earnings.	Retained earnings that are restricted in accordance with contractual requirements, board of directors' policy, or the apparent necessity of the moment.
Change in accounting principle.	The use of a principle in the current year that is different from the one used in the preceding year.
Comprehensive income.	An income amount that includes all revenues and gains, expenses and losses reported in net income, and, in addition it includes gains and losses that bypass net income but affect stockholders' equity.
Changes in estimates.	Normal, recurring corrections and adjustments.
Corrections of errors.	Mathematical mistakes, mistakes in the application of accounting principles, or oversight or misuse of facts that existed at the time financial statements were prepared.
Discontinued operations.	The disposal of a significant segment of a business.
Earnings per share.	The net income earned by each ordinary share outstanding.
Intraperiod tax allocation.	The procedure of associating income taxes with the specific item that directly affects the income taxes for the period.
Prior period adjustments.	Items of income or loss related to corrections of errors in the financial statements of a prior period.

CHAPTER OUTLINE

Fill in the outline presented below.

(L.O. 1) Usefulness and Limitations of the Income Statement

(L.O. 2 and 3) Content and Format of the Income Statement

(L.O. 4) Reporting Items in the Income Statement

Classification of Expenses

Discontinued Operations

Changes in Accounting Principle

Changes in Estimate

Corrections of Errors

(L.O. 5) Earnings per Share

(L.O. 6) Intraperiod Tax Allocation

(L.O. 7) Reporting Changes and Errors

(L.O. 8)   Retained Earnings Statement

(L.O. 9)   Comprehensive Income

REVIEW QUESTIONS AND EXERCISES

TRUE-FALSE

Indicate whether each of the following is true (T) or false (F) in the space provided.

_____   1. (L.O. 1) One of the limitations of the income statement is that items that cannot be measured reliably are not reported in the income statement.

_____   2. (L.O. 1) Earnings management refers to the planned timing of income and expenses to smooth out bumps in earnings.

_____   3. (L.O. 1) The transaction approach focuses on income-related activities that have occurred during the period.

_____   4. (L.O. 2) IFRS requires that companies disclose gross margin on their income statements.

_____   5. (L.O. 2) One component of the income statement is an allocation of net income to the non-controlling interest.

_____   6. (L.O. 5) A manufacturer of computer hardware who sells all computer manufacturing facilities located in foreign countries can record the transaction as a disposal of a segment.

_____   7. (L.O. 5) Phasing out of a product line or class of service is a disposal of assets that qualifies as a disposal of a segment of a business.

_____   8. (L.O. 5) The results of operations of a segment that has been or will be disposed of need not be separated from the results of continuing operations as long as the gain or loss from the disposal is shown separately.

_____   9. (L.O. 5) Earnings per share is computed as (net income – preference dividends)/weighted average of preference shares outstanding.

_____   10. (L.O. 5) Companies must disclose earnings per share on the face of the income statement.

_____   11. (L.O. 4) The function-of-expense method of classifying expenses is viewed as less arbitrary and less relevant than the nature-of-expense method.

_____   12. (L.O. 4) When expenses are classified using the function-of-expense method, functions include cost of goods sold, selling expenses, and administrative expenses.

_____   13. (L.O. 7) Adjustments that grow out of the use of estimates in accounting are not classified as prior period adjustments.

_____   14. (L.O. 7) The effect on net income of adopting a new accounting principle should be disclosed as a separate item following extraordinary items in the income statement.

_____   15. (L.O. 7) A change in accounting principle is considered appropriate only when it is demonstrated that the newly adopted principle is preferable to the old one.

_____   16. (L.O. 7) A correction of an error should not be made to prior year statements even if shown for comparative purposes since the error was discovered and corrected in the current period.

_____   17. (L.O. 6) Intraperiod tax allocation causes a reduction in total income tax expense for the period in which it is used.

_____   18. (L.O. 5) Earnings per share measures the number of dollars earned by each ordinary share.

_____   19. (L.O. 5) The presentation of earnings per share is affected by the existence of prior period adjustments.

_____   20. (L.O. 8) The statement of retained earnings provides a reconciliation of the retained earnings account from the beginning of the year to the end of the year.

_____   21. (L.O. 8) The statement of retained earnings shows the total change in stockholders' equity for a specified period.

_____   22. (L.O. 7) A prior period adjustment results from the correction of an error in the financial statements of a prior period discovered subsequent to their issuance.

_____   23. (L.O. 7) Prior period adjustments should be charged or credited to the opening balance of retained earnings and, thus, excluded from the determination of net income for the current period.

_____   24. (L.O. 9) According to the IASB, displaying comprehensive income as a part of the statement of stockholders' equity is one of the acceptable ways of presenting comprehensive income items.

MULTIPLE CHOICE

Select the best answer for each of the following items and enter the corresponding letter in the space provided.

_____   1. (L.O. 1) Which of the following would represent the least likely use of an income statement prepared for a business enterprise?

      A.   Use by customers to determine a company's ability to provide needed goods and services.

      B.   Use by labor unions to examine earnings closely as a basis for salary discussions.

      C.   Use by government agencies to formulate tax and economic policy.

      D.   Use by investors interested in the financial position of the entity.

_____   2. (L.O. 1) The primary reason the income statement is so important to investors and creditors relates to its ability to provide information helpful in

      A.   determining the honesty of those involved in managing the enterprise.

      B.   assessing the financial position of the entity at a point in time.

      C.   predicting the amount, timing, and uncertainty of future cash flows.

      D.   determining the amount of future income the entity may generate from current operations.

_____ 3. (L.O. 1) The income statement reveals:

  A. resources and equities of a firm at a point in time.
  B. resources and equities of a firm for a period of time.
  C. net earnings (net income) of a firm at a point in time.
  D. net earnings (net income) of a firm for a period of time.

_____ 4. (L.O. 3) During the year 2012, Siska Corporation had the following information available related to its income statement:

Disbursements for purchases	$630,000
Increase in trade accounts payable	80,000
Decrease in merchandise inventory	25,000

  Cost of goods sold for 2012 amounted to

  A. $735,000
  B. $685,000
  C. $575,000
  D. $525,000

_____ 5. (L.O. 3) The occurrence that most likely would have no effect on 2012 net income is the:

  A. sale in 2012 of an office building contributed by a stockholder in 1984.
  B. collection in 2012 of a dividend from an investment.
  C. correction of an error in the financial statements of a prior period discovered subsequent to their issuance.
  D. stock purchased in 2002 deemed worthless in 2012.

_____ 6. (L.O. 2) Which of the following is not among the items required to be presented on the income statement?

  A. Gross margin.
  B. Tax expense.
  C. Net income.
  D. Finance costs or interest expense..

_____ 7. (L.O. 1) The element of financial statements known as income includes

	Gains	Losses
A.	Yes	Yes
B.	No	No
C.	Yes	No
D.	No	Yes

_____ 8. (L.O. 5) Which of the following asset disposals would qualify as a discontinued operation?

  A. Phasing out of a product line or class of service.
  B. Changes occasioned by a technological improvement.
  C. Sale by an auto parts manufacturer of one of its five parts-manufacturing subsidiaries.
  D. Sale by a transportation company of its bus operations but not its airline operations.

_____ 9. (L.O. 5) Material gains or losses resulting from the disposition of a segment of the business should be reported separately as a component of income

  A. after net income but before comprehensive income.
  B. after results from continuing operations and before net income.
  C. before results from continuing operations and as part of administrative expenses.
  D. before results from continuing operations and after cost of goods sold.

_____ 10. (L.O. 4) To be classified on an income statement as an extraordinary item, the transaction or event must be material in nature and

	Unusual	Occur Infrequently
A.	Yes	Yes
B.	No	Yes
C.	Yes	No
D.	No	No

_____ 11. (L.O. 5) Shannon, Inc. decided to discontinue its plastics division during the current year. For the current year, the plastics division lost $600,000. Shannon sold the division at the end of the year at a loss of $1,000,000. Shannon, Inc.'s tax rate is 40%. Under "Discontinued operations" on the income statement, what amount will Shannon, Inc. report as gain or loss from disposal of the plastics division?

    A. $1,600,000 loss.
    B. $960,000 loss.
    C. $240,000 gain.
    D. $2,240,000 loss.

_____ 12. (L.O. 5) Shannon, Inc. decided to discontinue its plastics division during the current year. For the current year, the plastics division lost $600,000. Shannon sold the division at the end of the year at a loss of $1,000,000. Shannon, Inc.'s tax rate is 40%. Shannon's income from continuing operations for the current year was $2,000,000 and the company has had 500,000 ordinary shares outstanding all year. What amount of EPS will Shannon, Inc. report on the face of its income statement for the current year?

    A. $4.00
    B. $0.48
    C. $2.40
    D. $0.80

_____ 13. (L.O. 6) The net profit or loss attributable to non-controlling shareholders is reported

    A.   in a separate section of the income statement between income from operations and income from income taxes.
    B.   as a separate item below net income or loss.
    C.   in a separate section of the income statement between income from continuing operations and net income.
    D.   as part of income from operations.

_____ 14. (L.O. 6) Which of the following items is reported in a separate section of the income statement between income from operations and income before income taxes?

    A.   The gain on disposal of a segment of a business.
    B.   Cost of goods sold.
    C.   Impairment loss on intangible assets.
    D.   Financing costs.

_____ 15. (L.O. 1) In general, the basic difference between the concepts of revenues and gains concerns:

    A.   the materiality of the item being considered.
    B.   whether the event giving rise to the item relates to the typical activity of the enterprise.
    C.   whether the item is taxable in the current year.
    D.   the effect on total assets of the enterprise.

_____ 16. (L.O. 1) When a manufacturing company sells one of its plant assets at a price in excess of its book value it should recognize

	Revenue	Gain
A.	No	Yes
B.	No	No
C.	Yes	No
D.	Yes	Yes

_____ 17. (L.O. 7) When a company changes from one accounting principle to another accounting principle:

    A.   the company does not have to disclose anything about it.

    B.   the current income statement should include only footnote disclosure so readers will be aware of the change.

    C.   a retrospective adjustment should be made to the financial statements.

    D.   it should always be reflected as a cumulative effect in the current year's financial statements.

_____ 18. (L.O. 7) Corrections of errors:

    A.   should only be reflected in the current year's financial statements if a company presents prior years' financial statement for comparative purposes even if the error effected prior years.

    B.   should be treated as prior period adjustments.

    C.   should only be disclosed in a footnote so readers will be aware of the errors.

    D.   should only be reflected in the current year's statement of financial position and never the income statement.

_____ 19. (L.O. 4) Which of the following items would be presented in the income statement only in the account affected (not in a separate section)?

    A.   Changes in estimates.

    B.   Earnings per share.

    C.   Financing costs.

    D.   Discontinued operations.

_____ 20. (L.O. 4) Changing the basis of inventory pricing from FIFO to average cost is an example of a(n):

    A.   Error correction.

    B.   Change in principle.

    C.   Change in estimate.

    D.   Discontinued operation.

_____ 21. (L.O. 7) Changes in estimate include all of the following except

    A.   change in revenue recognition for long-term construction contracts..

    B.   change in the realizability of receivables and inventories..

    C.   change in estimated useful lives of equipment.

    D.   change in estimated liability for warranty costs.

_____ 22. (L.O. 7) A change in estimate

	Is accounted for prospectively	**Corrects improper accounting**
A.	No	No
B.	Yes	Yes
C.	No	Yes
D.	Yes	No

_____ 23. (L.O. 5) Earnings per share must always be shown separately for:

    A.   net income.

    B.   pretax income.

    C.   non-controlling interest.

    D.   All of the choices are correct.

_____   24. (L.O. 9) Which of the following is **not** one of the items disclosed in the statement of changes in equity?

  A.   Comprehensive income for the period.
  B.   Earnings per share for the period.
  C.   Contributions (issuances of shares) and distributions (dividends) to owners.
  D.   Reconciliation of the carrying amount of each component of equity from the beginning to the end of the period.

REVIEW EXERCISES

1. (L.O. 3 and 4) Kubitz Co. had the following amounts in its income statements:

	2011	**2012**	**2013**
Sales	46,800		78,000
Cost of Goods Sold		48,000	
Gross Margin	10,800	14,400	18,000
Administrative Expenses			6,000
Income Before Tax	8,800		
Tax Expense (40%)		2,560	
Net Income (Net Loss)		3,840	

Instructions: Complete the tabulation by filling in the missing amounts.

2. (L.O. 3 and 4) Schmitt, Inc., a retail store, has the following data for the year ended December 31, 2012:

Sales	$90,000
Cost of goods sold	55,000
Interest expense	1,000
Selling expenses	11,000
Income tax expense	4,400
Administrative expenses	3,000

Weighted-average number of ordinary shares outstanding during the year, 10,000

Instructions:

Develop an income statement for Schmitt, Inc. for the year ended December 31, 2012.

3.   (L.O. 5 and 6) The following items are presented on financial statements:
     A.   Changes in estimates.
     B.   Changes in principle.
     C.   Correction of errors.
     D.   Discontinued operations.
     E.   Non-controlling interest.

Instructions: For each of the items listed above, describe (a) the criteria used to identify the item and (b) its placement on the financial statements. Assume that each item is material.

4. (L.O. 4) The following accounts are taken from the adjusted trial balance of Tamara Company as of December 31, 2012.

Ordinary Shares (100,000 shares)	$ 300,000	Accounts Payable	$ 85,600
Transportation-in	12,600	Sales Returns	15,900
Rent Revenue	28,500	Purchase Discounts	12,100
Administrative Expense (Total)	145,800	Gain on Sale of Land	18,300
Cost of Goods Sold	464,800	Selling Expense (Total)	186,800
Sales Discounts	9,500	Accounts Receivable	96,200
Bond Interest Expense	14,300	Retained Earnings (1/1)	226,900
Sales	1,265,000	Dividend Income	17,700

All income is taxed at a uniform rate of 42%.

Instructions:

Prepare a multiple-step income statement for Tamara Company for the year ended December 31, 2012.

_____

_____

_____

_____

_____

_____

_____

_____

_____

_____

5. (L.O. 4, 5, 6, 7 and 8) Presented below is financial information of the Mickey Corporation for 2012.

Beginning Retained Earnings, 1/1/12	$ 950,000
Gain on the sale of investments	110,000
Sales for the year	30,000,000
Loss due to flood damage	125,000
Cost of goods sold	21,000,000
Loss on disposal of retail division	450,000*
Interest revenue	70,000
Loss on operations of retail division	460,000*
Selling and administrative expenses	5,500,000
Dividends declared on ordinary shares	230,000
Impairment of goodwill	520,000
Dividends declared on preference shares	80,000
Income tax on operations for 2012	1,600,000

Mickey Corporation decided to discontinue its retail operations and to retain their manufacturing operations. On August 15, Mickey sold the retail operations to Schoen Company. During 2012, there were 250,000 ordinary shares outstanding all year.

net of tax

Instructions:
Prepare an income statement and retained earnings statement.

5.   *(continued)*

SOLUTIONS TO REVIEW QUESTIONS AND EXERCISES

TRUE-FALSE

1. (T)

2. (T)

3. (T)

4. (F)   IFRS requires certain minimum disclosures on the income statement, but gross margin is not among them. Required are revenue, tax expense, interest expense, share of profit/loss associated with the equity method, discontinued operations, and net income or loss.

5. (T)

6. (T)

7. (F)   Phasing out of a product line or class of service does **not** qualify as the disposal of a segment of a business. The IASB defines a discontinued operation as a component of an entity that either has been disposed of, or is classified as held-for-sale, and: 1. Represents a major line of business or geographical area of operations, or 2. Is part of a single, co-coordinated plan to dispose of a major line of business or geographical area of operations, or 3. Is a subsidiary acquired exclusively with a view to resell.

8. (F)   Companies report as discontinued operations (in a separate income statement category) the gain or loss from disposal of a component of a business. In addition, companies report the results of operations of a component that has been or will be disposed of separately from continuing operations. Companies show the effects of discontinued operations net of tax as a separate category, after continuing operations.

9. (F)   Earnings per share is computed as (net income – preference dividends)/weighted average of ordinary shares outstanding.

10. (T)

11. (F)   The function-of-expense method of classifying expenses is viewed as both more arbitrary and more relevant than the nature-of-expense method.

12. (T)

13. (T)

14. (F)   A company recognizes a change in accounting principle by making a retrospective adjustment to the financial statements and the cumulative effect of the change for prior periods as an adjustment to beginning retained earnings of the earliest year presented.

15. (T)

16. (F)   A correction of an error should be made to prior years' financial statements when such an error effects those prior years and the prior years are shown for comparative purposes.

17. (F)   Intraperiod tax allocation is a method designed to relate the income tax expense of the fiscal period to the items that affect the amount of the tax provision. Use of this method does not affect the income tax expense for the period, merely the manner in which the income tax expense is presented.

18.   (T)

19.   (F)   Because prior period adjustments are carried directly to retained earnings, the presentation of earnings per share, which is included in the income statement, is unaffected.

20.   (T)

21.   (F)   The statement of retained earnings presents a reconciliation of the balance of the retained earnings account from the beginning to the end of the year. This statement does not include information about the other accounts that appear in an entity's equity section.

22.   (T)

23.   (T)

24.   (F)   The IASB decided that companies must display the components of other comprehensive income in one of two ways: (1) a second income statement or (2) a combined statement of comprehensive income.

MULTIPLE CHOICE

1.   (D)   Customers, labor unions, and government agencies may well make use of the income statement for the reasons noted in alternatives A, B, and C respectively. However, the income statement reports results of operations, not financial position. To determine financial position of an entity the investor would have to refer to the information in a statement of financial position.

2.   (C)   Investors and creditors are most interested in the ability of the entity to generate cash flows into the future. Accurate predictions of future cash flows help investors assess the economic value of the enterprise and creditors determine the probability of repayment of their claims against the enterprise. The honesty of management or future income from current operations are not items primarily measured by the income statement. Also, financial position is a statement of financial position concept.

3.   (D)   The income statement is defined as the financial statement of a business entity that reveals net earnings for a period of time.

4.   (A)   Cash payments for purchases totaled $630,000, but the amount of merchandise purchased in 2012 exceeded this amount by the $80,000 increase in trade accounts payable. Merchandise inventory decreased by $25,000, which means beginning inventory exceeded ending inventory by this amount. Thus, this amount would have to be added to the cash payment amount to arrive at cost of goods sold as follows:

Amount paid for purchases..	$630,000
Add increase in trade payables	80,000
Add decrease in inventory	25,000
2012 Cost of goods sold	$735,000

5.   (C)   Prior period adjustments should be charged or credited to the opening balance of retained earnings and, thus, excluded from the determination of net income.

6.   (A)   IFRS requires certain minimum disclosures on the income statement, but gross margin is not among them. Required are revenue, tax expense, interest expense, share of profit/loss associated with the equity method, discontinued operations, and net income or loss.

7.   (C)   The element of financial statements known as income includes both revenues and gains. The element of financial statements known as expenses includes expenses and losses.

8. (D)   The only disposal that qualifies as a disposal of a segment is the disposal by the transportation company of its entire bus operations. This company remains in the transportation business, but an entire segment of the business has been terminated. Items (A), (B), and (C) are examples of asset disposals that do not qualify as discontinued operations because the company has not disposed of or classified as held-for-sale a major line of business or a geographic area of operations..

9. (B)   The effects of discontinued operations are shown net of tax as a separate category in the income statement after continuing operations but before net income.

10. (A)   Extraordinary items are events and transactions that are distinguished by their unusual nature and by the infrequency of their occurrence. **Both** of these criteria must be met to classify an event or transaction as an extraordinary item.

11. (B)   Discontinued operations:

Loss from operation of discontinued plastics division...............	($600,000)
Loss from disposal of plastics division.....................................	(1,000,000)
Income tax benefit ($600,000 + 1,000,000) × 40%)..................	640,000
Loss from disposal of plastics division.....................................	(<u>$960,000</u>)

12. (B)   The company will report EPS of $.48 per share computed as ($2,000,000 − 1,000,000 − 600,000) = $400,000 × 60% = $240,000 after tax net income. $240,000/500,000 = $.48.

13. (B)   The net profit or loss attributable to non-controlling shareholders is reported as a separate item below net income or loss as an allocation of the net income or loss (not as an item of income or expense).

14. (D)   Financing costs (interest expense) are reported in a separate section of the income statement between income from operations and income before income taxes

15. (B)   Revenues represent inflows from activities that constitute the entity's ongoing major or central operations. Gains, on the other hand, represent increases in equity from peripheral or incidental transactions of an entity. The concepts of materiality (A) or taxability (C) have nothing to do with distinguishing revenues from gains.

16. (A)   Gains are increases in equity (net assets) resulting from peripheral or incidental transactions of an entity. The sale of plant assets by a manufacturing company is not a part of its regular operations and thus results in a gain rather than revenue.

17. (C)   When a company changes from one accounting principle to another accounting principle a retrospective adjustment should be made to the financial statements.

18. (B)   Corrections of errors should be treated as prior period adjustments, the accounting for which is similar to the accounting for changes in accounting principles.

19. (A)   Changes in estimates are presented in the income statement only in the account affected. Alternatives (B), (C) and (D) are all items that would be presented in a separate section of the income statement.

20. (B) Changing the basis of inventory pricing from FIFO to average cost is an example of a change in principle.

21. (A) A change in the method of revenue recognition for long-term construction contracts (to or from percentage-of-completion) is accounted for as a change in principle. The other examples all relate to changes in estimates.

22. (D) Changes in estimate are accounted for prospectively and are used to account for changes in good faith estimates of such things as useful lives of assets or bad debt expectations. Corrections of errors, which require prior period adjustments, are used to correct improper accounting.

23. (A) Earnings per share must be disclosed on the face of the income statement for net income. EPS is not shown for pretax income or non-controlling interest.

24. (B) Earnings per share for the period is not one of the required disclosures on the statement of changes in equity. All the other choices are disclosed on the statement of changes in equity.

REVIEW EXERCISES

		2011	2012	2013
1.	Sales	46,800	**62,400**	78,000
	Cost of Goods Sold	**36,000**	48,000	**60,000**
	Gross Margin of Profit	10,800	14,400	18,000
	Administrative Expenses	**2,000**	**8,000**	6,000
	Income Before Tax	8,800	**6,400**	**12,000**
	Tax Expense (40%)	**3,520**	2,560	**4,800**
	Net Income (Net Loss)	**5,280**	3,840	**7,200**

2.

Schmitt Inc.

Income Statement

Year Ending December 31, 2012

Sales	$90,000	
Cost of goods sold	55,000	
Gross profit		$35,000
Selling expenses	11,000	
Administrative expenses	3,000	14,000
Income from operations		21,000
Interest expense		1,000
Income before tax		20,000
Income tax		4,400
Net income		$15,600
Earnings per share:		
Net income ($15,600 ÷ 10,000)		1.56

3.

Item	**Criteria**	**Placement**
A. Changes in estimates	Normal, recurring corrections or adjustments to estimate.	Change in income statement only in the account affected.
B. Changes in principle	Change from one accounting principle to another.	Retrospective adjustment to all years that are presented.
C. Corrections of errors	Mathematical mistakes, mistakes in application of principles, or oversight or misuse of facts.	Retrospective adjustment to all years that are presented.
D. Discontinued operations	Disposal of a segment of a business constituting a separate line of business or a class of customer.	Separate section in the income statement after continuing operations but before extra-ordinary items.
E. Non-controlling interest	Net profit or loss attributable to non-controlling shareholders.	Report as a separate item below net income or loss as an allocation of the net income or loss (not as an item of income or expense).

4.

Tamara Company
Income Statement
For the Year Ended December 31, 2012

Revenues

Sales...		$1,265,000
Less: Sales discounts	$ 9,500	
Sales returns	15,900	25,400
Net sales..		1,239,600
Cost of goods sold		464,800
Gross profit on sales		774,800
Selling Expenses...	186,800	
Administrative Expenses	145,800	332,600

Other Income and Expense

Rent revenue	28,500	
Dividend income...	17,700	
Gain on sale of land..	18,300	64,500
Income from operations..		506,700
Bond interest expense		14,300
Income before tax		492,400
Income tax ($492,400 × .42)......................................		206,808
Net income for the year		$285,592
Earnings per share ($285,592 ÷ 100,000)......................		$2.86

5.

Mickey Corporation
Income Statement
For The Year Ended December 31, 2012

Sales..		$30,000,000
Cost of goods sold		21,000,000
Gross profit..		9,000,000
Selling and administrative expenses...............................		5,500,000
Other income and expense:		
Interest revenue	$ 70,000	
Gain on sale of investments......................................	110,000	
Loss from flood...	125,000	
Impairment of goodwill...	520,000	465,000
Income before income tax...		3,035,000
Income tax		1,600,000
Income from continuing operations..................................		1,435,000
Discontinued operations		
Loss from operations, net of tax................................	460,000	
Loss from disposition, net of tax...............................	450,000	910,000
Net income...		$ 525,000
Earnings per share:		
Income from continuing operations...........................		$5.42a
Discontinued operations:		
Loss from operations (net of tax)...........................	$(1.84)	
Loss from disposition (net of tax)	(1.80)	(3.64)
Net income		$1.78b

Mickey Corporation
Retained Earnings Statement
For the Year Ended December 31, 2012

Beginning balance of retained earnings.........................		$ 950,000
Add Net income..		525,000
Subtotal...		1,475,000
Less dividends:		
Preference shares...	$ 80,000	
Ordinary shares..	230,000	310,000
Ending balance of retained earnings.............................		$1,165,000

a: $\dfrac{\$1,435,000 - \$80,000}{250,000 \text{ shares}}$ = $5.42

b: $\dfrac{\$525,000 - \$80,000}{250,000 \text{ shares}}$ = $1.78

5

Statement of Financial Position and Statement of Cash Flows

CHAPTER LEARNING OBJECTIVES

1. Explain the uses and limitations of a statement of financial position.

2. Identify the major classifications of the statement of financial position.

3. Prepare a classified statement of financial position using the report and account formats.

4. Indicate the purpose of the statement of cash flows.

5. Identify the content of the statement of cash flows.

6. Prepare a basic statement of cash flows.

7. Understand the usefulness of the statement of cash flows.

8. Determine additional information requiring note disclosure.

9. Describe the major disclosure techniques for financial statements.

*10. Identify the major types of financial ratios and what they measure.

CHAPTER REVIEW

1.   Chapter 5 presents a detailed discussion of the concepts and techniques that underlie the preparation and analysis of the statement of financial position. Along with the mechanics of preparation, acceptable disclosure requirements are examined and illustrated. A brief introduction to the statement of cash flows is also presented. At the end of Chapter 5, a multi-page illustration of the financial statements and accompanying notes of a corporation is presented. This illustration may be referred to throughout your study of intermediate accounting as it includes information relevant to many of the topics discussed in subsequent chapters.

Uses and Limitations of the Statement of Financial Position

2.   (L.O. 1) The statement of financial position can be a very useful and versatile financial statement. If a statement of financial position is examined carefully, users can gain a considerable amount of information related to **liquidity, solvency** and **financial flexibility.** Liquidity is generally related to the amount of time that is expected to elapse until an asset is realized or otherwise converted into cash or until a liability has to be paid. Solvency refers to the ability of an enterprise to pay its debts as they mature. Financial flexibility is the ability of an enterprise to take effective action to alter the amounts and timing of cash flow so that it can respond to unexpected needs and opportunities.

* *Note: All asterisked (*) items relate to material contained in the Appendix to the chapter.*

3. Criticism of the statement of financial position has revolved around the limitations of the information presented therein. These limitations include: (a) failure to reflect current value information, (b) the extensive use of estimates, and (c) failure to include items of financial value that cannot be recorded objectively.

4. The problem with current value information concerns the reliability of such information. The estimation process involved in developing current-value type information causes a concern about the objectivity of the resulting financial information. The use of estimates is extensive in the development of statement of financial position data. These estimates are required by IFRS, but reflect a limitation of the statement of financial position. The limitation concerns the fact that the estimates are only as good as the understanding and objectivity of the person(s) making the estimates. The final limitation of the statement of financial position concerns the fact that some significant assets of the entity are not recorded. Items such as human resources (employee workforce), managerial skills, customer base, and reputation are not recorded because such assets are difficult to quantify.

Classification in the Statement of financial position

5. (L.O. 2) The **major classifications** used in the statement of financial position are **assets, equity,** and **liabilities.** These items were defined in the discussion presented in Chapter 2. To provide the financial statement reader with additional information, these major classifications are divided into several **subclassifications.** Assets are further classified as **noncurrent** or **current,** with the noncurrent divided among long-term investments; property, plant, and equipment; intangible assets; and other assets. Equity includes share capital, share premium, and retained earnings. Liabilities are classified as **noncurrent** or **current.** These items are defined as follows:

Assets. Resources controlled by the entity as a result of past events and from which future economic benefits are expected to flow to the entity.
Liabilities. Present obligations of the entity arising from past events, the settlement of which is expected to result in an outflow from the entity of resources embodying economic benefits.
Equity. Residual interest in the assets of an entity that remains after deducting its liabilities.

Noncurrent Assets

Long-Term Investments

6. Items classified as **long-term investments** in the assets section of the statement of financial position normally are one of four types. These include:

   a.   Investments in securities, such as stock, bonds, or long-term notes.
   b.   Investments in tangible fixed assets not currently used in operations.
   c.   Investments set aside in special funds (sinking, pension, plant expansion, etc.) and cash surrender value of life insurance.
   d.   Investments in nonconsolidated subsidiaries or affiliated companies.

Long-term investments are rather permanent in nature as they are not normally disposed of for a long period of time.

Property, Plant and Equipment

7. **Property, plant and equipment** are properties of a durable nature that are used in the regular operations of the enterprise. Examples include land, buildings, machinery, furniture, tools, and wasting resources with the exception of land, these assets are either depreciable or depletable.

Intangible Assets

8.   **Intangible assets** lack physical substance; however, their benefit lies in the rights they convey to the holder. Examples include patents, copyrights, franchises, goodwill, trademarks, trade names, and secret processes.

9.   **Limited-life** intangible assets are amortized over their useful lives. **Indefinite-life** intangibles (such as goodwill) are not amortized but, instead, are assessed periodically for impairment.

Other Assets

10.   Many companies include an **"Other Assets"** classification in the statement of financial position after Property, Plant, and Equipment. This section includes a wide variety of items that do not appear to fall clearly into one of the other classifications. Some of the more common items included in this section are: long-term prepaid expenses, noncurrent receivables, assets in special funds, and property held for sale.

Current Assets

11.   **Current assets** are cash and other assets expected to be converted into cash, sold, or consumed either in one year or in the operating cycle, whichever is longer. There are some exceptions to a literal interpretation of the current asset definition. These exceptions involve prepaid expenses, investments in common stock, and the subsequent years' depreciation of fixed assets. These exceptions are recognized in the accounting process and are understood by most financial statement users. Current assets normally include inventories, receivables, prepaid expenses, short-term investments, and cash.

12.   For a proper presentation of **inventories,** the basis of valuation (i.e., lower-of-cost-or-net realizable value) and the method of costing (FIFO or average cost) should be disclosed. Any anticipated loss due to uncollectibles, the amount and nature of any nontrade **receivables,** and any receivables designated as collateral should be clearly identified. **Prepaid expenses** are expenditures already made for benefits (usually services) to be received within one year or the operating cycle, whichever is longer. **Short-term investments** are usually categorized as held-to-maturity, trading, or available-for-sale. Any restrictions on the general availability of **cash** or any commitments on its probable disposition must be disclosed.

Equity

13.   The **equity section** of the statement of financial position includes information related to shares, retained earnings, accumulated other comprehensive income, and non-controlling interest. Preparation of the equity section should be done carefully because of the various restrictions imposed by corporation laws, liability agreements, and voluntary actions of the board of directors.

14.   The equity section is typically divided into six different sections:
   a.   Share capital consists of the par or stated value of shares issued, including ordinary shares and preference shares. Companies must disclose the par value, authorized, issued and outstanding share amounts for ordinary shares.
   b.   Share premium is the excess amounts paid in over the stated or par value.
   c.   Retained earnings is the corporation's undistributed earnings; can be divided into unappropriated (available for dividends) and restricted.
   d.   Accumulated other comprehensive income is the aggregate of comprehensive income items.
   e.   Treasury shares are those ordinary shares repurchased by the corporation, shown as a reduction of equity.
   f.   Non-controlling interest is the portion of the equity of subsidiaries not owned by the reporting company.

Non-Current Liabilities

15. **Non-current liabilities** are obligations whose settlement date extends beyond the normal operating cycle or one year, whichever is longer. Examples include bonds payable, notes payable, lease obligations, and pension obligations. Generally, the disclosure requirements for non-current liabilities are quite substantial as a result of various covenants and restrictions included for the protection of the lenders. Non-current liabilities that mature within the current operating cycle are classified as current liabilities if their liquidation requires use of current assets. Non-current liabilities generally fall into one of the three following categories:

   a. Obligations arising from specific financing situations, such as the issuance of bonds, long-term lease obligations, and long-term notes payable.

   b. Obligations arising from the ordinary operations of the enterprise such as pensions and deferred income taxes.

   c. Obligations that are dependent upon the occurrence or non-occurrence of one or more future events to confirm the amount payable such as warranties and other contingencies; these items are often called provisions.

Current Liabilities

16. **Current liabilities** are the obligations that are reasonably expected to be liquidated either through the use of current assets or the creation of other current liabilities. Items normally shown in the current liabilities section of the statement of financial position include notes and accounts payable, advances received from customers, current maturities of long-term debt, taxes payable, and accrued liabilities. Obligations due to be paid during the next year may be excluded from the current liability section if the item is refinanced through long-term debt or the item will be paid out of noncurrent assets. Companies do not report current liabilities in any consistent order. In general, though, companies most commonly list notes payable, accounts payable, or short-term debt as the first item. Income tax payables or other current liabilities are commonly listed last.

17. **Working capital** is the excess of current assets over current liabilities. This concept, sometimes referred to as net working capital, represents the net amount of a company's relatively liquid resources. By reference to this amount, a financial statement user is able to assess the entity's ability to meet financial demands during the operating cycle. While the amount of working capital has a definite relationship to liquidity, the reader must analyze the composition of the current assets to determine their nearness to cash.

Statement of Financial Position Format

18. (L.O. 3) IFRS does not specify either a particular order of presentation for items in the statement of financial position, nor the format of the statement. The account format of a statement of financial position lists assets by sections on the left side and equity and liabilities by sections on the right side. The report format lists equity and liabilities directly below assets on the same page.

Statement of Cash Flows

19. (L.O. 4) The primary purpose of a statement of cash flows is to provide relevant information about the cash receipts and cash payments of an enterprise during a period. The statement of cash flows reports (1) cash effects of operations during the period, (2) investing transactions, (3) financing transactions, and (4) net increase or decrease in cash during the period.

20. (L.O. 5) In accomplishing its purpose, the statement focuses attention on three different activities related to cash flows.

    a.   **Operating activities** involve the cash effects of transactions that enter into determination of net income.

    b.   **Investing activities** include making and collecting loans and acquiring and disposing of debt and equity investments and property, plant, and equipment.

    c.   **Financing activities** involve liability and equity items and include (1) obtaining capital from owners and providing them with return on (and return of) their investment and (2) borrowing money from creditors and repaying the amounts borrowed.

The basic format of the statement of cash flows is shown below.

Statement of Cash Flows

Cash flows from operating activities	$XXX
Cash flows from investing activities	XXX
Cash flows from financing activities	XXX
Net increase (decrease) in cash	XXX
Cash at beginning of year	XXX
Cash at end of year	$XXX

21. (L.O. 6) The information to prepare the statement of cash flows comes from three sources: (a) comparative statements of financial position, (b) the current income statement, and (c) selected transaction data. Preparation of the statement of cash flows involves the following steps.

    a.   Determine the cash provided or used by operations.

    b.   Determine the cash provided by or used in investing and financing activities.

    c.   Determine the change (increase or decrease) in cash during the period.

    d.   Reconcile the change in cash with the beginning and the ending cash balances.

22. Significant non-cash activities include transactions such as issuing ordinary shares to purchase an asset, converting bonds into ordinary shares, issuing debt to purchase assets, or exchanging long-lived assets. Significant financing and investing activities that do not affect cash are not reported in the body of the statement of cash flows, they are reported in a separate note to the financial statements.

Usefulness of the Statement of Cash Flows

23.   (L.O. 7) Creditors look for answers to the following questions in the company's cash flow statement:

a.   How successful is the company in generating net cash provided by operating activities?
b.   What are the trends in net cash flow provided by operating activities over time?
c.   What are the major reasons for the positive or negative net cash provided by operating activities?

Financial Liquidity

24.   The **current cash debt coverage ratio** is:

$$\frac{\text{Net Cash Provided}}{\text{by Operating Activities}} \div \frac{\text{Average Current}}{\text{Liabilities}} = \frac{\text{Current Cash Debt}}{\text{Coverage Ratio}}$$

Financial Flexibility

25.   The cash debt coverage ratio is:

$$\frac{\text{Net Cash Provided}}{\text{by Operating Activities}} \div \frac{\text{Average Total}}{\text{Liabilities}} = \frac{\text{Cash Debt}}{\text{Coverage Ratio}}$$

Free Cash Flow

26.   **Free cash flow** is the amount of discretionary cash flow a company has for purchasing additional investments, retiring its debt, purchasing treasury stock, or simply adding to its liquidity.

$$\frac{\text{Net Cash Provided}}{\text{by Operating Activities}} - \frac{\text{(Capital Expenditures}}{\text{+ Dividends)}} = \text{Free Cash Flow}$$

Financial Statements and Notes

27.   (L.O. 8) A complete set of financial statements comprise the following.

a.   A statement of financial position at the end of the period;
b.   A statement of comprehensive income for the period to be presented either as:
   (i) One single statement of comprehensive income.
   (ii) A separate income statement and statement of comprehensive income.
c.   A statement of changes in equity;
d.   A statement of cash flows; and
e.   Notes, comprising a summary of significant accounting policies and other explanatory information.

28.   Notes are integral to the financial statements and are necessary to help users of the financial statements understand and evaluate financial statement components and their relationships. The **Summary of Significant Accounting Policies** is generally the first note to the financial statements. The IASB recommends disclosure for all significant accounting principles and methods that involve selection from among alternatives or those that are peculiar to a given industry. In many cases, IFRS requires specific disclosures; for example, items of PP&E are disaggregated into classes (such as land and building) with related accumulated depreciation reported where applicable.

Techniques of Disclosure

29.   (L.O. 9)   Effective communication of the information required to be disclosed in financial statements is an important consideration. Accountants have developed certain methods that have proven useful in disclosing pertinent information. The methods are **parenthetical explanations, cross reference and contra items**. Numerous examples of the techniques of disclosure are presented in the text. These examples should be reviewed as they represent concepts referred to in subsequent chapter material.

*Ratio Analysis

*30.   (L.O. 10) **Appendix 5A Ratio Analysis--A Reference** demonstrates various ratios used to analyze financial performance.

GLOSSARY

Accounting policies.	Explanations of the basic assumptions made concerning inventory valuations, depreciation methods, investments in subsidiaries, etc.
Current assets.	Cash and other assets expected to be converted into cash, sold, or consumed either in one year or in the operating cycle, whichever is longer.
Current liabilities.	Obligations that are reasonably expected to be liquidated either through the use of current assets or the creation of other current liabilities within the longer of 1 year or the operating cycle.
Financial flexibility.	The ability of an enterprise to take effective actions to alter the amounts and timing of cash flows so it can respond to unexpected needs and opportunities.
Liquidity.	The amount of time that is expected to elapse until an asset is realized or otherwise converted into cash or until a liability has to be paid.
Non-current liabilities.	Obligations that are not reasonably expected to be liquidated within a year or the normal operating cycle, whichever is longer, but instead, are payable at some date beyond that time.
Retained earnings.	The corporation's undistributed earnings.
Share capital.	The par or stated value of the shares issues.
Share premium.	The excess of amounts paid in over par or stated value.
Solvency.	The ability of an enterprise to pay its debts as they mature.
Working capital.	The excess of total current assets over total current liabilities.

CHAPTER OUTLINE

Fill in the outline presented below.

(L.O. 1) Usefulness of the Statement of Financial Position

Limitations of the Statement of Financial Position

(L.O. 2) Major Classifications

Long-term Investments

Property, Plant, and Equipment

Intangible Assets

Other Assets

Current Assets

Chapter Outline *(continued)*

          Equity

          Share Capital

          Share Premium

          Retained Earnings

          Non-current Liabilities

          Current Liabilities

    (L.O. 3) Preparing a Statement of Financial Position

    (L.O. 4) Purpose of the Statement of Cash Flows

    (L.O. 5) Content of the Statement of Cash Flows

(L.O. 6) Preparation of a Basic Statement of Cash Flows

(L.O. 7) Usefulness of a Statement of Cash Flows

(L.O. 8) Note Disclosures

(L.O. 9) Disclosure Techniques

*(L.O. 10) Ratio Analysis

REVIEW QUESTIONS AND EXERCISES

TRUE-FALSE

Indicate whether each of the following is true (T) or false (F) in the space provided.

_____   1. (L.O. 1) The statement of financial position reflects a corporation's results of operations for a specified period of time.

_____   2. (L.O. 1) Liquidity is the ability of an enterprise to take effective actions to alter the amounts and timing of cash flows so it can respond to unexpected needs and opportunities.

_____   3. (L.O. 1) One of the limitations of the statement of financial position is that many items of financial value are omitted.

_____   4. (L.O. 2) The statement of financial position has 3 elements, assets, liabilities, and retained earnings.

_____   5. (L.O. 2) The non-controlling interest, the portion of equity of subsidiaries not owned by the reporting corporation, is reported as a non-current liability.

_____   6. (L.O. 2) Current assets include only assets expected to be sold within one year or the operating cycle, whichever is longer.

_____   7. (L.O. 2) If cash is restricted for purposes other than the liquidation of current obligations, it should not be classified as a current asset.

_____   8. (L.O. 2) Available-for-sale investments are debt securities that the enterprise has the positive intent and ability to hold to maturity.

_____   9. (L.O. 2) Trading securities are reported at fair value in the current asset section.

_____   10. (L.O. 2) Proper presentation of inventories for a manufacturing concern includes disclosure of the basis of valuation, the method of pricing, and the stage of completion.

_____   11. (L.O. 2) Reserves, as used on a statement of financial position, refers to accumulated other comprehensive income.

_____   12. (L.O. 2) Securities classified as available-for-sale should be reported at cost.

_____   13. (L.O. 2) The use of an other-asset section varies widely in practice. It should be restricted to unusual items that are different from assets included elsewhere.

_____   14. (L.O. 2) Current liabilities are the obligations that are reasonably expected to be liquidated either by creation of other current liabilities or through the use of current assets.

_____   15. (L.O. 2) Long-term liabilities are obligations that are not reasonably expected to be liquidated within one year or the normal operating cycle, whichever is longer.

_____   16. (L.O. 2) The equity accounts used by a corporation are the same as those used in accounting for a partnership or proprietorship.

_____   17. (L.O. 3) IFRS specifies that companies use the account format for the statement of financial position since this format most accurately reflects a company's true accounting position.

_____   18. (L.O. 8) It is recommended that there be a disclosure for all significant accounting principles and methods that involve selection from among alternatives or those that are peculiar to a given industry.

_____   19. (L.O. 8) A maturity analysis for receivables is an IFRS-required disclosure.

_____   20. (L.O. 8) Notes disclosures are voluminous under IFRS, many times including over 20 pages of notes to the financial statements.

_____   21. (L.O. 9) One advantage of using a parenthetical disclosure is that it brings the information into the body of the statement.

_____   22. (L.O. 4) The primary purpose of the statement of cash flows is to provide relevant information about the cash receipts and cash payments of an enterprise during a period.

_____   23. (L.O. 6) Determination of cash flows from operating activities requires predicting the amount of cash the entity will collect from customers who purchase the entity's product on account.

_____   24. (L.O. 6) The sale of 12,000 of its ordinary shares by Xerax Company for $22,000 cash would be classified as an investing activity due to the increased investment by company shareholders.

_____   25. (L.O. 6) To arrive at cash provided by operations, an increase in accounts receivable must be deducted from net income, and an increase in accounts payable must be added back to net income.

MULTIPLE CHOICE

Select the best answer for each of the following items and enter the corresponding letter in the space provided.

_____ 1. (L.O. 1) The statement of financial position contributes to financial reporting by providing a basis for all of the following **except**

    A.   computing rates of return.
    B.   evaluating the capital structure of the enterprise.
    C.   determining the increase in cash due to operations.
    D.   assessing the liquidity and financial flexibility of the enterprise.

_____ 2. (L.O. 1) Solvency refers to:

    A.   the ability of an enterprise to pay its debts as they mature.
    B.   the amount of time that is expected to elapse until an asset is realized.
    C.   the amount of time that is expected to elapse until a liability has to be paid.
    D.   the amount of time that is expected to elapse until an asset is converted into cash.

_____ 3. (L.O. 1) One criticism not normally aimed at a statement of financial position prepared using current accounting and reporting standards is:

    A.   failure to reflect current value information.
    B.   the extensive use of separate classifications.
    C.   an extensive use of estimates.
    D.   failure to include items of financial value that cannot be recorded objectively.

_____ 4. (L.O. 1) The primary purpose of the statement of financial position is to reflect

    A.   the firm's potential for growth in stock values in the stock market.
    B.   items of value, debts, and net worth.
    C.   the value of items owned by the firm.
    D.   the status of the firm's assets in case of forced liquidation of the firm.

_____ 5. (L.O. 2) For accounting purposes the "operating cycle concept"

    A.   has become obsolete.
    B.   affects the income statement but not the statement of financial position.
    C.   permits some assets to be classified as current even though they are more than one year removed from becoming cash.
    D.   causes the distinction between current and noncurrent items to depend on whether they will affect cash within one year.

_____ 6. (L.O. 2) If $1,240 cash and a $4,760 note are given in exchange for a delivery truck to be used in a business:

    A.   assets and liabilities will change by the same amount.
    B.   equity will be increased.
    C.   assets will increase and liabilities decrease.
    D.   assets and liabilities will increase but by different amounts.

_____   7. (L.O. 2) Which of the following is not a current asset?

A.   Prepaid property taxes that relate to the next operating period.
B.   The cash surrender value of a life insurance policy carried by a corporation on its president.
C.   Marketable securities purchased as a temporary investment of cash.
D.   Installment notes receivable due over 15 months in accordance with normal trade practices.

_____   8. (L.O. 2) Of the following statements, which best illustrates the fact that the formal distinction made between current and noncurrent assets is somewhat arbitrary?

A.   Cash in a checking account is a current asset, while cash in a savings account is more permanent and is normally classified as noncurrent.
B.   Inventory that may be sold next year, or in the subsequent year as demand dictates may be classified as current or noncurrent.
C.   Accounts receivable due in less than one year or the operating cycle are classified as current assets, while accounts receivable due in longer than one year or the operating cycle are classified as noncurrent.
D.   An amount equal to the current depreciation charge on buildings should be placed in the current assets section at the beginning of the year, because it will be consumed in the next operating cycle.

_____   9. (L.O. 2) Which of the following items should never be included in the current section of the statement of financial position?

A.   Receivable from a customer outstanding for more than a year.
B.   Deferred income taxes resulting from interperiod tax allocation.
C.   Three-year premium for fire insurance on plant and equipment.
D.   A pension fund.

_____   10. (L.O. 2) Of the following items, the one which should be classified as a current asset is

A.   trade installment receivables normally collectible in 20 months.
B.   a deposit on equipment ordered, delivery of which will be made within 7 months.
C.   cash designated for the redemption of callable bonds.
D.   cash surrender value of a life insurance policy of which the company is a beneficiary.

_____   11. (L.O. 2) Prepaid expenses are included in the current assets section of the statement of financial position because

A.   they will be converted into cash within one year or the operating cycle, whichever is longer.
B.   if they had not been already paid they would require the use of cash during the next year or operating cycle.
C.   they were already included in operating expenses on the income statement in the year cash was expended.
D.   they reflect payments that were made in a prior period that will not be charged to expense in the current period.

_____   12. (L.O. 2) One of the main reasons for separating liabilities into current and long-term is:

A.   to provide decision makers with information regarding currently maturing debts.
B.   to separate large and small debts.
C.   to separate capital into its component parts.
D.   to separate total equity into its two basic parts.

_____ 13. (L.O. 2) A liability to be paid next year would not be included in the current liability section of the statement of financial position if

    A.   the operating cycle is less than one year.
    B.   the liability is to be paid with cash that the company expects to earn during the next year.
    C.   the debt is to be retired out of noncurrent assets.
    D.   the liability is the result of a nonoperating debt instrument due with the next year.

_____ 14. (L.O. 2) A characteristic of all assets and liabilities comprising working capital is that they are

    A.   monetary.
    B.   marketable.
    C.   current.
    D.   cash equivalents.

_____ 15. (L.O. 2) If a company converted a short-term note payable into a long-term note payable, this transaction would

    A.   increase both working capital and net income.
    B.   decrease only working capital.
    C.   increase only working capital.
    D.   decrease both working capital and equity.

_____ 16. (L.O. 2) How are the following items handled in computing the total equity section of the statement of financial position?

	Treasury Stock	Share Premium
A.	Added	Added
B.	Added	Subtracted
C.	Subtracted	Added
D.	Subtracted	Subtracted

_____ 17. (L.O. 8) Which of the following statement of financial position classifications would normally require the greatest amount of supplementary disclosure?

    A.   Current assets.
    B.   Current liabilities.
    C.   Plant assets.
    D.   Non-current liabilities.

_____ 18. (L.O. 2) Which of the following reflects proper use of the term "reserve" in the preparation of financial statements?

    A.   The term used to describe amounts deducted from assets, such as "reserve for depreciation."
    B.   The initial term used in connection with an estimated liability, such as "estimated reserve for product warranty."
    C.   The term used to describe the setting aside of funds for the subsequent payment of an existing liability, such as "reserve for bonds payable."
    D.   The term used to describe an all-inclusive account for retained earnings, share premium, and accumulated other comprehensive income.

_____ 19. (L.O. 4) The statement of cash flows provides answers to all of the following questions except:

    A.   Where did the cash come from during the period?
    B.   What was the cash used for during the period?
    C.   What is the impact of inflation on the cash balance at the end of the year?
    D.   What was the change in the cash balance during the period?

_____ 20. (L.O. 6) Which of the following would not be considered a basic source of information useful in preparing a statement of cash flows?

    A.   Selected transaction data.
    B.   Comparative statement of financial positions.
    C.   An analysis of sales by territory.
    D.   The current income statement.

_____ 21. (L.O. 6) The payment of cash dividends to the ordinary shareholders would be reported on a company's statement of cash flows under the classification of

    A.   Operating Activities.
    B.   Financing Activities.
    C.   Investing Activities.
    D.   Significant Transactions.

_____ 22. (L.O. 6) How would the two items shown below be handled in arriving at cash provided by operations in the statement of cash flows?

	Increase in **Accounts Receivable**	**Increase in** **Accounts Payable**
A.	Add to net income	Add to net income
B.	Deduct from net income	Deduct from net income
C.	Add to net income	Deduct from net income
D.	Deduct from net income	Add to net income

_____ 23. (L.O. 7) One of the benefits of the statement of cash flows is that it helps users evaluate financial flexibility. Which of the following explanations is a description of financial flexibility?

    A.   The nearness to cash of assets and liabilities.
    B.   The firm's ability to respond and adapt to financial adversity and unexpected needs and opportunities.
    C.   The firm's ability to pay its debts as they mature.
    D.   The firm's ability to invest in a number of projects with different objectives and costs.

_____ *24. (L.O. 10) Amy Carlson Company had current assets of $12,000, current liabilities of $20,000, net sales of $40,000, cost of goods sold of $24,000, and net income of $8,000. What is Amy Carlson's profit margin on sales?

    A.   80%.
    B.   60%.
    C.   50%.
    D.   20%.

_____ *25. (L.O. 10) Lindsey Corp. is concerned with measuring its ability to meet interest payments as they come due. Lindsey Corp. would most likely use which following ratio?

    A.   Payout ratio.
    B.   Inventory turnover.
    C.   Times interest earned.
    D.   Price earnings ratio.

REVIEW EXERCISES

1. (L.O.1) Schwigert Corporation had a balance in accounts receivable on September 1, 2012, of $33,000. All sales are made on account. During September the corporation collected $30,800 from customers, and at the end of September the accounts receivable totaled $27,500.

Instructions: Compute the amount of sales for September.

2.   (L.O.1 and 2) On December 31, 2012, the total assets of Allen, Inc. were $91,000, and liabilities were $48,000. Allen, Inc. began business January 1, 2008, and had an average net income of $16,000 per year. Total dividends paid for the five-year period were $63,850.

> **Instructions:** Compute Allen, Inc.'s equity balance as of December 31, 2012 and the amount of its original investment.

_____
_____
_____
_____
_____
_____
_____
_____
_____
_____
_____
_____

3.   (L.O.2) Indicate the most preferred statement of financial position classification of each item in Group B by inserting the appropriate letter from Group A in the space provided.

Group A		Group B
A. Current assets.	_____ 1.	Cash fund for plant expansion
B. Property, plant and Equipment	_____ 2.	Preference shares
	_____ 3.	Franchise
C. Long-term investments	_____ 4.	Accrued interest on customers' notes
D. Intangible assets	_____ 5.	Dividend payable in cash
E. Other assets	_____ 6.	Premium ordinary shares
F. Current liabilities	_____ 7.	Net sales
G. Long-term liabilities	_____ 8.	Advances to suppliers
H. Share capital	_____ 9.	Accrued employee wages
I. Share premium	_____ 10.	Unexpired insurance
J. Unappropriated retained earnings	_____ 11.	Ten-year bonds issued to finance plant acquisition
K. Appropriated retained earnings	_____ 12.	Land
	_____ 13.	Uncertain outcome of a pending lawsuit
L. Footnote disclosure	_____ 14.	Undistributed portion of current year's net income
M. Not shown on statement of financial position		
	_____ 15.	Accumulated depreciation
	_____ 16.	Share dividend distributable
	_____ 17.	Discount on bonds payable
	_____ 18.	Sinking fund for bond retirement
	_____ 19.	Patent
	_____ 20.	Purchase commitment (3 years)

4. (L.O.3) The following accounts appeared on the trial balance of Elbert Company at December 31, 2012. All accounts have normal balances.

Notes Payable	$ 64,000	Accounts Receivable	$ 172,800
Accumulated Depreciation — Bldg.	261,000	Prepaid Expenses	18,750
Supplies on Hand	12,600	Customers' Deposits	1,250
Accrued Salaries and Wages	11,400	Ordinary Shares***	375,000
Investments in Debt Securities*	93,800	Unappropriated Retained Earnings	?
Cash	56,750	Inventories (average cost)	526,750
Bonds Payable Due 1/1/2016	400,000	Land at Cost	155,000
Allowance for Doubtful Accts.	2,600	Trading Securities****	24,400
Franchise	64,300	Accrued Interest on Notes	
Notes Receivable	46,000	Payable	650
Income Taxes Payable	52,000	Buildings at Cost	642,000
Preference Shares**	250,000	Accounts Payable	136,650
Appropriated Retained Earnings	98,000	Share Premium	54,600

*   *The company intends to hold the securities until maturity, which is in ten years.*
**   *8% cumulative; $10 par value; 25,000 shares authorized and outstanding.*
*** *$1 par value 400,000 shares authorized; 375,000 shares issued and outstanding.*
**** *The company intends to sell the trading securities in the next year.*

Instructions:
Prepare a classified statement of financial position for Elbert Company at December 31, 2012.

4. *(continued)*

5.   (L.O.8) The information shown below is taken from the accounts of the Robinson Corporation for the year ended December 31, 2012.

Net income	$209,000
Amortization of intangible (franchise)	12,000
Proceeds from issuance of ordinary shares	103,000
Increase in inventory	18,000
Sale of building at a $10,000 gain	85,000
Increase in accounts payable	15,000
Purchase of computer equipment	125,000
Payment of cash dividends	24,000
Depreciation expense	35,000
Increase in accounts receivable	23,000
Payment of mortgage	52,000
Decrease in short-term notes payable	8,000
Sale of land at a $5,000 loss	26,000
Purchase of delivery truck	33,000
Cash at beginning of year	173,000

Instructions:

Prepare a statement of cash flows for Robinson Corporation for the year ended December 31, 2012.

SOLUTIONS TO REVIEW QUESTIONS AND EXERCISES

TRUE-FALSE

1. (F) The statement of financial position reflects a corporation's financial position for a point in time. This accounts for the heading on a statement of financial position, which states "December 31, 20X1," rather than "For the year ended December 31, 20X1."

2. (F) Liquidity describes the amount of time that is expected to elapse until an asset is realized or otherwise converted into cash or until a liability has to be paid. Financial flexibility is the ability of an enterprise to take effective actions to alter the amounts and timing of cash flows so it can respond to unexpected needs and opportunities.

3. (T)

4. (F) The statement of financial position has 3 elements, assets, liabilities, and equity.

5. (F) The non-controlling interest, the portion of equity of subsidiaries not owned by the reporting corporation, is reported as part of equity.

6. (F) Current assets are cash and other assets that are expected to be converted into cash, sold, or consumed either in one year or in the operating cycle, whichever is longer.

7. (T)

8. (F) Held-to-maturity investments are debt securities that the enterprise has the positive intent and ability to hold to maturity. Trading investments are securities bought and held primarily for sale in the near term to generate income on short-term price differences. Available-for-sale investments are securities not classified as held-to-maturity or trading securities.

9. (T)

10. (T)

11. (T)

12. (F) Securities classified as available-for-sale should be reported at fair value. Securities classified as held-to-maturity are reported at cost.

13. (T)

14. (T)

15. (T)

16. (F) A partnership or proprietorship uses individual capital accounts for each owner in the equity section of the statement of financial position. A corporation's equity section shows share capital accounts representing ownership and a retained earnings account that reflects undistributed earnings of the corporation.

17. (F) IFRS does not specify the order or the format in which companies present items in the statement of financial position.

18. (T)

19. (T)

20. (T)

21. (T)

22. (T)

23. (F)   Cash flow from operating activities refers to the amount of cash inflow and cash outflow which result from the activities an entity enters into for the purpose of generating net income. Because an income statement is prepared on an accrual basis, it includes revenues earned and expenses incurred in earning revenues without regard for the receipt or payment of cash. To compute cash flow from operating activities you must add to or deduct from net income those items in the income statement which did not generate or require the use of cash.

24. (F)   When an entity sells its shares for cash it is considered to have entered into a transaction designed to aid in financing the entity's operation. Thus, this transaction would be classified as a financing activity on Xerax Company's statement of cash flows. Investing activities refer to those activities designed to utilize cash to acquire debt and equity investments of other companies (bonds and shares) as well as property, plant, and equipment.

25. (T)

MULTIPLE CHOICE

1. (C)   The statement of financial position provides a basis for computing rates of return based on asset growth. The statement of financial position also includes information used in evaluating capital structure (equity section) and assessing the liquidity and financial flexibility (assets and liabilities) of the enterprise. However, to determine the increase in cash due to operations one should refer to the statement of cash flows.

2. (A)   Solvency refers to the ability of an enterprise to pay its debts as they mature. Alternatives (B), (C) and (D) are all part of the definition of liquidity.

3. (B)   The statement of financial position is criticized for its failure to reflect current value (A), the extensive use of estimates in its preparation (C), and its failure to include items of financial value that cannot be measured objectively (D). The statement of financial position is rarely, if ever, criticized for its division of items into separate classifications.

4. (B)   The primary purpose of the statement of financial position is to reflect items of value, debts, and net worth. The three classes of items that appear on the statement of financial position are assets (items of value measured by historical costs or net realizable values), liabilities (debts and obligations of the firm which represent creditor claims to the assets of the firm), and equity (the net worth of the owners as represented by their claims to the firm's assets). The statement of financial position reflects these items as of a particular date.

5. (C)   The operating cycle concept is used as a basis for classifying current items. The operating cycle of a firm is the length of time elapsed from the time cash is expended for such items as inventory to the time it converts the inventory back to cash. When the operating cycle is longer than 12 months, the longer period should be used. Therefore, the operating cycle concept does allow some assets to be classified as current even though their conversion into cash will not take place within one year.

6. (A)   This transaction causes assets to increase by $4,760. The asset account truck increases by $6,000 (the purchase price), but assets also decrease by $1,240 due to the cash payment. Liabilities increase by $4,760 as a result of the issuance of the note.

7. (B)   Generally, the rule is that if an asset is to be turned into cash, sold, or consumed either in one year or the operating cycle, whichever is longer, it is classified as current. The cash surrender value of a life insurance policy is not expected to be turned into cash, etc. within a year or the operating cycle. This item is normally shown in the long-term investments section of the statement of financial position.

8. (D)   Cash is a current asset whether it is in a checking or savings account. Inventory is a current asset at the time the statement of financial position is prepared even though it may not all be sold in the subsequent year, as it is held for sale in the normal course of business. The accounts receivable that are not collectible in the coming year should be classified as a noncurrent asset. However, while the theoretical treatment of next year's depreciation should be shown as a current asset, common practice is to ignore the formal distinction in this case.

9. (D)   A pension fund is an investment made by a company for the retirement benefits of its employees. These funds will not be converted to cash for use in the business nor will they be used to liquidate current liabilities. The other three alternatives (A, B, and C) include items that, although somewhat unusual, could be classified as current.

10. (A)   A current asset is either cash, something that will be converted into cash or consumed in one year or the operating cycle, whichever is longer. If installment sales are a normal part of operations, they may be classified as current assets because they will be converted into cash within the company's normal operating cycle. Answer (B) is incorrect because the cash deposit is a part of the cost of the machinery ordered and should be classified as a noncurrent asset. Answer (C) is incorrect because cash that is restricted for an indefinite period of time should be classified as a noncurrent asset. Answer (D) is incorrect because a life insurance policy is not likely to be canceled in the near future; therefore, its cash surrender value would be most appropriately reported in the long-term investment section of the statement of financial position.

11. (B)   Prepaid expenses are expenditures already made for benefits to be received within one year or the operating cycle, whichever is longer. The cash has already been expended, but its inclusion on the income statement will not occur until the benefit has been received by the company.

12. (A)   Alternative (B) is incorrect because dividing liabilities between current and long-term has nothing to do with the amount of the debt. Alternative (C) is incorrect because the term "capital" is not a correct term to use in describing debt. Alternative (D) is incorrect because total equity includes both debt and equity.

13. (C)   When the operating cycle is less than one year and/or the debt will be paid with cash (alternatives A & B) the item is properly classified as a current liability. Also, all debt acquired or assumed by a company is a liability of that company. However, when the debt is retired out of noncurrent assets it should not be classified as current even if it meets the operating cycle/one year criteria.

14. (C)   A characteristic of all assets and liabilities comprising working capital is that they are current. The accounting profession defines working capital as the excess of current assets over current liabilities. Answers (A), (B), and (D) are incorrect because not all working capital assets and liabilities are monetary (e.g., inventory), marketable (e.g., federal income taxes payable), or cash equivalents (e.g., prepaid expenses).

15. (C)   Conversion of a short-term note payable (current liability) into a long-term note payable (noncurrent liability) would increase working capital. Working capital is the difference between current assets and current liabilities. Conversion of the short-term note payable reduces current liabilities and does not affect current assets. Answers (A) and (D) are incorrect because there is no effect on net income or equity.

16. (C)   Treasury stock (the company's own stock reacquired and not canceled) is shown as a reduction of equity, while share premium is added to the equity section of the statement of financial position.

17. (D)   Non-current liabilities normally require the greatest amount of supplementary disclosure. This is because the terms of all non-current liability agreements, including maturity date or dates, rate of interest, nature of obligation, and any security pledged to support the debt, should be disclosed. The other classifications do require supplementary disclosure, but rarely is it as extensive as that required for non-current liabilities.

18. (D)   Many companies reporting under IFRS often use the term "reserve" as an all-inclusive catch-all for items such as retained earnings, share premium, and accumulated other comprehensive income.

19. (C) The statement of cash flows does not adjust the cash balance for the effects of inflation or deflation during the period. Such an amount can be determined by the use of certain indices, but this is not a function of the statement of cash flows.

20. (C) A statement of cash flows deals with gross inflows and outflows of cash. An analysis of sales by territory would generate no information about the cash flow from the sales.

21. (B) Financing activities involve liability and equity items. They include (1) obtaining capital from owners and providing them with a return on (and a return of) their investment and (b) borrowing money from creditors and repaying the amounts borrowed.

22. (D) To arrive at cash provided by operation, the increase in accounts receivable must be deducted from net income, and the increase in accounts payable must be added back to net income.

23. (B) Financial flexibility refers to a firm's ability to respond and adapt to financial adversity and unexpected needs and opportunities. Alternative "D" is an indication of flexibility, but does not take into account adversity and unexpected needs. The nearness to cash of assets and liabilities is a firm's liquidity, and the firm's ability to pay its debts refers to solvency.

*24. (D) The profit margin on sales is 20%. Profit margin on sales is calculated by dividing net income by net sales ($8,000 ÷ $40,000).

*25. (C) The times interest earned ratio measures the ability of a company to meet its interest payments as they come due.

REVIEW EXERCISES

1.
Beginning Receivable balance..	$33,000
Ending Receivable balance..	27,500
Net change	($5,500)

Collection during September...	$30,800
Less decrease in Receivables...	(5,500)
September Sales...	$25,300

2. December 31, 2012:

Assets	=	Liabilities	+	Equity
$91,000	=	$48,000	+	$43,000

Original Investment:

12-31-12 Equity..		$43,000
Net Income 1-1-08—12-31-12 (16,000 × 5)	$80,000	
Less Dividends Paid	63,850	
Increase in Equity from Operations.......................................		16,150
Original Investment		$26,850

3.

1.	(C)	6.	(I)	11.	(G)	16.	(H)
2.	(H)	7.	(M)	12.	(B)	17.	(G)
3.	(D)	8.	(A)	13.	(L)	18.	(C)
4.	(A)	9.	(F)	14.	(J)	19.	(D)
5.	(F)	10.	(A)	15.	(B)	20.	(L) or (M)

4.

Elbert Company
Statement of Financial Position
December 31, 2012

Assets

Non-Current Assets
Long-term investments

Securities to be held-to-maturity		$ 93,800

Property, plant, and equipment

Land	$155,000	
Building	$642,000	
Less accumulated depreciation	261,000	381,000
Total property, plant and equipment..........		536,000

Intangible assets

Franchise		64,300
Total non-current assets		694,100

Current Assets

Inventories at average cost		526,750
Accounts receivable..	172,800	
Less allowance for doubtful accounts................	2,600	170,200
Notes receivable		46,000
Prepaid expenses		18,750
Trading securities		24,400
Supplies on hand		12,600
Cash		56,750
Total current assets		855,450
Total assets..		$1,549,550

Equity and Liabilities

Equity

Share capital - preference, 8% cumulative, $10 par value, 25,000 shares authorized and outstanding		$250,000
Share capital – ordinary, $1 par value, 400,000 shares authorized, 375,000 shares issued and outstanding		375,000
Share premium..		54,600
Retained Earnings		
Appropriated	$ 98,000	
Unappropriated	106,000	204,000
Total equity		$ 883,600

Long-term debt

Bonds payable - due 1/1/2016...................................	400,000	
Total non-current liabilities		400,000

Current liabilities

Notes payable	64,000	
Accounts payable	136,650	
Accrued interest on notes payable............................	650	
Income tax payable...	52,000	
Accrued salaries and wages......................................	11,400	
Customers' deposits	1,250	
Total current liabilities......................................		265,950
Total equity and liabilities..........................		$1,549,550

5.

Robinson Corporation
Statement of Cash Flows
For the Year Ended December 31, 2012

Cash flows from operating activities

Net income		$209,000
Adjustments to reconcile net income to net		
cash provided by operating activities:		
Depreciation expense	$35,000	
Amortization expense	12,000	
Gain on sale of building	(10,000)	
Loss on sale of land	5,000	
Increase in inventory	(18,000)	
Increase in accounts payable	15,000	
Decrease in short-term notes	(8,000)	
Increase in accounts receivable	(23,000)	8,000
Net cash provided by operations		217,000
Cash flows from investing activities		
Sale of building	85,000	
Sale of land	26,000	
Purchase of computer equipment	(125,000)	
Purchase of delivery truck	(33,000)	
Net cash used by investing activities		(47,000)
Cash flows from financing activities		
Issuance of ordinary shares	103,000	
Payment of cash dividends	(24,000)	
Payment of mortgage	(52,000)	
Net cash provided by financing activities		27,000
Net increase in cash		197,000
Cash at beginning of year		173,000
Cash at end of year		$370,000

6

Accounting and the Time Value of Money

CHAPTER LEARNING OBJECTIVES

1. Identify accounting topics where the time value of money is relevant.
2. Distinguish between simple and compound interest.
3. Use appropriate compound interest tables.
4. Identify variables fundamental to solving interest problems.
5. Solve future and present value of 1 problems.
6. Solve future value of ordinary and annuity due problems.
7. Solve present value of ordinary and annuity due problems.
8. Solve present value problems related to deferred annuities and bonds.
9. Apply expected cash flows to present value measurement.

CHAPTER REVIEW

1. (L.O. 1) Chapter 6 discusses the essentials of compound interest, annuities and present value. These techniques are being used in many areas of financial reporting where the relative values of cash inflows and outflows are measured and analyzed. The material presented in Chapter 6 will provide a sufficient background for application of these techniques to topics presented in subsequent chapters.

2. **Compound interest, annuity, and present value** techniques can be applied to many of the items found in financial statements. In accounting, these techniques can be used to measure the relative values of cash inflows and outflows, evaluate alternative investment opportunities, and determine periodic payments necessary to meet future obligations. Some of the accounting items to which these techniques may be applied are: (a) **notes receivable and payable,** (b) **leases,** (c) **pensions,** (d) **long-term assets,** (e) **sinking funds,** (f) **business combinations,** (g) **disclosures,** and (h) **installment contracts.**

Nature of Interest

3. (L.O. 2) **Interest** is the payment for the use of money. It is normally stated as a percentage of the amount borrowed (principal), calculated on a yearly basis. For example, an entity may borrow $5,000 from a bank at 7% interest. The yearly interest on this loan is $350. If the loan is repaid in six months, the interest due would be 1/2 of $350, or $175. This type of interest computation is known as **simple interest** because the interest is computed on the amount of the principal only. The formula for simple interest can be expressed as $p \times i \times n$ where p is the principal, i is the rate of interest for one period, and n is the number of periods.

Compound Interest

4. (L.O. 2) **Compound interest** is the process of computing interest on the principal plus any interest previously earned. Referring to the example in (2) above, if the loan was for two years with interest compounded annually, the second year's interest would be $374.50 (principal plus first year's interest multiplied by 7%). Compound interest is most common in business situations where large amounts of capital are financed over long periods of time. Simple interest is applied mainly to short-term investments and debts due in one year or less. The frequency with which interest is compounded can make a substantial difference in the level of return achieved.

5. In discussing compound interest, the term **period** is used in place of **years** because interest may be compounded daily, weekly, monthly, and so on. Thus, to convert the **annual interest rate** to the **compounding period interest rate,** divide the annual interest rate by the number of compounding periods in a year. Also, the number of periods over which interest will be compounded is calculated by multiplying the number of years involved by the number of compounding periods in a year.

Time Value of Money Tables

6. (L.O. 3) Compound interest tables have been developed to aid in the computation of present values and annuities. Careful analysis of the problem as to which compound interest tables will be applied is necessary to determine the appropriate procedures to follow.

7. The following is a summary of the contents of the five types of compound interest tables:

"Future value of 1" table. Contains the amounts to which 1 will accumulate if deposited now at a specified rate and left for a specified number of periods.

"Present value of 1" table. Contains the amount that must be deposited now at a specified rate of interest to amount to 1 at the end of a specified number of periods.

"Future value of an ordinary annuity of 1" table. Contains the amount to which periodic rents of 1 will accumulate if the rents are invested at a specified rate of interest and are continued for a specified number of periods. (This table may also be used as a basis for converting to the amount of an annuity due of 1.)

"Present value of an ordinary annuity of 1" table. Contains the amounts that must be deposited now at a specified rate of interest to permit withdrawals of 1 at the end of regular periodic intervals for the specified number of periods.

"Present value of an annuity due of 1" table. Contains the amounts that must be deposited now at a specified rate of interest to permit withdrawals of 1 at the beginning of regular periodic intervals for the specified number of periods.

8.   (L.O. 4) Certain concepts are fundamental to all compound interest problems. These concepts are:

   a.   **Rate of Interest.** The annual rate that must be adjusted to reflect the length of the compounding period if less than one year.
   b.   **Number of Time Periods.** The number of compounding periods (a period may be equal to or less than a year).
   c.   **Future Amount.** The value at a future date of a given sum or sums invested assuming compound interest.
   d.   **Present Value.** The value now (present time) of a future sum or sums discounted assuming compound interest.

9.   (L.O. 5) The remaining review paragraphs pertain to **present values** and **future amounts.** The text material covers the following six major time value of money concepts:

   a.   Future value of a single sum.
   b.   Present value of a single sum.
   c.   Future value of an ordinary annuity.
   d.   Future value of an annuity due.
   e.   Present value of an ordinary annuity.
   f.   Present value of an annuity due.

10.   Single-sum problems generally fall into one of two categories. The first category consists of problems that require the computation of the **unknown future amount** of a known single sum of money that is invested now for a certain number of periods at a certain interest rate. The second category consists of problems that require the computation of the **unknown present value** of a known single sum of money in the future that is discounted for a certain number of periods at a certain interest rate.

Present Value

11.   The concept of **present value** is described as the amount that must be invested now to produce a known future value. This is the opposite of the compound interest discussion in which the present value was known and the future value was determined. An example of the type of question addressed by the present value method is: What amount must be invested today at 6% interest compounded annually to accumulate $5,000 at the end of 10 years? In this question the present value method is used to determine the initial dollar amount to be invested. The present value method can also be used to determine the **number of years** or the **interest rate** when the other facts are known.

\Future Amount of an Annuity

12.   (L.O. 6) An **annuity** is a series of equal periodic payments or receipts called **rents.** An annuity requires that the rents be paid or received at equal time intervals, and that compound interest be applied. The **future amount of an annuity** is the sum (future value) of all the rents (payments or receipts) plus the accumulated compound interest on them. If the rents occur at the end of each time period, the annuity is known as an **ordinary annuity.** If rents occur at the beginning of each time period, it is an **annuity due.** Thus, in determining the amount of an annuity for a given set of facts, there will be one less interest period for an ordinary annuity than for an annuity due.

Present Value of an Annuity

13.   (L.O. 7) The **present value of an annuity** is a sum of money invested today at compound interest that will provide for a series of equal withdrawals for a specified number of future periods. If the annuity is an **ordinary annuity,** the initial sum of money is invested at the beginning of the first period and withdrawals are made at the end of each period. If the annuity is an **annuity due,** the initial sum of money is invested at the beginning of the first period and withdrawals are made at the beginning of each

period starting with the first period. Thus, the first rent withdrawn in an annuity due occurs on the day after the initial sum of money is invested. When computing the present value of an annuity, for a given set of facts, there will be one less discount period for an annuity due than for an ordinary annuity.

Deferred Annuities

14. (L.O. 8) A **deferred annuity** is an annuity in which two or more periods must pass, after it has been arranged, before the rents will begin. For example, an ordinary annuity of 10 annual rents deferred five years means that no rents will occur during the first five years, and that the first of the 10 rents will occur at the end of the sixth year. An annuity due of 10 annual rents deferred five years means that no rents will occur during the first five years, and that the first of the 10 rents will occur at the beginning of the sixth year. The fact that an annuity is a deferred annuity affects the computation of the present value. However, the **future amount of a deferred annuity** is the same as the amount of an annuity not deferred because there is no accumulation or investment on which interest may accrue.

15. A long-term bond produces two cash flows: (1) periodic interest payments during the life of the bond, and (2) the principal (face value) paid at maturity. At the date of issue, bond buyers determine the present value of these two cash flows using the market rate of interest.

16. (L.O. 9) *International Accounting Standard t No. 36* introduces an expected cash flow approach that uses a range of cash flows and incorporates the probabilities of those cash flows to provide a more relevant measurement of present value. The IASB takes the position that after the expected cash flows are computed, they should be discounted by the **risk-free rate of return,** which is defined as **the pure rate of return plus the expected inflation rate.**

Financial Calculators

*17. Business professionals, after mastering the above concepts, will often use a financial (business) calculator to solve time value of money problems. When using financial calculators, the five most common keys used to solve time value of money problems are:

$$\boxed{N} \quad \boxed{I} \quad \boxed{PV} \quad \boxed{PMT} \quad \boxed{FV}$$

where:
N =   number of periods.
I =   interest rate per period (some calculators use I/YR or i).
PV =   present value (occurs at the beginning of the first period).
PMT =   payment (all payments are equal, and none are skipped).
FV =   future value (occurs at the end of the last period).

DEMONSTRATION PROBLEMS

1.   Compute the future amount of 10 periodic payments of $5,000 each made at the beginning of each period and compounded at 6%.

Solution:

1.	Future amount of ordinary annuity for 10 periods of 6% (Table 6-3)	13.18079
2.	Factor (1 + .06)	× 1.06
3.	Future amount of annuity due for 10 periods of 12%	13.97164
4.	Periodic payment (rent)	$ 5,000
5.	Future amount	$69,858.19

Solution:

Inputs: Set payments to "Begin"

10	6	0	-5,000	?
N	I	PV	PMT	FV

Answer: $69,858.19

2.   Compute the present value of 14 receipts of $800 each received at the beginning of each period, discounted at 10% compound interest.

Solution:

This is the present value of an annuity due of $800 payments for 14 periods at 10%.

1.	Present value of an annuity due for 14 periods at 10% (Table 6-5)	8.10336
2.	Periodic receipt (rent)	× $800
3.	Present value	$6,482.69

Solution:

Inputs: Set payments to "Begin"

14	10	?	−800	0
N	I	PV	PMT	FV

Answer: $6,482.69

3.   How much must be invested at the end of each year to accumulate a fund of $50,000 at the end of 10 years, if the fund earns 9% interest, compounded annually?

Solution:

Known final amount (a)	$ 50,000
Divide (a) by the amount of an ordinary annuity of $1 for	
10 years at 9% (Table 6-3)	÷ 15.19293
The result is the periodic rent that would accumulate $50,000 at the end of	
10 years at 9% interest	$ 3,291

Solution:

Inputs: Set payments to "End"

     10   9   0   ?   50,000

     N   I   PV   PMT   FV

Answer: <u>$3,291</u>

4. An asset has a cash price of $9,593.37. The purchaser agrees to pay $2,000 down and 4 annual payments of $2,500 at the end of each year. Assuming compounding on an annual basis, what is the stated interest rate of this transaction?

Solution:

Cash price	$9,593.37
Down payment	2,000.00
Net amount due	$7,593.37

$$\$7{,}593.37 \div \$2{,}500 = 3.03735$$

Go to Table 6-4 and find the factor 3.03735 in row 4 and read up to the top of the column to find the appropriate interest rate which is **12%**.

Inputs: Set payments to "End"

     4   ? $7,593.37   –2,500   0

     N   I   PV   PMT   FV

Answer:

$$\$9{,}593.37 - \$2{,}000 = \underline{\$7{,}593.37}$$

5. A fund of $25,000 is deposited in a savings account earning a 12% stated rate but interest is compounded quarterly (3%). What is the maximum amount that could be withdrawn quarterly at the end of each quarter for the next 10 years?

Solution:

$$PV = R (PVF\text{-}OA_{n,i})$$
$$\$25{,}000 = R (PVF\text{-}OA_{40,\,3\%})$$
$$\$25{,}000 = R (23.11477)$$
$$\$1{,}081.56 = R$$

Thus, $1,081.56 can be withdrawn at the end of each quarter for the next 10 years. The solution requires that the 12% interest rate be divided by 4 and that the 10 years be multiplied by 4 due to the quarterly compounding. Use the 3% column in Table 6-4 for 40 periods.

Solution:

Inputs: Set payments to "End"

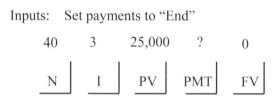

40	3	25,000	?	0
N	I	PV	PMT	FV

Answer: $1,081.56

GLOSSARY

Annuity.	A series of equal dollar amounts (rents) that are paid or received periodically at equal intervals of time.
Annuity due.	An annuity whereby each rent is payable (receivable) at the beginning of the period.
Compound interest.	Interest accrues on the unpaid interest of past periods as well as on the principal.
Credit risk rate of interest.	The amount of interest that depends on the financial stability, profitability, etc., of a business enterprise.
Deferred annuity.	An annuity in which the rents begin after a specified number of periods.
Expected inflation rate of interest.	The amount of interest that is based on inflationary or deflationary expectations.
Future value.	The value at a future date of a given sum or sums invested assuming compound interest.
Future value of 1 table.	Contains the amounts to which 1 will accumulate if deposited now at a specified rate and left for a specified number of periods.
Future value of an ordinary annuity of 1 table.	Contains the amounts to which periodic rents of 1 will accumulate if the payments are invested at the **end** of each period at a specified rate of interest for a specified number of periods.
Interest.	Payment for the use of money.
Ordinary annuity.	An annuity whereby each rent is payable (receivable) at the end of the period.
Present value.	The value now (present time) of a future sum or sums discounted assuming compound interest.
Present value of 1 table.	Contains the amounts that must be deposited now at a specified rate of interest to equal 1 at the end of a specified number of periods.

Present value of an annuity due of 1 table.	Contains the amounts that must be deposited now at a specified rate of interest to permit withdrawals of 1 at the **beginning** of regular periodic intervals for the specified number of periods.
Present value of an ordinary annuity of 1 table.	Contains the amounts that must be deposited now at a specified rate of interest to permit withdrawals of 1 at the **end** of regular periodic intervals for the specified number of periods.
Principal.	The amount borrowed or invested.
Pure rate of interest.	The amount at lender would charge if there were no possibilities of default and no expectation of inflation.
Simple interest.	Interest on principal only, regardless of interest that may have accrued in the past.

CHAPTER OUTLINE

Fill in the outline presented below.

(L.O. 1) Present Value-Based Accounting Measurements

Nature of Interest

(L.O. 2) Simple Interest

Compound Interest

(L.O. 4) Fundamental Variables

(L.O. 5) Future Amount of a Single Sum

Present Value of a Single Sum

(L.O. 6) Future Amount of an Ordinary Annuity

Chapter Outline *(continued)*

Future Amount of an Annuity Due

(L.O. 7) Present Value of an Ordinary Annuity

Present Value of an Annuity Due

(L.O. 8) Deferred Annuities and Bonds

(L.O. 9) Expected Cash Flows

REVIEW QUESTIONS AND EXERCISES

TRUE-FALSE

Indicate whether each of the following is true (T) or false (F) in the space provided.

_____ 1. (L.O. 1) Present value techniques can be used in valuing receivables and payables that carry no stated interest rate.

_____ 2. (L.O. 2) The amount of interest on a $1,000, 6%, 6-month note is the same as the amount of interest on a $1,000, 3%, 1-year note.

_____ 3. (L.O. 2) In the formula for compound interest, the number of periods refers to the number of months an obligation will be outstanding.

_____ 4. (L.O. 2) The major difference between compound interest and simple interest lies in the fact that compound interest is computed twice each year, whereas simple interest is computed only once.

_____ 5. (L.O. 2) The growth in principal is the same under both compound and simple interest if only one compounding period is involved.

_____ 6. (L.O. 3) If interest is compounded quarterly and the annual interest rate is 8%, the compounding period interest rate is 4%.

_____ 7. (L.O. 4) Present value is the amount that must be invested now to produce a known future amount.

_____ 8. (L.O. 6) An annuity requires that periodic rents always be the same even though the interval between the rents may vary.

_____ 9. (L.O. 6) An annuity is classified as an ordinary annuity if the rents occur at the end of the period; it is classified as an annuity due if the rents occur at the beginning of the period.

_____ 10. (L.O. 6) The ordinary annuity table may be used to compute the periodic rents when the desired future amount and the present value of the annuity are not known.

_____ 11. (L.O. 6) Periodic interest earnings under an ordinary annuity will always be lower by one period's interest than the interest earned by an annuity due.

_____ 12. (L.O. 7) The present value of an ordinary annuity is the present value of series of rents to be made at equal intervals in the future.

_____ 13. (L.O. 7) The number of rents exceeds the number of discount periods under the present value of an ordinary annuity.

_____ 14. (L.O. 7) The future amount of a deferred annuity is normally greater than the future amount of an annuity not deferred.

_____ 15. (L.O. 7) The valuation of a sum as of an earlier date involves a determination of present value; the valuation of a sum as of a later date involves a determination of a future value.

MULTIPLE CHOICE

Select the best answer for each of the following items and enter the corresponding letter in the space provided.

_____ 1. (L.O. 3) Which of the following tables would show the largest value for an interest rate of 10% for 8 periods?

    A. Future amount of 1 table.
    B. Present value of 1 table.
    C. Future amount of an ordinary annuity of 1 table.
    D. Present value of an ordinary annuity of 1 table.

_____ 2. (L.O. 3) On June 1, 2012, Walsh Company sold some equipment to Fischer Company. The two companies entered into an installment sales contract at a rate of 8%. The contract required 8 equal annual payments with the first payment due on June 1, 2012. What type of compound interest table is appropriate for this situation?

    A. Present value of an annuity due of 1 table.
    B. Present value of an ordinary annuity of 1 table.
    C. Future amount of an ordinary annuity of 1 table.
    D. Future amount of 1 table.

_____ 3. (L.O. 3) Which of the following transactions would best use the present value of an annuity due of 1 table.

    A. Diamond Bar, Inc. rents a truck for 5 years with annual rental payments of $20,000 to be made at the beginning of each year.

    B. Michener Co. rents a warehouse for 7 years with annual rental payments of $120,000 to be made at the end of each year.

    C. Durant, Inc. borrows $20,000 and has agreed to pay back the principal plus interest in three years.

    D. Babbitt, Inc. wants to deposit a lump sum to accumulate $50,000 for the construction of a new parking lot in 4 years.

_____ 4. (L.O. 5) Bob Geimer plans on going on vacation to Asia in four years. The trip will cost $4,000. He proposes to finance the trip by investing a sum of money now at 9% compound interest. How much should Bob invest now in order to obtain his goal of $4,000?

    A. $2,474.67
    B. $2,654.35
    C. $2,833.72
    D. $3,088.72

_____ 5. (L.O. 5) What amount should be deposited in a bank today at an interest rate of 10% to grow to $2,000 four years from today?

    A. $2,000/0.68301
    B. $2,000 × 0.90909 × 3
    C. ($2,000 × 0.90909) + ($2,000 × 0.82645) + ($2,000 × 0.75132) + ($2,000 × 0.68301)
    D. $2,000 × 0.68301

_____ 6. (L.O. 5) What amount should Spencer Forman have in his 6% bank account today before withdrawal if he needs $3,000 each year for three years with the first withdrawal to be made today and each subsequent withdrawal at one-year intervals? (He is to have exactly a zero balance in his bank account after the third withdrawal.)

    A. $3,000 + ($3,000 × 0.94340) + ($3,000 × 0.89000)
    B. ($3,000/0.83962) × 3
    C. ($3,000 × 0.94340) ∣ ($3,000 × 0.89000) + ($3,000 × 0.83962)
    D. ($3,000/0.94340) × 3

_____ 7. (L.O. 5) If J.J. Morse put $1,000 in a 12% savings account today, what amount of cash would be available 3 years from now?

    A. $1,000 × .71178
    B. $1,000 × .71178 × 3
    C. $1,000/.71178
    D. ($1,000/.89286) × 3

_____ 8. (L.O. 6) Kimberly Nelson, a computer programmer, wishes to create her own retirement fund. Kimberly deposits $4,000 today in a fixed rate savings account that earns 5% interest. She plans to deposit $4,000 every year for the next 24 years (total of 25 deposits). How much cash will she have accumulated in her retirement account when she retires in 25 years?

   A. $186,908
   B. $190,908
   C. $194,908
   D. $200,454

_____ 9. (L.O. 6) Jeanie Pearson plans to buy a golf course in 10 years. Because of cash flow problems, Jeanie is able to budget deposits of $900,000 that are expected to earn 10% annually only at the end of the seventh, eighth, ninth, and tenth periods. What future amount will Jeanie accumulate at the end of the tenth year?

   A. $3,600,000
   B. $3,960,000
   C. $4,176,900
   D. $6,902,631

_____ 10. (L.O. 7) Sharon Walsh has developed and patented a computer chip that allows telecommunications in race cars to become more efficient. She agrees to sell the patent to Pensca for five annual payments of $50,000 each. The payments are to begin three years from today. Given an annual rate of 6%, what is the present value of the five payments?

   A. $176,839
   B. $187,450
   C. $210,618
   D. $218,820

REVIEW EXERCISES

1.   Listed below are a series of questions. These questions can be answered using the methods presented in Chapter 6.

Instructions:

a.   Match each question with the method listed below that would be used in providing a solution.
.
b.   Compute the answer to each of the 10 questions listed below and on the right.

METHOD

A.   Present Value or Future Value of a Single Sum
B.   Future Value of an Ordinary Annuity
C.   Future Value of an Annuity Due
D.   Present Value of an Ordinary Annuity
E.   Present Value of an Annuity Due
F.   Present Value of a Deferred Annuity

QUESTIONS

_____ 1. How much will Tom receive if he invests $1,000 for 1 year at 5%?

_____ 2. How much should Bob deposit at the end of each 6-month period to accumulate $20,000 when he graduates in 4 years assuming that he can earn an annual rate of 10% compounded semiannually?

_____ 3. What rate of interest must Connie earn on an investment of $60,000 to be able to withdraw $9,000 at the beginning of each year for the next 10 years?

_____ 4. What amount should Ray invest now at 12% to provide 5 payments of $5,000 at the end of each ycar, starting 3 years from now?

_____ 5. How many years will it take to accumulate $20,000 if Brent invests $1,845 at 10%?

_____ 6. If Daisy invests $3,000 at 8%, with interest computcd on the principal plus undistributed interest, how much will she have at the end of 10 years (annual compounding)?

_____ 7. If Pat has $15,000 in a bank earning 6% interest compounded annually, how much can he withdraw at the end of each year for the next 8 years?

_____ 8. At what annually compounded interest rate must Dave invest $25,331 to provide $50,000 at the end of 6 years?

_____ 9. How much should Karen deposit on each birthday beginning on her twentieth birthday to accumulate $50,000 on her 50th birthday, assuming that she can earn 12% interest compounded annually (no deposit on her fiftieth birthday)?

_____ 10. How much should Mark set aside now, assuming that he can earn 8% interest compounded annually, so he can withdraw $10,000 at the end of each year for the next 10 years?

SOLUTIONS TO REVIEW QUESTIONS

TRUE-FALSE

1. (T)

2. (T)

3. (F)   In the formula for compound interest the number of periods refers to the number of times interest is compounded. Interest is generally expressed in terms of an annual rate; however, in many business circumstances, the compounding period is less than a year (daily, monthly, quarterly, semiannually, etc.). In such circumstances the annual interest rate must be converted to correspond to the length of the period. This is done by dividing the annual rate by the number of compounding periods per year.

4. (F)   Simple interest is the term used to describe interest that is computed on the amount of the principal only. Compound interest is the term used to describe interest that is compounded on principal and on any interest earned that has not been paid or withdrawn.

5. (T)

6. (F)   In this case the compounding interest rate is 2% rather than 4%. This is computed by dividing the annual rate (8%) by the number of compounding periods per year (4).

7. (T)

8. (F)   An annuity requires that (a) the periodic payments or receipts (called rents) always be the same, (b) the interval between such rents always be the same, and (c) the interest be compounded once each interval.

9. (T)

10. (F)   If the desired future amount or present value of an annuity are not known, the periodic rents cannot be computed.

11. (T)

12. (T)

13. (F)   The present value of an ordinary annuity is the present value of a series of rents equal to the number of discount periods.

14. (F)   Because there is no accumulation or investment on which interest may accrue, the future amount of a deferred annuity is the same as the future amount of an annuity not deferred.

15. (T)

MULTIPLE CHOICE

1. (C)   The future amount of an ordinary annuity of 1 table would show the largest value for an interest rate of 10% for 8 periods. Answer (A) is incorrect because the future amount of 1 table only calculates the future amount of a single sum whereas the future amount of an ordinary annuity of 1 table calculates the future amount of a stream of payments. Answer (B) is incorrect because the present value of 1 table includes values of less than 1 whereas the future amount of an ordinary annuity of 1 table includes values greater than 1. Answer (D) is incorrect because the present value of an ordinary annuity of 1 table calculates a stream of payments back to the present whereas the future value of an ordinary annuity of 1 table calculates a stream of payments forward to the future; thus the future amount is greater than the present amount because it is earning more interest.

2. (A)   The present value of an annuity due of 1 table would be the appropriate table for this situation. The present value of an annuity due involves the present value of equal future annual payments due **at the beginning** of the annual period. Answer (B) is incorrect because it concerns the present value of equal future annual payments due at the end of the annual period (ordinary annuity). Answers (C) and (D) are incorrect because they involve accumulations of an annuity and of a single amount, respectively, into some future value.

3. (A)   The present value of annuity due of 1 table involves equal periodic rents which become due **at the beginning** of regular periodic intervals. Therefore a lease which requires the initial rental payment to be made upon signing the lease would be the correct answer. Answer (B) is incorrect because it would use the present value of an ordinary annuity of 1 table because the rental payments are due at the end of the regular periodic intervals. Answer (C) is incorrect because it involves the future amount of a single sum. Answer (D) is incorrect because it involves the present value of a single sum.

4. (C)   This problem involves the present value of a single sum. Using Table 6-2 for 9% at 4 periods, the value of .70843 is multiplied by $4,000 to obtain the amount of $2,833.72.

5. (D)   The amount to be deposited today (present value) to grow to $2,000 (future value) four years from now if the bank pays 10% annual compound interest can be calculated by multiplying the desired future value ($2,000) by the present value factor for 4 periods at 10% per period (0.68301). The correct answer is $2,000 × 0.68301.

6. (A)   The requirement is to find the amount Spencer Forman should have in his bank account today (present value) if he desires to withdraw $3,000 each year for 3 years with the first $3,000 withdrawal occurring today. Normally the present value of an annuity due table for 1 could be used for this problem; however, such an answer was not provided in the choices given. Instead, the present value of this future series of withdrawals can be calculated by using the present value of 1 table and summing the present value of $3,000 to be received now ($3,000) and, the present value of $3,000 to be received 1 period from now ($3,000 × 0.94340) and the present value of $3,000 to be received 2 periods from now ($3,000 × 0.89000). This series of withdrawals follows the pattern of an annuity due; that is, the withdrawals of the amounts take place at the beginning of an interest period. Consequently the first withdrawal does not earn interest. Answer (C) is incorrect because it describes an ordinary annuity situation where the withdrawals are made at the end of the interest period; that is, the first withdrawal would have had to be made one interest period from now.

7.   (C)   The requirement is to determine the calculation needed to find the future value of $1,000 deposited in the bank today. The appropriate table to use would be the future amount of 1 table; however, the answers do not provide that answer so the present value of 1 table can be used to calculate the future value in the following manner:

Present value = Future Value × Present Value Factor for 3 Periods

Let X = Future Value

$1,000 = X(0.71178)

$1,000/0.71178 = X

8.   (D)   Using the future value of an ordinary annuity of 1 table, the solution is computed as follows:

Future value of an ordinary annuity of 1 for 25 periods at 5%	47.72710
Factor (1 + .05)	× 1.05
Future value of an annuity due of 1 for 25 periods at 5%	50.11350
Periodic payment	× $4,000
Accumulated amount at the end of 25 years	$200,454

9.   (C)   The amount accumulated is determined by using the standard formula for the future amount of an ordinary annuity for 4 periods at 10%:

X   = $900,000 × 4.64100
X   = $4,176,900.

10.   (B)   To compute the present value of a deferred annuity, compute the present value of an ordinary annuity of 1 as if the rents had occurred for the entire period, and then subtract the present value of rents which were not received during the deferral period.

Using only Table 6-4 as follows:

Each periodic rent		$50,000
Present value of an ordinary annuity		
of 1 for total periods (7) [number of rents (5)		
plus number of deferred periods (2)] at 6%	5.58238	
Less: Present value of an ordinary annuity of 1		
for the number of deferred periods (2) at 6%	1.83339	
Difference		× 3.74899
		$187,449.50

REVIEW EXERCISES

a.   1.   (A)   6.   (A)

      2.   (B)   7.   (D)

      3.   (E)   8.   (A)

      4.   (F)   9.   (C)

      5.   (A)   10.   (D)

b.   1. $1,000 × 1.05 = $1,050

      2. $20,000 ÷ 9.54911 = $2,094.44 (From Table 6-3, 5% for 8 periods.)

      3. $60,000 ÷ $9,000 = 6.667 (From Table 6-5 for 10 periods,
          the interest rate is between 10% and 11%.)

      4.   Each periodic rent $5,000
         Present value of an ordinary annuity of 1 for total
           periods (8) involved [number of rents (5) plus number
           of deferred periods (3)] at 12%..   4.96764
         Less: Present value of an ordinary annuity of 1 for
           the number of deferred periods (3) at 12%...........................   2.40183
         Difference ....   × 2.56581
         Present value of 5 rents of $5,000.. $12,829.05

      5. $20,000 ÷ $1,845 = 10.84010 (From Table 6-1, in the 10% column
          the number 10.84010 falls between 25 and 26 years.)

      6. $3,000 × 2.15892 = $6,476.76 (From Table 6-1, 8% for 10 years).

      7. $15,000 ÷ 6.20979 = $2,415.54 (From Table 6-4).

      8. $25,331 ÷ $50,000 = .50662 (From Table 6-2, this amount is found
          for 6 years at 12% interest.)

      9.   Future amount of an ordinary annuity of 1 for 30 years at 12%...........................   241.33268
         Factor (1 + .12) ....   ×   1.12
         Future amount of an annuity due for 30 years at 12%...   270.29260
                     $50,000 ÷ 270.29260= $184.98

    10. $10,000 × 6.71008 = $67,100.80 (From Table 6-4).

Table 6-1 FUTURE VALUE OF 1

$$\text{FVF}_{n,\,i} = (1 + i)^n$$

(n) Periods	2%	2-1/2%	3%	4%	5%	6%
1	1.02000	1.02500	1.03000	1.04000	1.05000	1.06000
2	1.04040	1.05063	1.06090	1.08160	1.10250	1.12360
3	1.06121	1.07689	1.09273	1.12486	1.15763	1.19102
4	1.08243	1.10381	1.12551	1.16986	1.21551	1.26248
5	1.10408	1.13141	1.15927	1.21665	1.27628	1.33823
6	1.12616	1.15969	1.19405	1.26532	1.34010	1.41852
7	1.14869	1.18869	1.22987	1.31593	1.40710	1.50363
8	1.17166	1.21840	1.26677	1.36857	1.47746	1.59385
9	1.19509	1.24886	1.30477	1.42331	1.55133	1.68948
10	1.21899	1.28008	1.34392	1.48024	1.62889	1.79085
11	1.24337	1.31209	1.38423	1.53945	1.71034	1.89830
12	1.26824	1.34489	1.42576	1.60103	1.79586	2.01220
13	1.29361	1.37851	1.46853	1.66507	1.88565	2.13293
14	1.31948	1.41297	1.51259	1.73168	1.97993	2.26090
15	1.34587	1.44830	1.55797	1.80094	2.07893	2.39656
16	1.37279	1.48451	1.60471	1.87298	2.18287	2.54035
17	1.40024	1.52162	1.65285	1.94790	2.29202	2.69277
18	1.42825	1.55966	1.70243	2.02582	2.40662	2.85434
19	1.45681	1.59865	1.75351	2.10685	2.52695	3.02560
20	1.48595	1.63862	1.80611	2.19112	2.65330	3.20714
21	1.51567	1.67958	1.86029	2.27877	2.78596	3.39956
22	1.54598	1.72157	1.91610	2.36992	2.92526	3.60354
23	1.57690	1.76461	1.97359	2.46472	3.07152	3.81975
24	1.60844	1.80873	2.03279	2.56330	3.22510	4.04893
25	1.64061	1.85394	2.09378	2.66584	3.38635	4.29187
26	1.67342	1.90029	2.15659	2.77247	3.55567	4.54938
27	1.70689	1.94780	2.22129	2.88337	3.73346	4.82235
28	1.74102	1.99650	2.28793	2.99870	3.92013	5.11169
29	1.77584	2.04641	2.35657	3.11865	4.11614	5.41839
30	1.81136	2.09757	2.42726	3.24340	4.32194	5.74349
31	1.84759	2.15001	2.50008	3.37313	4.53804	6.08810
32	1.88454	2.20376	2.57508	3.50806	4.76494	6.45339
33	1.92223	2.25885	2.65234	3.64838	5.00319	6.84059
34	1.96068	2.31532	2.73191	3.79432	5.25335	7.25103
35	1.99989	2.37321	2.81386	3.94609	5.51602	7.68609
36	2.03989	2.43254	2.89828	4.10393	5.79182	8.14725
37	2.08069	2.49335	2.98523	4.26809	6.08141	8.63609
38	2.12230	2.55568	3.07478	4.43881	6.38548	9.15425
39	2.16474	2.61957	3.16703	4.61637	6.70475	9.70351
40	2.20804	2.68506	3.26204	4.80102	7.03999	10.28572

8%	9%	10%	12%	15%	(n) Periods
1.08000	1.09000	1.10000	1.12000	1.15000	1
1.16640	1.18810	1.21000	1.25440	1.32250	2
1.25971	1.29503	1.33100	1.40493	1.52088	3
1.36049	1.41158	1.46410	1.57352	1.74901	4
1.46933	1.53862	1.61051	1.76234	2.01136	5
1.58687	1.67710	1.77156	1.97382	2.31306	6
1.71382	1.82804	1.94872	2.21068	2.66002	7
1.85093	1.99256	2.14359	2.47596	3.05902	8
1.99900	2.17189	2.35795	2.77308	3.51788	9
2.15892	2.36736	2.59374	3.10585	4.04556	10
2.33164	2.58043	2.85312	3.47855	4.65239	11
2.51817	2.81267	3.13843	3.89598	5.35025	12
2.71962	3.06581	3.45227	4.36349	6.15279	13
2.93719	3.34173	3.79750	4.88711	7.07571	14
3.17217	3.64248	4.17725	5.47357	8.13706	15
3.42594	3.97031	4.59497	6.13039	9.35762	16
3.70002	4.32763	5.05447	6.86604	10.76162	17
3.99602	4.71712	5.55992	7.68997	12.37545	18
4.31570	5.14166	6.11591	8.61276	14.23177	19
4.66096	5.60441	6.72750	9.64629	16.36654	20
5.03383	6.10881	7.40025	10.80385	18.82152	21
5.43654	6.65860	8.14028	12.10031	21.64475	22
5.87146	7.25787	8.95430	13.55235	24.89146	23
6.34118	7.91108	9.84973	15.17863	28.62518	24
6.84847	8.62308	10.83471	17.00000	32.91895	25
7.39635	9.39916	11.91818	19.04007	37.85680	26
7.98806	10.24508	13.10999	21.32488	43.53532	27
8.62711	11.16714	14.42099	23.88387	50.06561	28
9.31727	12.17218	15.86309	26.74993	57.57545	29
10.06266	13.26768	17.44940	29.95992	66.21177	30
10.86767	14.46177	19.19434	33.55511	76.14354	31
11.73708	15.76333	21.11378	37.58173	87.56507	32
12.67605	17.18203	23.22515	42.09153	100.69983	33
13.69013	18.72841	25.54767	47.14252	115.80480	34
14.78534	20.41397	28.10244	52.79962	133.17552	35
15.96817	22.25123	30.91268	59.13557	153.15185	36
17.24563	24.25384	34.00395	66.23184	176.12463	37
18.62528	26.43668	37.40434	74.17966	202.54332	38
20.11530	28.81598	41.14479	83.08122	232.92482	39
21.72452	31.40942	45.25926	93.05097	267.86355	40

TABLE 6-2 PRESENT VALUE OF 1

$$PVF_{n,\,i} = \frac{1}{(1+i)^n} = (1+i)^{-n}$$

(n) Periods	2%	2-1/2%	3%	4%	5%	6%
1	.98039	.97561	.97087	.96154	.95238	.94340
2	.96117	.95181	.94260	.92456	.90703	.89000
3	.94232	.92860	.91514	.88900	.86384	.83962
4	.92385	.90595	.88949	.85480	.82270	.79209
5	.90573	.88385	.86261	.82193	.78353	.74726
6	.88797	.86230	.83748	.79031	.74622	.70496
7	.87056	.84127	.81309	.75992	.71068	.66506
8	.85349	.82075	.78941	.73069	.67684	.62741
9	.83676	.80073	.76642	.70259	.64461	.59190
10	.82035	.78120	.74409	.67556	.61391	.55839
11	.80462	.76214	.72242	.64958	.58468	.56279
12	.78849	.74356	.70138	.62460	.55684	.49697
13	.77303	.72542	.68095	.60057	.53032	.46884
14	.75788	.70773	.66112	.57748	.50507	.44230
15	.74301	.69047	.64186	.55526	.48102	.41727
16	.72845	.67362	.62317	.53391	.45811	.39365
17	.71416	.65720	.60502	.51337	.43630	.37136
18	.70016	.64117	.58739	.49363	.41552	.35034
19	.68643	.62553	.57029	.47464	.39573	.33051
20	.67297	.61027	.55368	.45639	.37689	.31180
21	.65978	.59539	.53755	.43883	.35894	.29416
22	.64684	.58086	.52189	.42196	.34185	.27751
23	.63416	.56670	.50669	.40573	.32557	.26180
24	.62172	.55288	.49193	.39012	.31007	.24698
25	.60593	.53939	.47761	.37512	.29530	.23300
26	.59758	.52623	.46369	.36069	.28124	.21981
27	.58586	.51340	.45019	.34682	.26785	.20737
28	.57437	.50088	.43708	.33348	.25509	.19563
29	.56311	.48866	.42435	.32065	.24295	.18456
30	.55207	.47674	.41199	.30832	.23138	.17411
31	.54125	.46511	.39999	.29646	.22036	.16425
32	.53063	.45377	.38834	.28506	.20987	.15496
33	.52023	.44270	.37703	.27409	.19987	.14619
34	.51003	.43191	.36604	.26355	.19035	.13791
35	.50003	.42137	.35538	.25342	.18129	.13011
36	.49022	.41109	.34503	.24367	.17266	.12274
37	.48061	.40107	.33498	.23430	.16444	.11579
38	.47119	.39128	.32523	.22529	.15661	.10924
39	.46195	.38174	.31575	.21662	.14915	.10306
40	.45289	.37243	.30656	.20829	.14205	.09722

8%	9%	10%	12%	15%	(n) Periods
.92593	.91743	.90909	.89286	.86957	1
.85734	.84168	.82645	.79719	.75614	2
.79383	.77218	.75132	.71178	.65752	3
.73503	.70843	.68301	.63552	.57175	4
.68058	.64993	.62092	.56743	.49718	5
.63017	.59627	.56447	.50663	.43233	6
.58349	.54703	.51316	.45235	.37594	7
.54027	.50187	.46651	.40388	.32690	8
.50025	.46043	.42410	.36061	.28426	9
.46319	.42241	.38554	.32197	.24719	10
.42888	.38753	.35049	.28748	.21494	11
.39711	.35554	.31863	.25668	.18691	12
.36770	.32618	.28966	.22917	.16253	13
.34046	.29925	.26333	.20462	.14133	14
.31524	.27454	.23939	.18270	.12289	15
.29189	.25187	.21763	.16312	.10687	16
.27027	.23107	.19785	.14564	.09293	17
.25025	.21199	.17986	.13004	.08081	18
.23171	.19449	.16351	.11611	.07027	19
.21455	.17843	.14864	.10367	.06110	20
.19866	.16370	.13513	.09256	.05313	21
.18394	.15018	.12285	.08264	.04620	22
.17032	.13778	.11168	.07379	.04017	23
.15770	.12641	.10153	.06588	.03493	24
.14602	.11597	.09230	.05882	.03038	25
.13520	.10639	.08391	.05252	.02642	26
.12519	.09761	.07628	.04689	.02297	27
.11591	.08955	.06934	.04187	.01997	28
.10733	.08216	.06304	.03738	.01737	29
.09938	.07537	.05731	.03338	.01510	30
.09202	.06915	.05210	.02980	.01313	31
.08520	.06344	.04736	.02661	.01142	32
.07889	.05820	.04306	.02376	.00993	33
.07305	.05340	.03914	.02121	.00864	34
.06763	.04899	.03558	.01894	.00751	35
.06262	.04494	.03235	.01691	.00653	36
.05799	.04123	.02941	.01510	.00568	37
.05396	.03783	.02674	.01348	.00494	38
.04971	.03470	.02430	.01204	.00429	39
.04603	.03184	.02210	.01075	.00373	40

TABLE 6-3 FUTURE VALUE OF AN ORDINARY ANNUITY OF 1

$$FVF-OA_{n,i} = \frac{(1+i)^n - 1}{i}$$

(n) Periods	2%	2-1/2%	3%	4%	5%	6%
1	1.00000	1.00000	1.00000	1.00000	1.00000	1.00000
2	2.02000	2.02500	2.03000	2.04000	2.05000	2.06000
3	3.06040	3.07563	3.09090	3.12160	3.15250	3.18360
4	4.12161	4.15252	4.18363	4.24646	4.31013	4.37462
5	5.20404	5.25633	5.30914	5.41632	5.52563	5.63709
6	6.30812	6.38774	6.46841	6.63298	6.80191	6.97532
7	7.43428	7.54743	7.66246	7.89829	8.14201	8.39384
8	8.58297	8.73612	8.89234	9.21423	9.54911	9.89747
9	9.75463	9.95452	10.15911	10.58280	11.02656	11.49132
10	10.94972	11.20338	11.46338	12.00611	12.57789	13.18079
11	12.16872	12.48347	12.80780	13.48635	14.20679	14.97164
12	13.41209	13.79555	14.19203	15.02581	15.91713	16.86994
13	14.68033	15.14044	15.61779	16.62684	17.71298	18.88214
14	15.97394	16.51895	17.08632	18.29191	19.59863	21.01507
15	17.29342	17.93193	18.59891	20.02359	21.57856	23.27597
16	18.63929	19.38022	20.15688	21.82453	23.65749	25.67253
17	20.01207	20.86473	21.76159	23.69751	25.84037	28.21288
18	21.41231	22.38635	23.41444	25.64541	28.13238	30.90565
19	22.84056	23.94601	25.11687	27.67123	30.53900	33.75999
20	24.29737	25.54466	26.87037	29.77808	33.06595	36.78559
21	25.78332	27.18327	28.67649	31.96920	35.71925	39.99273
22	27.29898	28.86286	30.53678	34.24797	38.50521	43.39229
23	28.84496	30.58443	32.45288	36.61789	41.43048	46.99583
24	30.42186	32.34904	34.42647	39.08260	44.50200	50.81558
25	32.03030	34.15776	36.45926	41.64591	47.72710	54.86451
26	33.67091	36.01171	38.55304	44.31174	51.11345	59.15638
27	35.34432	37.91200	40.70963	47.08421	54.66913	63.70577
28	37.05121	39.85980	42.93092	49.96758	58.40258	68.52811
29	38.79223	41.85630	45.21885	52.96629	62.32271	73.63980
30	40.56808	43.90270	47.57542	56.08494	66.43885	79.05819
31	42.37944	46.00027	50.00268	59.32834	70.76079	84.80168
32	44.22703	48.15028	52.50276	62.70147	75.29883	90.88978
33	46.11157	50.35403	55.07784	66.20953	80.06377	97.34316
34	48.03380	52.61289	57.73018	69.85791	85.06696	104.18376
35	49.99448	54.92821	60.46208	73.65222	90.32031	111.43478
36	51.99437	57.30141	63.27594	77.59831	95.83632	119.12087
37	54.03425	59.73395	66.17422	81.70225	101.62814	127.26812
38	56.11494	62.22730	69.15945	85.97034	107.70955	135.90421
39	58.23724	64.78298	72.23423	90.40915	114.09502	145.05846
40	60.40198	67.40255	75.40126	95.02552	120.79977	154.76197

8%	9%	10%	12%	15%	(n) Periods
1.00000	1.00000	1.00000	1.00000	1.00000	1
2.08000	2.09000	2.10000	2.12000	2.15000	2
3.24640	3.27810	3.31000	3.37440	3.47250	3
4.50611	4.57313	4.64100	4.77933	4.99338	4
5.86660	5.98471	6.10510	6.35285	6.74238	5
7.33592	7.52334	7.71561	8.11519	8.75374	6
8.92280	9.20044	9.48717	10.08901	11.06680	7
10.63663	11.02847	11.43589	12.29969	13.72682	8
12.48756	13.02104	13.57948	14.77566	16.78584	9
14.48656	15.19293	15.93743	17.54874	20.30372	10
16.64549	17.56029	18.53117	20.65458	24.34928	11
18.97713	20.14072	21.38428	24.13313	29.00167	12
21.49530	22.95339	24.52271	28.02911	34.35192	13
24.21492	26.01919	27.97498	32.39260	40.50471	14
27.15211	29.36092	31.77248	37.27972	47.58041	15
30.32428	33.00340	35.94973	42.75328	55.71747	16
33.75023	36.97371	40.54470	48.88367	65.07509	17
37.45024	41.30134	45.59917	55.74972	75.83636	18
41.44626	46.01846	51.15909	63.43968	88.21181	19
45.76196	51.16012	57.27500	72.05244	102.44358	20
50.42292	56.76453	64.00250	81.69874	118.81012	21
55.45676	62.87334	71.40275	92.50258	137.63164	22
60.89330	69.53194	79.54302	104.60289	159.27638	23
66.76476	76.78981	88.49733	118.15524	184.16784	24
73.10594	84.70090	98.34706	133.33387	212.79302	25
79.95442	93.32398	109.18177	150.33393	245.71197	26
87.35077	102.72314	121.09994	169.37401	283.56877	27
95.33883	112.96822	134.20994	190.69889	327.10408	28
103.96594	124.13536	148.63093	214.58275	377.16969	29
113.28231	136.30754	164.49402	241.33268	434.74515	30
123.34587	149.57522	181.94343	271.29261	500.95692	31
134.21354	164.03699	201.13777	304.84772	577.10046	32
145.95062	179.80032	222.25154	342.42945	644.66553	33
158.62667	196.98234	245.47670	384.52098	765.36535	34
172.31680	215.71076	271.02437	431.66350	881.17016	35
187.10215	236.12472	299.12681	484.46312	1014.34568	36
203.07032	258.37595	330.03949	543.59869	1167.49753	37
220.31595	282.62978	364.04343	609.83053	1342.62216	38
238.94122	309.06646	401.44778	684.01020	1546.16549	39
259.05652	337.88245	442.59256	767.09142	1779.09031	40

TABLE 6-4 PRESENT VALUE OF AN ORDINARY ANNUITY OF 1

$$PVF - OA_{n,i} = \frac{1 - \dfrac{1}{(1+i)^n}}{i} = \frac{1 - v^n}{i}$$

(n) Periods	2%	2-1/2%	3%	4%	5%	6%
1	.98039	.97561	.97087	.96154	.95238	.94340
2	1.94156	1.92742	1.91347	1.88609	1.85941	1.83339
3	2.88388	2.85602	2.82861	2.77509	2.72325	2.67301
4	3.80773	3.76197	3.71710	3.62990	3.54595	3.46511
5	4.71346	4.64583	4.57971	4.45182	4.32948	4.21236
6	5.60143	5.50813	5.41719	5.42414	5.07569	4.91732
7	6.47199	6.34939	6.23028	6.00205	5.78637	5.58238
8	7.32548	7.17014	7.01969	6.73274	6.46321	6.20979
9	8.16224	7.97087	7.78611	7.43533	7.10782	6.80169
10	8.98259	8.75206	8.53020	8.11090	7.72173	7.36009
11	9.78685	9.51421	9.25262	8.76048	8.30641	7.88687
12	10.57534	10.25776	9.95400	9.38507	8.86325	8.38384
13	11.34837	10.98319	10.63496	9.98565	9.39357	8.85268
14	12.10625	11.69091	11.29607	10.56312	9.89864	9.29498
15	12.84926	12.38138	11.93794	11.11839	10.37966	9.71225
16	13.57771	13.05500	12.56110	11.65230	10.83777	10.10590
17	14.29187	13.71220	13.16612	12.16567	11.27407	10.47726
18	14.99203	14.35336	13.75351	12.65930	11.68959	10.82760
19	15.67846	14.97889	14.32380	13.13394	12.08532	11.15812
20	16.35143	15.58916	14.87747	13.59033	12.46221	11.46992
21	17.01121	16.18455	15.41502	14.02916	12.82115	11.76408
22	17.65805	16.76541	15.93692	14.45112	13.16300	12.04158
23	18.29220	17.33211	16.44361	14.85684	13.48857	12.30338
24	18.91393	17.88499	16.93554	15.24696	13.79864	12.55036
25	19.52346	18.42438	17.41315	15.62208	14.09394	12.78336
26	20.12104	18.95061	17.87684	15.98277	14.37519	13.00217
27	20.70690	19.46401	18.32703	16.32959	14.64303	13.21053
28	21.28127	19.96489	18.76411	16.66306	14.89813	13.40616
29	21.84438	20.45355	19.18845	16.98371	15.14107	13.59072
30	22.39646	20.93029	19.60044	17.29203	15.37245	13.76483
31	22.93770	21.39541	20.00043	17.58849	15.59281	13.92909
32	23.46833	21.84918	20.38877	17.87355	15.80268	14.08404
33	23.98856	22.29188	20.76579	18.14765	16.00255	14.23023
34	24.49859	22.72379	21.13184	18.41120	16.19290	14.36814
35	24.99862	23.14516	21.48722	18.66461	16.37419	14.49825
36	25.48884	23.55625	21.83225	18.90828	16.54685	14.62099
37	25.96945	23.95732	22.16724	19.14258	16.71129	14.73678
38	26.44064	24.34860	22.49246	19.36786	16.86789	14.84602
39	26.90259	24.73034	22.80822	19.58448	17.01704	14.94907
40	27.35548	25.10278	23.11477	19.79277	17.15909	15.04630

8%	9%	10%	12%	15%	(n) **Periods**
.92593	.91743	.90909	.89286	.86957	1
1.78326	1.75911	1.73554	1.69005	1.62571	2
2.57710	2.53130	2.48685	2.40183	2.28323	3
3.31213	3.23972	3.16986	3.03735	2.85498	4
3.99271	3.88965	3.79079	3.60478	3.35216	5
4.62288	4.48592	4.35526	4.11141	3.78448	6
5.20637	5.03295	4.86842	4.56376	4.16042	7
5.74664	5.53482	5.33493	4.96764	4.48732	8
6.24689	5.99525	5.75902	5.32825	4.77158	9
6.71008	6.41766	6.14457	5.65022	5.01877	10
7.13896	6.80519	6.49506	5.93770	5.23371	11
7.53608	7.16073	6.81369	6.19437	5.42062	12
7.90378	7.48690	7.10336	6.42355	5.58315	13
8.24424	7.78615	7.36669	6.62817	5.72448	14
8.55948	8.06069	7.60608	6.81086	5.84737	15
8.85137	8.31256	7.82371	6.97399	5.95424	16
9.12164	8.54363	8.02155	7.11963	6.04716	17
9.37189	8.75563	8.20141	7.24967	6.12797	18
9.60360	8.95012	7.36492	7.36578	6.19823	19
9.81815	9.12855	8.51356	7.46944	6.25933	20
10.01680	9.29224	8.64869	7.56200	6.31246	21
10.20074	9.44243	8.77154	7.64465	6.35866	22
10.37106	9.58021	8.88322	7.71843	6.39884	23
10.52876	9.70661	8.98474	7.78432	6.43377	24
10.67478	9.82258	9.07704	7.84314	6.46415	25
10.80998	9.92897	9.16095	7.89566	6.49056	26
10.93516	10.02658	9.23722	7.94255	6.51353	27
11.05108	10.11613	9.30657	7.98442	6.53351	28
11.15841	10.19828	9.36961	8.02181	6.55088	29
11.25778	10.27365	9.42691	8.05518	6.56598	30
11.34980	10.34280	9.47901	8.08499	6.57911	31
11.43500	10.40624	9.52638	8.11159	6.59053	32
11.51389	10.46444	9.56943	8.13535	6.60046	33
11.58693	10.51784	9.60858	8.15656	6.60910	34
11.65457	10.56682	9.64416	8.17550	6.61661	35
11.71719	10.61176	9.67651	8.19241	6.62314	36
11.77518	10.65299	9.70592	8.20751	6.62882	37
11.82887	10.69082	9.73265	8.22099	6.63375	38
11.87858	10.72552	9.75697	8.23303	6.63805	39
11.92461	10.75736	9.77905	8.24378	6.64178	40

TABLE 6-5 PRESENT VALUE OF AN ANNUITY DUE OF 1

$$PVF - AD_{n,\,i} \;=\; 1 + \frac{1 - \dfrac{1}{(1+i)^{n-1}}}{i} = (1+i) + \left(\frac{1-v^n}{i}\right) = (1+i)\left(a_{\overline{n}|i}\right)$$

(n) Periods	2%	2-1/2%	3%	4%	5%	6%
1	1.00000	1.00000	1.00000	1.00000	1.00000	1.00000
2	1.98039	1.97561	1.97087	1.96154	1.95238	1.94340
3	2.94156	2.92742	2.91347	2.88609	2.85941	2.83339
4	3.88388	3.85602	3.82861	3.77509	3.72325	3.67301
5	4.80773	4.76197	4.71710	4.62990	4.54595	4.46511
6	5.71346	5.64583	5.57971	5.45182	5.32948	5.21236
7	6.60143	6.50813	6.41719	6.24214	6.07569	5.91732
8	7.47199	7.34939	7.23028	7.00205	6.78637	6.58238
9	8.32548	8.17014	8.01969	7.73274	7.46321	7.20979
10	9.16224	8.97087	8.78611	8.43533	8.10782	7.80169
11	9.98259	9.75206	9.53020	9.11090	8.72173	8.36009
12	10.78685	10.51421	10.25262	9.76048	9.30641	8.88687
13	11.57534	11.25776	10.95400	10.38507	9.86325	9.38384
14	12.34837	11.98319	11.63496	10.98565	10.39357	9.85268
15	13.10625	12.69091	12.29607	11.56312	10.89864	10.29498
16	13.84926	13.38138	12.93794	12.11839	11.37966	10.71225
17	14.57771	14.05500	13.56110	12.65230	11.83777	11.10590
18	15.29187	14.71220	14.16612	13.16567	12.27407	11.47726
19	15.99203	15.35336	14.75351	13.65930	12.68959	11.82760
20	16.67846	15.97889	15.32380	14.13394	13.08532	12.15812
21	17.35143	16.58916	15.87747	14.59033	13.46221	12.46992
22	18.01121	17.18455	16.41502	15.02916	13.82115	12.76408
23	18.65805	17.76541	16.93692	15.45112	14.16300	13.04158
24	19.29220	18.33211	17.44361	15.85684	14.48857	13.30338
25	19.91393	18.88499	17.93554	16.24696	14.79864	13.55036
26	20.52346	19.42438	18.41315	16.62208	15.09394	13.78336
27	21.12104	19.95061	18.87684	16.98277	15.37519	14.00317
28	21.70690	20.46401	19.32703	17.32959	15.64303	14.21053
29	22.28127	20.96489	19.76411	17.66306	15.89813	14.40616
30	22.84438	21.45355	20.18845	17.98371	16.14107	14.59072
31	23.39646	21.93029	20.60044	18.29203	16.37245	14.76483
32	23.93770	22.39541	21.00043	18.58849	16.59281	14.92909
33	24.46833	22.84918	21.38877	18.87355	16.80268	15.08404
34	24.98856	23.29188	21.76579	19.14765	17.00255	15.23023
35	25.49859	23.72379	22.13184	19.41120	17.19290	15.36814
36	25.98862	24.14516	22.48722	19.66461	17.37419	15.49825
37	26.48884	24.55625	22.83255	19.90828	17.54685	15.62099
38	26.96945	24.95732	23.16724	20.14258	17.71129	15.73678
39	27.44064	25.34860	23.49246	20.36786	17.86789	15.84602
40	27.90259	25.73034	23.80822	20.58448	18.01704	15.94907

8%	9%	10%	12%	15%	(n) Periods
1.00000	1.00000	1.00000	1.00000	1.00000	1
1.92593	1.91743	1.90909	1.89286	1.86957	2
2.78326	2.75911	2.73554	2.69005	2.62571	3
3.57710	3.53130	3.48685	3.40183	3.28323	4
4.31213	4.23972	4.16986	4.03735	3.85498	5
4.99271	4.88965	4.79079	4.60478	4.35216	6
5.62288	5.48592	5.35526	5.11141	4.78448	7
6.20637	6.03295	5.86842	5.56376	5.16042	8
6.74664	6.53482	6.33493	5.96764	5.48732	9
7.24689	6.99525	6.75902	6.32825	5.77158	10
7.71008	7.41766	7.14457	6.65022	6.01877	11
8.13896	7.80519	7.49506	6.93770	6.23371	12
8.53608	8.16073	7.18369	7.19437	6.42062	13
8.90378	8.48690	8.10336	7.42355	6.58315	14
9.24424	8.78615	8.36669	7.62817	6.72448	15
9.55948	9.06069	8.60608	7.81086	6.84737	16
9.85137	9.31256	8.82371	7.97399	6.95424	17
10.12164	9.54363	9.02155	8.11963	7.04716	18
10.37189	9.75563	9.20141	8.24967	7.12797	19
10.60360	9.95012	9.36492	8.36578	7.19823	20
10.81815	10.12855	9.51356	8.46944	7.25933	21
11.01680	10.29224	9.64869	8.56200	7.31246	22
11.20074	10.44243	9.77154	8.64465	7.35866	23
11.37106	10.58021	9.88322	8.71843	7.39884	24
11.52876	10.70661	9.98474	8.78432	7.43377	25
11.67478	10.82258	10.07704	8.84314	7.46415	26
11.80998	10.92897	10.16095	8.89566	7.49056	27
11.93518	11.02658	10.23722	8.94255	7.51353	28
12.05108	11.11613	10.30657	8.98442	7.53351	29
12.15841	11.19828	10.36961	9.02181	7.55088	30
12.25778	11.27365	10.42691	9.05518	7.56598	31
12.34980	11.34280	10.47901	9.08499	7.57911	32
12.43500	11.40624	10.52638	9.11159	7.59053	33
12.51389	11.46444	10.56943	9.13535	7.60046	34
12.58693	11.51784	10.60858	9.15656	7.60910	35
12.65457	11.56682	10.64416	9.17550	7.61661	36
12.71719	11.61176	10.67651	9.19241	7.62314	37
12.77518	11.65299	10.70592	9.20751	7.62882	38
12.82887	11.69082	10.73265	9.22099	7.63375	39
12.87858	11.72552	10.75697	9.23303	7.63805	40

7

Cash and Receivables

CHAPTER LEARNING OBJECTIVES

1. Identify items considered cash.
2. Indicate how to report cash and related items.
3. Define receivables and identify the different types of receivables.
4. Explain accounting issues related to recognition of accounts receivable.
5. Explain accounting issues related to valuation of accounts receivable.
6. Explain accounting issues related to recognition of notes receivable.
7. Explain accounting issues related to valuation of notes receivable.
8. Understand special topics related to receivables.
9. Describe how to report and analyze receivables.
*10. Explain common techniques employed to control cash.
*11. Describe the accounting for a loan impairment.

CHAPTER REVIEW

1. (L.O. 1) Chapter 7 presents a detailed discussion of two of the primary liquid assets of a business enterprise, cash and receivables. Cash is the most liquid asset held by a business enterprise and possesses unique problems in its management and control. Receivables are composed of both accounts and notes receivables. Chapter coverage of accounts receivable places emphasis on trade receivables. In covering notes receivables, the chapter includes both short-term and long-term notes.

Nature of Cash

2.   **Cash** is a financial asset and a financial instrument. A financial instrument is defined as any contract that gives rise to a financial asset of one entity and a financial liability or equity interest of another entity. Cash consists of coin, currency, bank deposits, and negotiable instruments such as money orders, checks, and bank drafts. Cash that has been designated for some specific use, other than for payment of currently maturing obligations, is segregated from the general cash account. This amount may be classified as a current asset if it will be disbursed within one year or the operating cycle, whichever is longer. Otherwise, the amount should be shown as a noncurrent asset.

*   *Note: All asterisked (*) items relate to material contained in the Appendix to the chapter.*

Restricted Cash

3.   (L.O. 2) It is common practice for an enterprise to have an agreement with a bank concerning credit and borrowing arrangements. When such an agreement exists, the bank usually requires the enterprise to maintain a minimum cash balance on deposit. This minimum balance is known as a **compensating   balance**. Compensating balances that result in legally restricted deposits must be separately classified in the statement of financial position. The nature of the borrowing arrangement determines whether the compensating balance is classified as a current asset or a noncurrent asset.

4.   Bank overdrafts occur when a check is written for more than the amount in the cash account. Bank overdrafts should be accounted for as accounts payable or, if material, separately disclosed. **Cash equivalents** are short-term, highly liquid investments that are both (**a**) readily convertible to known amounts of cash and (**b**) so near their maturity that they present insignificant risk of changes in interest rates. In the future it is likely they will have to be recorded as temporary investments.

Accounts Receivable

5.   (L.O. 3) **Receivables** are financial assets and also financial instruments and are defined as claims held against customers and others for money, goods, or services. Receivables may generally be classified as **trade** or **non-trade**. Trade receivables (accounts receivable and notes receivable) are the most significant receivables an enterprise possesses. Accounts receivable are oral promises of the purchaser to pay for goods and services sold. Notes receivable are written promises to pay a certain sum of money on a specified future date. Non-trade receivables arise from a variety of transactions and can be written promises either to pay or to deliver. Non-trade receivables are generally classified and reported as separate items in the statement of financial position.

6.   (L.O. 4) In most receivable transactions, the amount to be recognized is the exchange price (amount due from the debtor) between two parties to a sales transaction. Two elements that must be considered in measuring receivables are (**a**) the availability of discounts and (**b**) the length of time between the sale and the payment due date (the interest factor).

7.   Two types of discounts that must be considered in determining the value of receivables are **trade discounts** and **cash discounts**. Trade discounts represent reductions from the list or catalog prices of merchandise. They are often used to avoid frequent changes in catalogs or to quote different prices for different quantities purchased. Cash discounts (also called sales discounts) are offered as an inducement for prompt payment and are communicated in terms that read, for example, 2/10, n/30 (2% discount if paid within 10 days of the purchase or invoice date, otherwise the gross amount is due in 30 days).

8.   (L.O. 5) It is highly unlikely that a company that extends credit to its customers will be successful in collecting all of its receivables. Thus, some method must be adopted to account for receivables that ultimately prove to be uncollectible. The two methods currently used are the **direct write-off method** and the **allowance method**. Under the direct write-off method, the receivable account is reduced and an expense is recorded when a specific account is determined to be uncollectible. The direct-write off method is theoretically deficient because it usually does not match costs and revenues of the period, nor does it result in receivables being stated at cash realizable value on the statement of financial position. The direct write-off method is not appropriate if the amount deemed uncollectible is material.

9.   Use of the allowance method requires a year-end estimate of expected uncollectible accounts based upon credit sales or outstanding receivables. The estimate is recorded by debiting an expense and crediting an allowance account in the period in which the sale is recorded. Then, in a subsequent period, when an account is deemed to be uncollectible, an entry is made debiting the allowance account and crediting accounts receivable.

10. Advocates of the allowance method contend that its use provides for a proper matching of revenues and expenses as well as reflecting a proper carrying value for accounts receivable at the end of the period. When the allowance method is used, the estimated amount of uncollectible accounts is normally based upon a percentage of sales or outstanding receivables. The **percentage-of-sales method** attempts to match costs with revenues, and is frequently referred to as the income statement approach. The **percentage-of-receivables approach** provides a reasonably accurate estimate of the cash realizable value of receivables shown on the statement of financial position. This approach is commonly referred to as the statement of financial position approach.

11. The method used to determine the amount of bad debts expense each year affects the amount of expense recorded. Under the percentage-of-sales method, the amount recorded as bad debts expense is the amount determined by multiplying the estimated percentage times the credit sales. However, under the percentage-of-receivables approach, the unadjusted ending balance in the allowance account must be considered in arriving at bad debts expense for the year.

Notes Receivable

12. (L.O. 6) The major differences between trade accounts receivables and **trade notes receivables** are (**a**) notes represent a formal promise to pay and (**b**) notes bear an interest element because of the time value of money. Notes are classified as notes bearing interest equal to the effective rate and those bearing interest different than the effective rate. **Interest-bearing notes** have a stated rate of interest, whereas **zero-interest bearing notes (noninterest-bearing)** include the interest as part of their face amount instead of stating it explicitly.

13. Short-term notes are generally recorded at face value (less allowances) because the interest implicit in the maturity value is immaterial. A general rule is that notes treated as cash equivalents (maturities of 3 months or less) are not subject to premium or discount amortization. Long-term notes receivable, however, are recorded at the present value of the future cash inflows. Determination of the present value can be complicated, particularly when a zero interest-bearing note or a note bearing an unreasonable interest rate is involved.

14. Long-term notes receivable should be recorded and reported at the present value of the cash expected to be collected. When the interest stated on an interest-bearing note is equal to the effective (market) rate of interest, the note sells at face value. When the stated rate is different from the market rate, the cash exchanged (present value) is different from the face value of the note. The difference between the face value and the cash exchanged, either a **discount** or a **premium**, is then recorded and amortized over the life of the note to approximate the effective interest rate. The discount or premium is shown on the statement of financial position as a direct deduction from or addition to the face of the note.

15. Whenever the face amount of a note does not reasonably represent the present value of the consideration given or received in the exchange, the accountant must evaluate the entire arrangement to record properly the exchange and the subsequent interest. Notes receivable are sometimes issued with zero interest rate stated or at a stated rate that is unreasonable. In such instances the present value of the note is measured by the cash proceeds to the borrower or fair value of the property, goods, or services rendered. The difference between the face amount of the note and the cash proceeds or fair value of the property represents the total amount of interest during the life of the note. If the fair value of the property, goods, or services rendered is not determinable, estimation of the present value requires use of an **imputed interest rate**. The choice of a rate may be affected specifically by the credit standing of the issuer, restrictive covenants, collateral, payment, and the existing prime interest rate. Determination of the imputed interest rate is made when the note is received; any subsequent changes in prevailing interest rates are ignored.

Valuation of Notes Receivables

16.   (L.O.7) Like accounts receivables, companies record and report short-term notes receivable at their cash realizable value - that is, at their face amount less all necessary allowances. Valuation of long-term receivables may involve estimation issues not present with short-term receivables. For example, impairment tests are often done on an individual basis rather than on a collective assessment basis as is done with short-term receivables.

Special Issues Related to Receivables

17.   (L.O. 8) Companies have the option to report receivables at fair value with unrealized holding gains and losses reported in net income. The fair value option must be elected at the time the receivable is originally recognized and used until the company no longer owns the receivable.

18.   Derecognition of receivables occurs when (a) the receivable no longer has value or (b) if the risks and rewards of ownership are transferred as a result of a sale. A secured borrowing occurs when a company uses receivables to collateralize a loan. In this case the borrowing company records a note payable and the receivables remain on the books of the borrower. A sale of the receivables without guarantee (recourse) results in the removal of the receivables from the books of the seller. In a sale of receivables with guarantee the accountant must determine whether substantially all the risks and rewards of ownership have been transferred; if not the transfer is recorded as a secured borrowing.

Presentation and Analysis

19.   (L.O. 9) The presentation of receivables in the statement of financial position includes the following considerations:. (a) Segregate and report the carrying amounts of the different categories of receivables. (b) Indicate the receivables classified as current and non-current in the statement of financial position. (c) Appropriately offset the valuation accounts for receivables that are impaired, including a discussion of individual and collectively determined impairments. (d) Disclose the fair value of receivables in such a way that permits it to be compared with its carrying amount. (e) Disclose information to assess the credit risk inherent in the receivables. (f) Disclose any receivables pledged as collateral. (g) Disclose all significant concentrations of credit risk arising from receivables.

20.   The ratio used to assess the liquidity of receivables is the receivables turnover ratio, which measures the number of times, on average, receivables are collected during the period.

$$\text{Accounts Receivable Turnover} = \frac{\text{Net Sales}}{\text{Average trade receivables (net)}}$$

$$\text{Days to collect Accounts receivable} = \frac{365}{\text{Accounts receivable turnover}}$$

*Cash Controls

*21.   (L.O. 10) Two problems associated with accounting for cash transactions for management: (1) Proper controls must be established to ensure that no unauthorized transactions are entered into by officers or employees; (2) Information necessary to the proper management of cash on hand and cash transactions must be provided.

*22.   Control over the handling of cash and cash transactions is an important consideration for any business enterprise. Among the control procedures that are used for cash transactions are the use of bank account such as a general checking account, imprest bank accounts and lockbox accounts.

*Petty Cash

*23.   In an imprest petty cash system, a petty cash custodian is given a small amount of currency from which to make small payments (minor office supplies, taxi, postage, etc.). Each time a disbursement is made, the petty cashier obtains a signed receipt for the payment. When cash in the fund runs low, the petty cashier submits the signed receipts to the general cashier and a check is prepared to replenish the petty cash fund. This process is designed to promote control over small cash disbursements which would be awkward to pay by check.

*Bank Reconciliation

*24.   A basic cash control is preparation of a monthly bank reconciliation. The bank reconciliation, when properly prepared, proves that the cash balance per bank and the cash balance per book are in agreement. The items that cause the bank and book balances to differ, and thus require preparation of a bank reconciliation, are the following:

   a.   **Deposits in Transit**. Deposits recorded in the cash account in one period but not received by the bank until the next period.
   b.   **Outstanding Checks.** Checks written by the depositor that have yet to be presented at the bank for collection.
   c.   **Bank Charges.** Charges by the bank for services that are deducted from the account by the bank and which the company learns of when it receives the bank statement.
   d.   **Bank Credits.** Collections or deposits in the company's account that the company is not aware of until receipt of the bank statement.
   e.   **Bank or Depositor Errors.** Errors made by the company or the bank that must be corrected for the reconciliation to balance.

*25.   Two forms of bank reconciliation may be prepared. One form reconciles from the bank statement balance to the book balance or vice versa. The other form is described as **the reconciliation of bank and book balances to corrected cash balance.** This form is composed of two separate sections that begin with the bank balance and book balance, respectively. Reconciling items that apply to the bank balance are added and subtracted to arrive at the corrected cash balance. Likewise, reconciling items that apply to the book balance are added and subtracted to arrive at the same corrected cash balance. The corrected cash balance is the amount that should be shown on the statement of financial position at the reconciliation date.

*Impairment of Receivables

*26.   Companies assess their receivables each period for impairment. The collective assessment approach is used for short-term receivables, whereas long-term receivables make use of the individual assessment approach. If a receivable is deemed impaired, the loss is measured as the difference between the carrying amount and the expected future cash flows discounted at the loan's **historical** effective-interest rate. A loss will only be recorded if some of the legally contracted cash flows are reduced. The impairment loss is recorded by debiting bad debt expense and crediting an allowance for doubtful accounts.

*27.   If events and circumstances change to the extent that the impairment loss decreases, some or all of the previously recorded impairment loss is reversed.

GLOSSARY

Accounts Receivable.	Oral promises of the purchaser to pay for goods and services sold.
Aging Schedule.	The analysis of customer balances by the length of time they have been unpaid.
Allowance Method.	A method for recording uncollectible receivables where an estimate is made of the expected uncollectible receivables.
Assignment of Receivables.	The owner of the receivables borrows cash from a lender by writing a promissory note designating or pledging the accounts receivable as collateral.
Bank Charges.	A fee charged by the bank for its services.
Bank Credits.	Collections or deposits by the bank for the benefit of the depositor that have not been recorded by the depositor.
Bank Overdrafts.	When a check is written for more than the amount in the cash account.
***Bank Reconciliation.**	A schedule explaining any differences between the company's record and the bank's record of the company's cash.
Cash.	Resources that consist of coin, currency, money orders, certified checks, cashier's checks, personal checks, and bank drafts.
Cash Equivalents.	Short-term, highly liquid temporary investments that are both (a) readily convertible to known amounts of cash, and (b) so near their maturity that they present insignificant risk of changes in interest rates.
Cash Realizable Value.	The net amount expected to be received in cash.
Cash (Sales) Discounts.	Discounts offered as an inducement for prompt payment communicated in terms that read, for example, 2/10, n/30.
Compensating Balances.	Minimum cash balances required by a bank in support of bank loans.
Deposits in Transit.	Deposits recorded by the depositor that have not been recorded by the bank.
Direct Write-Off Method.	A method for recording uncollectible receivables where no entry is made until a specific account has been established as uncollectible.
Dishonored Notes.	A note that is not paid in full at maturity.

Factoring Receivables.	When a finance company or bank buys receivables from a business for a fee and then collects the remittances directly from the customers.
*Imprest Petty Cash System.	A cash fund used to pay relatively small amounts.
*Lockbox Account.	An account where customer remittances are mailed to a local post office box and a local bank is authorized to pick up the remittances mailed to it.
Notes Receivable.	Written promises to pay a certain sum of money on a specified future date.
*Not-Sufficient-Funds (NSF) Check.	A check that is not paid by a bank because of insufficient funds in a customer's bank account.
*Outstanding Checks.	Checks issued and recorded by a company that have not been paid by the bank.
Percentage-of-Receivables (Statement of Financial Position) Approach.	Management establishes a percentage relationship between the amount of receivables and the expected losses from uncollectible accounts.
Percentage of Sales (Income Statement) Approach.	Management establishes a percentage relationship between the amount of credit sales and expected losses from uncollectible accounts.
Promissory Note.	A negotiable instrument signed by a maker promising to pay a certain sum of money at a specified future date to a designated payee.
Receivables.	Claims held against customers and others for money, goods, or services.
Sales Returns and Allowances.	When a customer returns goods to the seller for credit or cash refund or when a customer has chosen to keep defective merchandise and receive a deduction from the selling price.
Trade Discount.	The difference between list or catalog prices and discounted prices which are used to avoid frequent changes in catalogs and to quote different prices for different quantities purchased.
Trade Receivables.	Amounts owed by customers for goods sold and services rendered as part of normal business operations.
Transfer Without Recourse.	When receivables are sold and the purchaser assumes the risk of collectibility and absorbs any credit losses.

Transfer With Recourse.	When receivables are sold and the seller guarantees payment to the purchaser in the event the debtor fails to pay.
Zero Interest Note.	A note which has no stated interest rate but has effective interest inherent in the instrument because of the difference in the present value of the note and its maturity value.

DEMONSTRATION PROBLEMS

1. (L.O. 5) The following account balances appeared on the trial balance of Cobb Company at 12/31:

	Dr.	Cr.
Accounts Receivable	$88,500	
Allowance for Doubtful Accounts		2,065
Sales		452,600
Sales Returns	3,200	

Required:

What amount would be debited or credited to Allowance for Doubtful Accounts if the company records bad debts expense based on:

a. 2% of net sales.
b. 8% of accounts receivable.

Solution:

a.	Net sales ([$452,600 – $3,200] × .02)	$8,988
	(The current balance in the "Allowance account is not considered. Thus, the "Allowance" account would have a balance of $11,053 ($8,988 + $2,065) after the entry)	
b.	$88,500 × .08	$7,080
	Less current "Allowance" balance	2,065
	Entry amount	$5,015

2. (L.O. 7) On December 31, 2012, Sondgeroth Construction Company accepted a promissory note from Morgan Enterprises for services rendered. The note has a face value of $475,000, is due December 31, 2019, and pays interest annually at a stated rate of 3%. The market rate of interest for a note of similar risk is 9%.

Required:

Compute the present value of the note and the amount of discount.

Solution:

Face value of the note		$475,000
Present value of $475,000 due in 7 years at 9%:		
$475,000 × .54703 (Table 6-2)	$259,839	
Present value of $14,250 payable annually for 7 years at 9%:		
$14,250 × 5.03295 (Table 6-4)	71,720	
Present value of the note		331,559
Discount		$143,441

Demonstration Problems *(continued)*

*3. (L.O. 10)   The following information applies to the cash account of the Nick Price Aviation Corporation as of August 31.

Balance per company books..	$7,165.84
Bank service charge for August	25.00
Note collected for the company by the bank...	1,200.00
August outstanding checks..	1,822.17
NSF* check returned with August bank statement	328.45
Balance per August bank statement...	8,438.56
Interest on the note collected by the bank	54.00
Receipts recorded on August 31 and sent to the bank that night.................................	1,450.00

* Not sufficient funds.

Required:

    A. Prepare a bank reconciliation for Price Aviation Corporation at August 31 that shows the correct cash balance as of that date.
    B. Prepare any necessary journal entries.

Solution:

A.

Price Aviation Corporation
Bank Reconciliation
August 31

Book balance		$7,165.84	Bank Balance		$8,438.56
Add:			Add:		
Note collected		1,200.00	Deposit in transit		1,450.00
Interest on note		54.00			9,888.56
		8,419.84			
Less:					
Service charge	25.00		Less:		
NSF check	328.45	353.45	Outstanding checks		1,822.17
Correct cash balance		$8,066.39			$8,066.39

B.	Miscellaneous expense	25.00	
	Accounts receivable	328.45	
	Cash		353.45
	Cash	1,254.00	
	Notes receivable		1,200.00
	Interest income		54.00

CHAPTER OUTLINE

Fill in the outline presented below.

(L.O. 1) Definition of Cash

       Items Considered to be Cash

       Items Considered to be Temporary Investments

       Other Items Not Considered to be Cash

(L.O. 2) Reporting Cash

       Restricted Cash

       Bank Overdrafts

       Cash Equivalents

(L.O. 3) Definitions of the Different Types of Receivables

(L.O. 4) Recognition of Accounts Receivable

Chapter Outline *(continued)*

        Trade Discounts

        Cash (Sales) Discounts

(L.O. 5) Valuation of Accounts Receivable

        Direct Write-Off Method

        Allowance Method

        Percentage-of-Sales Approach

        Percentage-of-Receivables Approach

(L.O. 6) Recognition of Notes Receivable

        Notes Bearing Interest

        Zero Interest or Unreasonable Interest-Bearing Notes

(L.O. 7) Valuation of Notes Receivable

(L.O. 8) Special Topics

           Fair Value

Disposition of Accounts and Notes Receivable

Secured Borrowing

Factoring of Accounts Receivable

Factoring Without Recourse

Factoring With Recourse

(L.O. 9) Statement of Financial Position Presentation of Receivables

*(L.O. 10) Management and Control of Cash

Petty Cash System

Bank Reconciliation

Reconciling Items for the Balance per Bank Statement

Reconciling Items for the Balance per Books

Four-Column Bank Reconciliation

*(L.O. 11) Impairments of Receivables

REVIEW QUESTIONS AND EXERCISES

TRUE-FALSE

Indicate whether each of the following is true (T) or false (F) in the space provided.

_____   1.   (L.O. 1) Cash consists of coin, currency, money market funds, certificates of deposit and other available funds on deposit at the bank.

_____   2.   (L.O. 1) Postage stamps on hand are classified as part of cash.

_____   3.   (L.O. 1) Because the bank has the legal right to demand notice before withdrawal, savings accounts usually are not classified on an entity's statement of financial position as cash.

_____   4.   (L.O. 2) Legally restricted deposits held as compensating balances against short-term borrowing arrangements should be stated separately among the cash and cash items in current assets.

_____   5.   (L.O. 2) Bond sinking fund cash should not be classified as a current asset because its use is restricted.

_____   6.   (L.O. 2) Bank overdrafts occur when a check is written for less than the amount in the cash account.

_____   7.   (L.O. 3) Accounts receivable are frequently accepted from customers who need to extend the payment period of an outstanding note receivable.

_____   8.   (L.O. 4) When a sale and the related receivable are initially recorded at the gross amount, sales discounts will be recognized in the accounts only when payment is received within the discount period.

_____   9.   (L.O. 5) The direct write-off method used in recording uncollectible accounts receivable allows the expense associated with bad debts always to be recorded in the accounting period in which the sale was made.

_____ 10.   (L.O. 5) When assessing the impairment of receivables, any receivable individually assessed that is not considered impaired should be included with a group of assets with similar credit-risk characteristics and collectively assessed for impairment.

_____ 11.   (L.O. 5) The percentage-of-receivables approach is also referred to as the income statement approach.

_____ 12.   (L.O. 5) It is improper to offset assets and liabilities in the statement of financial position, except where a right of offset exists.

_____ 13.   (L.O. 6) Zero-interest-bearing notes receivable include interest as part of their face amount.

_____ 14.   (L.O. 7) A trade receivable due two years hence should never be classified as a current asset.

_____ 15.   (L.O. 8) Factoring is the term used to describe the pledging of receivables as collateral for a loan.

_____ 16.   (L.O. 8) If receivables are sold with recourse, the seller guarantees payment to the purchaser in the event the debtor does not pay.

_____ 17.   (L.O. 8) The present value of a note is measured by the fair value of the property, goods, or services exchanged for the note or by an amount that reasonably approximates the market value of the note.

_____ 18. (L.O. 8) The essence of a transfer of receivables in a borrowing transaction is that the transferor retains the same risks and rewards related to the receivables after the transaction that it had before the transaction.

_____ *19. (L.O. 10) The replenishment of the petty cash fund under an imprest system requires a debit to the Petty Cash account for the amount of the replenishment.

_____ *20. (L.O. 10) If cash proves out short in a petty cash fund, the shortage is debited to the Cash Over and Short account.

_____ *21. (L.O. 10) A bank reconciliation is an integral part of the system of internal control over cash.

_____ *22. (L.O. 10) Of the two bank reconciliation formats used by a business entity, the form more widely used reconciles both the bank balance and the book balance to a correct cash balance.

_____ *23. (L.O. 10) When preparing a bank reconciliation for the purpose of arriving at a correct cash balance, NSF (not sufficient funds) checks are subtracted from the balance per books.

_____ *24. (L.O. 11) If a receivable is deemed to be individually impaired, the impairment loss is measured as the difference between the carrying value of the receivable and its fair value.

MULTIPLE CHOICE

Select the best answer for each of the following items and enter the corresponding letter in the space provided.

_____ 1. (L.O. 1) Which of the following is properly classified as cash?

      A.   Customer's postdated checks on hand.
      B.   Certificates of deposit.
      C.   Savings accounts.
      D.   Bond sinking fund cash.

_____ 2. (L.O. 1) Kari, Inc.'s book balance on December 31, 2012, was $5,000. In addition, Kari had the following items on its premises on December 31:

Check payable to Kari, Inc., dated January 3, 2013, included in December 31 book balance	$ 200
Postage stamps on hand not included in December 31 book balance	100
Cashier's check payable to Kari, Inc., dated December 28, 2012, not included in December 31 book balance	1,300

The proper amount to be shown as Cash on Kari's statement of financial position at December 31, 2012, is

      A. $6,100
      B. $6,200
      C. $6,300
      D. $6,400

_____ 3. (L.O. 2) Etheredge Company held an IOU at December 31, 2012. The IOU should be reported as

      A.   an investment.
      B.   petty cash.
      C.   cash.
      D.   a receivable.

_____ 4. (L.O. 2) A compensating balance is best reflected by which of the following?

    A.   A savings account maintained at the bank equal to the amount of all outstanding loans.

    B.   An amount of capital stock held in the company's treasury equal to outstanding loan commitments.

    C.   The portion of any demand deposit, time deposit, or certificate of deposit maintained by a corporation which constitutes support for existing borrowing arrangements of the corporation with the lending institution.

    D.   A balance held in a time or demand deposit account that is equal to the interest currently due on a loan.

_____ 5. (L.O. 2) A cash equivalent is a short-term, highly liquid investment that is readily convertible into known amounts of cash that

    A.   is acceptable as a means to pay current liabilities.

    B.   has a current market value that is greater than its original cost.

    C.   bears an interest rate that is at least equal to the prime rate of interest at the date of liquidation.

    D.   in the future will likely be recorded as temporary investments.

_____ 6. (L.O. 3) What is the preferable presentation of accounts receivable from officers, employees, or affiliated companies on a statement of financial position?

    A.   As offsets to capital.

    B.   By means of footnotes only.

    C.   As assets but separately from other receivables.

    D.   As trade notes and accounts receivable if they otherwise qualify as current assets.

_____ 7. (L.O. 4) When a customer purchases merchandise inventory from a business organization, she may be given a discount which is designed to induce prompt payment. Such a discount is called a(n)

    A.   trade discount.

    B.   nominal discount.

    C.   enhancement discount.

    D.   cash discount.

_____ 8. (L.O. 5) The advantage of relating a company's bad debt expense to its accounts receivable is that this approach:

    A.   gives a reasonably correct measure of receivables in the statement of financial position.

    B.   relates bad debt expense to the period of sale.

    C.   is the only acceptable method of valuing accounts receivable.

    D.   makes estimates of uncollectible accounts unnecessary.

_____ 9. (L.O. 5) Which of the following statements is **not** correct regarding uncollectible accounts receivable?

    A.   The direct write-off method records the bad debt in the year that it is determined that a specific receivable cannot be collected.

    B.   The allowance method is based on the assumption that the percentage of receivables that will not be collected can be predicted from past experiences, present market conditions, and an analysis of outstanding balances.

    C.   The direct write-off method will provide for a proper matching of costs with revenues of the period when the average monthly accounts receivable balance is consistent throughout the year.

    D.   An uncollectible account receivable is a loss of revenue that requires—through proper entry in the accounts—a decrease in the asset accounts receivable and a related decrease in income and stockholders' equity.

_____ 10. (L.O. 5) For the month of December 2012, the records of Turling Corporation show the following information:

Cash sales	$20,000
Cash received on accounts receivable	25,000
Accounts receivable, December 1, 2012	70,000
Accounts receivable, December 31, 2012	64,000
Accounts receivable written off as uncollectible	1,000

The Turling Corporation uses the direct write-off method in accounting for uncollectible accounts receivable. What are the gross sales for the month of December 31, 2012?

A. $39,000
B. $40,000
C. $45,000
D. $52,000

_____ 11. (L.O. 5) The allowance method is preferable to the direct write-off method because the allowance method

A. relies on estimates which are always accurate and stable among years.
B. reflects the real facts.
C. recognizes the expense of a bad debt in the year in which the account is determined to be uncollectible.
D. recognizes the expense of a bad debt in the same period as the sale.

_____ 12. (L.O. 5) Green Company wrote off a client's account receivable of $400 as uncollectible. What will be the effect on net income under each of the following methods of recognizing bad debt expense?

	Direct Write-Off	Allowance
A.	None	Decrease
B.	Decrease	None
C.	None	None
D.	Decrease	Decrease

_____ 13. (L.O. 5) Gardin Corporation uses the allowance method of accounting for uncollectible accounts. During 2012 Gardin had charges to Bad Debts Expense of $20,000 and wrote off as uncollectible, accounts receivable totaling $16,000. These transactions decreased working capital by:

A. $20,000
B. $16,000
C. $ 4,000
D. $ 0

_____ 14. (L.O. 5) The basic accounting issues for both accounts receivable and notes receivable would center around which of the following?

	Recognition	Valuation
A.	Yes	No
B.	Yes	Yes
C.	No	Yes
D.	No	No

_____ 15. (L.O. 6) Moluf Corporation receives a 5-year, $20,000 zero interest-bearing note, the present value of which is $11,348.60. What is the implicit interest rate that equates the total cash to be received to the present value of the future cash flows?

    A.   8%
    B.   9%
    C.   10%
    D.   12%

_____ 16. (L.O. 7) Pinkowski sold land to Ewell for $100,000 cash and a zero interest-bearing note with a face amount of $400,000. The fair value of the land at the date of sale was $450,000. Pinkowski should value the note receivable at:

    A. $450,000.
    B. $400,000.
    C. $350,000.
    D. $500,000.

_____ 17. (L.O. 7) Vonesh Company sold a drill press to Mary Company, taking in exchange a zero interest-bearing note. The drill press had a fair market value of $12,000 and the face amount of the note was $13,000. In a statement of financial position prepared immediately after receipt of the note, Vonesh should present the note at its face amount

    A.   plus implicit interest.
    B.   plus the anticipated net earnings related to the note.
    C.   less implicit interest.
    D.   without adjustment.

_____ 18. (L.O. 8) Which of the following statements is incorrect regarding the classification of accounts and notes receivable?

    A.   Segregation of the different types of receivables is required if they are material.
    B.   Disclose any loss contingencies that exist on the receivables.
    C.   Any discount or premium resulting from the determination of present value in notes receivable transactions is an asset or liability respectively.
    D.   Valuation accounts should be appropriately offset against the proper receivable accounts.

_____ 19. (L.O. 8) Thresher Corporation sold its accounts receivable outright to Kari Company, a financing company which normally buys accounts receivable of other companies without recourse. The accounts receivable have been

    A.   collateralized.
    B.   pledged.
    C.   factored.
    D.   assigned.

_____ 20. (L.O. 8) The fair value option for valuing receivables requires that unrealized holding gains and losses be reported as

	Part of Net Income	A Separate Component of Equity
A.	Yes	Yes
B.	Yes	No
C.	No	Yes
D.	No	No

_____ 21. (L.O. 9) The accounts receivable turnover ratio

  A. Provides information about how many days it takes to collect accounts receivable.
  B. Is computed as Net income/Accounts receivable.
  C. Shows how successful a company is in collecting its outstanding receivables.
  D. All of the choices are correct.

_____ 22. (L.O. 10) Which of the following journal entries is appropriate to establish an imprest petty cash fund?

A.	Petty Cash Fund	500	
	Cash		500
B.	Petty Cash Expense	500	
	Cash		500
C.	Administrative Expense	100	
	Selling Expense	200	
	Operating Expense	200	
	Cash		500
D.	Miscellaneous Expense	500	
	Cash		500

_____ *23. (L.O. 10) When preparing a bank reconciliation for the purpose of arriving at the correct cash balance:

  A. outstanding checks can be added to the balance per books.
  B. NSF checks should be deducted from the balance per books.
  C. deposits in transit are deducted from the balance per bank.
  D. notes collected by the bank should be added to the balance per bank.

_____ *24. (L.O. 10) In a bank reconciliation that attempts to reconcile the bank balance to the corrected cash balance, the following items would affect the reconciliation in what way?

	Outstanding Checks	**Deposits In Transit**
A.	Added	Added
B.	Subtracted	Added
C.	Added	Subtracted
D.	Subtracted	Subtracted

_____ *25. (L.O. 10) In preparing its bank reconciliation for the month of September 2012, Moran Company has available the following information:

Balance per bank statement, 9/30/12	$42,000
Deposits in transit, 9/30/12	7,200
Outstanding checks, 9/30/12	6,500
Bank service charges for September	25

What should be the correct balance of cash at September 30, 2012?

  A. $41,275
  B. $41,300
  C. $42,675
  D. $42,700

REVIEW EXERCISES

1. (L.O. 5) A trial balance for Foerch Company shows the following balances at December 31:

	Debit	Credit
Accounts Receivable	$120,000	
Allowance for Doubtful Accounts		$ 200
Sales		360,000
Sales Discounts	10,000	

Instructions:
Prepare the adjusting entry necessary at December 31 to provide for estimated uncollectibles under each of the following independent assumptions.

a. Foerch Company uses the percentage of sales method of accounting for uncollectible accounts. Company experience indicates that 1% of net sales will prove uncollectible.

b. Foerch bases its estimate of uncollectible accounts on an aging of accounts receivable. The aging at December 31 indicates uncollectible accounts of $4,000.

a.

General Journal			J1
Date	**Account Title**	**Debit**	**Credit**

b.

General Journal			J1
Date	**Account Title**	**Debit**	**Credit**

2.   (L.O. 8) The following transactions of Relias Company occurred during 2012.

August 14   --   Sold merchandise on account to Erml Company for $10,000.

September 5   --   Received a $10,000, 6%, 60-day note dated September 5 from Erml Company for the sale made on August 14.

September 5   --   Factored the note receivable from Erml Company at McEllen State Bank. The transfer was without recourse and had a finance charge of 4% of the amount of the note and the Bank retained an amount equal to 5% of the note.

Instructions:

Prepare the journal entries necessary to record the above transactions for Relias Company.

General Journal			
			J1
Date	**Account Title**	**Debit**	**Credit**

3.   (L.O. 6 and 7) DeFilippo Company agreed to loan Morreale Glass Corporation $400,000. Morreale Glass Corporation gave a zero interest-bearing note due in 4 years. A 12% interest rate is an appropriate rate for both companies.

Instructions:

a. Prepare the journal entry DeFilippo Company would make to record this transaction.

b. Prepare an amortization schedule for the note using the effective interest method.

a.

General Journal			J1
Date	**Account Title**	**Debit**	**Credit**

b.

Year	Cash Interest	Effective Interest	Discount Amortized	Unamortized Discount	Note Present Value
1					
2					
3					
4					

4.   (L.O. 8) Ehrlich Company factors $175,000 of accounts receivable with Vegas Finance Corporation on a without recourse basis on July 1, 2012. All the records related to the receivables are transferred to Vegas Finance as it will receive the collections. Vegas Finance assesses a finance charge of 2% of the amount of accounts receivable and retains an amount equal to 5% of accounts receivable to cover sales discounts, returns, and allowances.

Instructions:

  a.   Prepare the journal entry that Ehrlich Company would make to record the sale of these receivables on July 1, 2012.
  b.   Prepare the journal entry that Vegas Finance Corporation would make to record the purchase of the receivables on July 1, 2012.

a.

General Journal			
			J1
Date	**Account Title**	**Debit**	**Credit**

b.

General Journal			
			J1
Date	**Account Title**	**Debit**	**Credit**

*5.   (L.O. 10) You are asked to prepare a bank reconciliation for Malikowski Company as of October 31, 2012. By placing the appropriate letter in the space provided, indicate whether the following items should be:

    A.   added to the balance per bank statement.
    B.   deducted from the balance per bank statement.
    C.   added to the balance per books.
    D.   deducted from the balance per books.
    E.   omitted from the bank reconciliation because the bank amount and the book amount are already in agreement with respect to this item.

_____   1.   Outstanding checks of Malikowski Company as of October 31, 2012; the checks were written in October 2012.

_____   2.   Outstanding checks of Malikowski Company as of October 31, 2012; the checks were written in September 2012.

_____   3.   A check of Mankowski Company had been charged by the bank against the account of Malikowski Company.

_____   4.   A certified check by Malikowski Company, dated October 10, 2012, is outstanding as of October 31.

_____   5.   Bank service charges for October.

_____   6.   Discovered that check No. 101 (one of the cancelled checks included with the bank statement) had been made out to Blue Company (a creditor) for $100. Malikowski Company had recorded the check in its Cash Payments Journal in the amount of $1,000.

_____   7.   Malikowski Company understated the amount of a customer's check in its Cash Receipts Journal. The check was received and deposited by Malikowski in October.

SOLUTIONS TO REVIEW QUESTIONS

TRUE-FALSE

1. (F)   Cash consists of coin, currency, and available funds on deposit at the bank. Money market funds, money market savings certificates, certificates of deposit (CDs), and similar types of deposits that provide small investors with an opportunity to earn high rates of interest are more appropriately classified as temporary investments.

2. (F)   Postage stamps on hand are classified as part of office supplies inventory or as a prepaid expense.

3. (F)   Banks rarely exercise the right to demand notice before withdrawal of funds from a savings account. Thus, these funds are normally classified as cash for financial reporting purposes.

4. (T)

5. (T)

6. (F)   Bank overdrafts occur when a check is written for more than the amount in the cash account.

7. (F)   Notes receivables are frequently accepted from customers who need to extend the payment period of an outstanding accounts receivable.

8. (T)

9. (F)   The direct write-off method does not always match costs with revenues of the period. This is because receivables recorded late in one year might be written off in a subsequent year under the direct write-off method.

10. (T)

11. (F)   The percentage-of-sales approach is also referred to as the income statement approach. The percentage-of-receivables approach is also referred to as the statement of financial position approach.

12. (T)

13. (T)

14. (F)   The rule about classification of current assets is that the item is classified as a current asset if it will be converted into cash within one year or the operating cycle, whichever is longer. Thus, if a company had an operating cycle of two years or longer, the trade receivable due in two years would be classified as a current asset.

15. (F)   Factoring is the sale of accounts receivable to factors. Factors are finance companies or banks that buy receivables from businesses for a fee and then collect remittances directly from the customer.

16. (T)

17.   (T)

18.   (T)

*19.   (F)   Entries are made to the Petty Cash account only to increase or decrease the size of the fund. When the petty cash fund is replenished, various expense accounts are debited and the cash account is credited.

*20.   (T)

*21.   (T)

*22.   (T)

*23.   (T)

*24.   (F)   When a receivable is determined to be individually impaired, the impairment loss is calculated as the difference between the carrying amount of the receivable and the expected future cash flows discounted at the loan's historical effective-interest rate.

MULTIPLE CHOICE

1.   (C)   A customer's postdated check is most appropriately classified as a receivable. Certificates of deposit provide investors with an opportunity to earn high rates of interest and should be classified as temporary investments rather than cash. Bond sinking fund cash is restricted and is classified either in the current asset or in the long-term asset section, depending on the date of disbursement. A savings account is the only item listed that is properly classified as cash.

2.   (A)   Kari should show cash of $6,100 on its December 31, 2012 statement of financial position. This corrected cash balance can be calculated as follows:

Unadjusted cash balance at 12/31/12		$5,000
Add:	Cashier's check	1,300
Less:	Postdated check	(200)
Correct cash balance at 12/31/12		$6,100

3.   (D)   IOUs should be reported as receivables. Only coin, currency, available funds on deposit at the bank, money orders, certified checks, cashier's checks, personal checks, and bank drafts should be reported as part of the cash balance.

4.   (C)   A compensating balance is "that portion of any demand deposit (or any time deposit or certificate of deposit) maintained by a corporation which constitutes support for existing borrowing arrangements of the corporation with a lending institution."

5.   (D)   Because of recent problems involved in converting cash equivalents as cash, in the future it is likely that they will have to be classified as temporary investments.

6.   (C)   Notes and accounts receivable from officers, employees, or affiliated companies may have different terms, such as due dates and interest rates, than trade receivables. Therefore, these receivables should be reported separately from other receivables on the statement of financial position if they are material.

7.   (D)   A cash discount (sometimes called a sales discount) is often offered as an inducement to prompt payment. Such discounts may be quoted as 2/10, n/30, which means a 2% discount is given if the price is paid within 10 days, otherwise the gross amount is due in 30 days. A trade discount is an amount taken off the price of merchandise as an inducement for customers to buy the merchandise. The other two terms, nominal and enhancement, have no formal definition as discount terminology.

8.   (A)   The objective of relating bad debts expense to accounts receivable is to report receivables in the statement of financial position at cash realizable value. Relating bad debts to accounts receivable is a statement of financial position approach. The other commonly used approach to the determination of bad debts expense is to take a percentage of credit sales for the period.

9.   (C)   The major problem with the direct write-off method is that it does not match costs with revenues of the period nor does it result in receivables being stated at estimated cash realizable value on the statement of financial position. The other three alternatives reflect accurate statements about uncollectible accounts receivable.

10. (B)   Turling Corporation's gross sales for December 2010 can be calculated as follows:

Gross sales:
Cash sales	$20,000
Credit sales (see T-account)	20,000
Total	$40,000

Accounts Receivable			
Dec. 1	$70,000		
		Cash received	$25,000
		Written off	1,000
Credit sales	**$20,000**		
Dec. 31	$64,000		

11. (D)   It is believed that matching the estimated expenses of bad debts against sales in the period of the sale gives the best matching of revenues and expense. Answer (C) is incorrect because a proper matching of revenues and expenses is not obtained under the direct write-off method.

12. (B)   The entries for the write off of an account receivable under each method would be:

Direct write-off method
  (Decrease net income):
Bad debts expense	400	
Accounts receivable		400

Allowance method
  (No effect on net income):
Allowance for uncollectible receivable	400	
Accounts receivable		400

From the above example entries, it can be seen that when a specific customer's account receivable is written off as uncollectible there is no effect on income if the allowance method is used. However, when the direct write-off method is used, writing off a specific customer's account decreases net income for the period.

13. (A)   The entry to record bad debts expense includes a credit to the Allowance for Doubtful Accounts account. Working capital is reduced by the credit to the account because it is a contra account to the current asset accounts receivable. The subsequent entry to write off $16,000 of accounts deemed uncollectible does not affect working capital because the net amount of accounts receivable (total receivables less the allowance) is unchanged. For example:

	Before Write-off	After Write-off
Accounts Receivable	$120,000	$104,000
Allowance	30,000	14,000
Net	$ 90,000	$ 90,000

14. (B)   The basic issues in accounting for notes and accounts receivable are essentially the same—recognition and valuation. When and where the item should be included in the financial statements along with the proper amount to record are the basic accounting issues surrounding the receivables accounts.

15. (D)   Present value – Cash to be received = P.V. factor for 5 years. ($11,348.60 ÷ $20,000 = .56743). In Table 6-2 the factor .56743 is the factor for 5 periods at 12%.

16. (C)   The note should be valued at the fair value of the asset exchanged. If the land has a fair value of $450,000 and $100,000 in cash is given, then the note is valued at $350,000. The additional $50,000 ($400,000 – $350,000) is an interest factor or discount that should be amortized over the life of the note.

17. (C)   The zero interest-bearing note received by Vonesh Company should be valued at the fair market value of the drill press sold. This value would equal the face of the note less imputed interest.

18. (C)   Premiums or discounts that arise from present value computations for notes receivable transactions are not assets or liabilities. The discount or premium accounts are reported in the statement of financial position as a direct deduction from or addition to the notes' face amount.

19. (C)   Accounts receivable are said to be factored when they are sold outright without recourse. Answers (B) and (D) are incorrect because accounts receivable are pledged or designated as collateral for borrowings. These transactions are not sales of the accounts receivable.

20. (B)   When the fair value option is used to value receivables unrealized holding gains and losses are reported as part of net income.

21. (C)   The accounts receivable turnover ratio is computed as net sales/average accounts receivable and shows how successful a company is in collecting its outstanding receivables. In order to compute how many days it takes to collect accounts receivable, the accounts receivable turnover ratio must be divided into 365 days.

22. (A)   The establishment of an imprest petty cash account requires the establishment of a fund that is recorded in an asset account. In an imprest petty cash system the fund is replenished by an entry debiting expense account(s) and crediting cash.

*23. (B)   When preparing a bank reconciliation for the purpose of arriving at a correct cash balance, NSF (not sufficient funds) checks should be deducted from the balance per books. This is because these checks were added to the book balance when received; however, as the maker is unable to pay the check, the cash book balance would be overstated if the amounts were not deducted.

*24. (B) Outstanding checks are checks that have been written by the company and have not cleared the bank as of the date of the reconciliation. Deposits in transit are deposits sent to the bank that have not cleared the bank as of the reconciliation date. Thus, the outstanding checks need to be deducted from the bank balance and the deposits in transit need to be added in arriving at the corrected cash balance.

*25. (D) Moran Company's correct cash balance at September 30, 2012, can be calculated as follows:

Balance per bank, 9/30/12		$42,000
Add:	Deposits in transit, 9/30/12	7,200
Less:	Outstanding checks, 9/30/12	(6,500)
Corrected balance per books, 9/30/12		$42,700

The bank service charge would not be deducted since the bank would have already accounted for it in its balance per bank.

REVIEW EXERCISES

1. a. Bad Debts Expense $3,500*
       Allowance for Doubtful Accounts............................... $3,500

   *.01 (360,000 – 10,000) = 3,500

   b. Bad Debts Expense $3,800*
       Allowance for Doubtful Accounts............................... $3,800

   *4,000 – 200 = 3,800

2. August 14   Accounts Receivable 10,000
                  Sales... 10,000

   September 5   Notes Receivable.. 10,000
                  Accounts Receivable 10,000

   September 5   Cash.. 9,100
                  Due from Factor 500*
                  Loss on Sale of Note 400*
                  Notes Receivable 10,000

   *(5% × $10,000)
   **(4% × $10,000)

3.   a.

Notes Receivable..	254,208	
Cash...		254,208

Calculation of discount:

Amount of loan		$400,000
Face amount of note..	$400,000	
P.V.* of 1 at 12%, 4 years..	× .63552	
Present value of the note		$ 254,208

*Present value.

b.

Year	Cash Interest	Effective Interest	Discount Amortized	Carrying Amount of Note
				$254,208
1	$0	$30,505	$30,505	$284,713
2	0	34,166	34,166	318,879
3	0	38,265	38,265	357,144
4	0	42,856	42,856	400,000*
		$145,792	$145,792	

*Rounded by $1.

4.   a.

Cash	162,750	
Due from Factor	8,750	
Loss on Sale of Receivables	3,500	
Accounts Receivable		175,000

(Finance Charge: $175,000 × .02 = $3,500)
(Due from Factor: $175,000 × .05 = $8,750)

b.

Accounts Receivable	175,000	
Due to Ehrlich Company		8,750
Financing Revenue		3,500
Cash		162,750

*5.   1.   (B)   5.   (D)
       2.   (B)   6.   (C)
       3.   (A)   7.   (C)
       4.   (E)

8

Valuation of Inventories:
A Cost Basis Approach

CHAPTER LEARNING OBJECTIVES

1. Identify major classifications of inventory.
2. Distinguish between perpetual and periodic inventory systems.
3. Identify the effects of inventory errors on the financial statements.
4. Understand the items to include as inventory cost.
5. Describe and compare the methods used to price inventories.
*6. Describe the LIFO cost flow assumption.
*7. Explain the significance and use of a LIFO reserve.
*8. Understand the effect of LIFO liquidations.
*9. Explain the dollar-value LIFO method.
*10. Explain the major advantages and disadvantages of LIFO.
*11. Understand why companies select given inventory methods.

CHAPTER REVIEW

1.   Careful attention is given to the inventory account by many business organizations because it represents one of the most significant assets held by the enterprise. Inventories are of particular importance to merchandising and manufacturing companies because they represent the primary source of revenue for the organization. Inventories are also significant because of their impact on both the statement of financial position and the income statement. Chapter 8 initiates the discussion of the basic issues involved in recording, classifying, and valuing items classified as inventory.

Inventory Issues

2.   (L.O. 1) Inventories are asset items held for sale in the ordinary course of business or goods that will be used or consumed in the production of goods to be sold. **Merchandise inventory** refers to the goods held for resale by a trading concern. The inventory of a **manufacturing firm** is composed of three separate items: **raw materials, work in process, and finished goods**.

3.   (L.O. 2) Inventory records may be maintained on a perpetual or periodic inventory system basis. **A perpetual inventory system** provides a means for generating up-to-date records related to inventory quantities. Under this inventory system, data are available at any time relative to the quantity of material or type of merchandise on hand. In a perpetual inventory system, purchases and sales of goods are recorded directly in the Inventory account as they occur. A Cost of Goods Sold account is used to accumulate the issuances from inventory. The balance in the Inventory account at the end of the year should represent the ending inventory amount.

   *   *Note: All asterisked (*) items relate to material contained in the Appendix to the chapter.*

4.   When the inventory is accounted for on a **periodic inventory system,** the acquisition of inventory is debited to a Purchases account. Cost of goods sold must be calculated each period when a periodic inventory system is in use. The computation of cost of goods sold is made by adding beginning inventory to net purchases and then subtracting ending inventory. Ending inventory is determined by a physical count at the end of the year under a periodic inventory system. Even in a perpetual inventory system, a physical inventory count at year-end is normally taken due to the potential for loss, error, or shrinkage of inventory during the year.

5.   Inventory **planning** and **control** is of vital importance to the success of a trading or manufacturing enterprise. If an excessive amount of inventory is accumulated, there is the danger of loss owing to obsolescence. If the supply of inventory is inadequate, the potential for lost sales exists. This dilemma makes inventory an asset to which management must devote a great deal of attention.

6.   Reconciliation between the recorded inventory amount and the actual amount of inventory on hand is normally performed at least once a year. This is called a **physical inventory** and involves counting all inventory items and comparing the amount counted with the amount shown in the detailed inventory records. Any errors in the records are corrected to agree with the physical count.

7.   The **cost of goods sold** during any accounting period is defined as all the **goods available for sale** during the period less any unsold goods on hand at the end of the period (**ending inventory**). The process of valuing inventory is complicated by the determination of (**a**) the physical goods to be included in inventory, (**b**) the costs to be included in inventory, and (**c**) the cost flow assumption to be used.

Physical Goods to be Included in Inventory

8.   Normally, goods are included in inventory when they are received from the supplier. However, at the end of the period, proper accounting requires that all goods to which the company has legal title be included in ending inventory. Goods in transit at the end of the period, shipped **f.o.b. shipping point**, should be included in the buyer's ending inventory. If goods are shipped **f.o.b. destination**, they belong to the seller until actually received by the buyer. Inventory out on **consignment** belongs to the consignor and is included in its inventory.

9.   In actual practice a few exceptions exist regarding the general rule that inventory is recorded by the company that has legal title to the merchandise. These exceptions are known as **special sale agreement**s. Three of the more common special sale agreements are (**a**) sales with buy back agreement, (**b**) sales with high rates of return, and (**c**) installment sales.

Effect of Inventory Errors

10.   (L.O. 3) Errors in recording inventory can affect the statement of financial position, the income statement, or both, because inventory is used in the preparation of both financial statements. For example, the failure to include certain inventory items in a year-end physical inventory count would result in the following items being overstated (O) or understated (U): ending inventory (U); working capital (U); cost of goods sold (O); and net income (U). If merchandise was not recorded as a purchase nor counted in the ending inventory, the result would be an understatement of inventory and accounts payable in the statement of financial position and an understatement of purchases and inventory in the income statement. Net income would be unaffected by this omission as purchases and ending inventory would be misstated by the same amount.

Costs Included in Inventory

11.   (L.O. 4) Inventories are recorded at cost when acquired. Cost in terms of inventory acquisition includes all expenditures necessary in acquiring the goods and converting them to a saleable condition. **Product costs** are those costs that "attach" to the inventory and are recorded in the inventory account. These costs include freight charges on goods purchased, other direct costs of acquisition, and labor and other production costs incurred in processing the goods up to the time of sale. **Period costs**, such as selling expenses and general and administrative expenses, are not considered inventoriable costs. The reason these costs are not included as a part of the inventory valuation concerns the fact that, in most instances, these costs are unrelated to the immediate production process.

12.   IFRS allow for the capitalization of interest costs related to assets constructed for internal use or assets produced as discrete projects (such as ships or real estate projects) for sale or lease. In the case of inventories that are routinely manufactured or produced in large quantities on a repetitive basis, interest costs should not be capitalized.

Purchase Discounts

13.   When purchases are recorded net of discounts, failure to pay within the discount period results in the treatment of lost discounts as a financial expense. If the **gross method** is used, purchase discounts should be reported as a deduction from purchases on the income statement. If the **net method** is used, purchase discounts lost should be considered a financial expense and reported in the "other expense and loss" section of the income statement.

Methods Used to Price Inventories

14.   (L.O. 5) Inventory cost flow assumptions include (**a**) specific identification, (**b**) average cost, and (**c**) first-in, first-out (FIFO). It should be remembered that these assumptions relate to the flow of costs and not the physical flow of inventory items into and out of the company.

15.   **Specific identification** calls for identifying each item sold and each item in inventory. The costs of the specific items sold are included in the cost of goods sold, and the costs of the specific items on hand are included in the inventory. IFRS requires the use of the specific identification method when inventory units are not interchangeable or for goods and services related to specific projects.The **average cost method** prices items in the inventory on the basis of the average cost of all similar goods available during the period.

FIFO

16.   Use of the **FIFO inventory method** assumes that the first goods purchased are the first used or sold. In all cases where FIFO is used, the inventory and cost of goods sold would be the same at the end of the month whether a perpetual or periodic system is used. A major advantage of the FIFO method is that the ending inventory is stated in terms of an approximate current cost figure. However, because FIFO tends to reflect current costs on the statement of financial position, a basic disadvantage of this method is that current costs are not matched against current revenues on the income statement.

LIFO

17. (L.O. 6) While the IASB prohibits the use of LIFO for financial reporting purposes, LIFO is permitted under U.S. GAAP for financial reporting purposes. Additionally, the U.S. and other countries permit LIFO for tax purposes which can result in significant tax savings. When LIFO is used, the most recent inventory costs are the first costs recorded for goods manufactured or sold. When inventory records are kept on a **periodic basis**, the ending inventory would be priced by using the total units as a basis of computation, disregarding the exact dates of purchases. The calculation of ending inventory and cost of sales changes somewhat when the LIFO method is used in connection with **perpetual inventory records**.

LIFO Reserve

18. (L.O. 7) Many U.S. companies use LIFO for tax and external reporting purposes, but maintain a FIFO, average cost, or standard cost system for internal reporting purposes. The difference between the inventory method used for internal reporting purposes and LIFO is referred to as the Allowance to Reduce Inventory to LIFO or the **LIFO Reserve.** The change in the allowance balance from one period to the next must be made each year.

LIFO Liquidation

19. (L.O. 8) When the LIFO inventory method is used, many companies combine inventory items into natural groups or **pools**. Each pool is assumed to be one unit for the purpose of costing the inventory. Any increment above beginning inventory is normally identified as a new inventory layer and priced at the average cost of goods purchased during the year. When the inventory is decreased, the most recently added inventory layer is the first layer eliminated (last-in, first-out). The **pooled approach** reduces record keeping and, accordingly, the cost of utilizing the LIFO inventory method.

Dollar-Value LIFO

20. (L.O. 9) Use of the pooled approach can result in problems for companies that often change the mix of their products, materials, and production methods. To overcome these problems, the **dollar-value LIFO method** has been developed. The important feature of the dollar-value LIFO method is that increases and decreases in a pool are determined and measured in terms of total dollar value, not the physical quantity of the goods as is done in the traditional LIFO pool approach.

21. In computing inventory under the dollar-value LIFO method, the ending inventory is first priced at the most current cost. Current cost is then restated to prices prevailing when LIFO was adopted. This is accomplished by using a **price index**. A new inventory layer is formed when the ending inventory, stated in base-year costs, exceeds the base-year costs of beginning inventory. Increases are priced at current cost. If the ending inventory, stated at base-year costs, is less than beginning inventory, the decrease is subtracted from the most recently added layer. A price index for the current year is computed by dividing **Ending Inventory for the Period at Current-Year Costs** by **Ending Inventory for the Period at Base-Year Costs**. The dollar-value method is a more practical way of valuing a complex, multiple-item inventory than the traditional LIFO method. The **Comprehensive Dollar-Value LIFO Example** in the text should be studied as it provides an excellent means of understanding the dollar-value LIFO computation.

Advantages and Disadvantages of LIFO

22. (L.O. 10) Proponents of the LIFO method advocate its use on the basis of its (**a**) proper matching of recent costs with current revenue, (**b**) tax benefits, (**c**) improved cash flow, and (**d**) future earnings hedge. Those opposed to the LIFO method claim that it (**a**) lowers reported earnings, (**b**) reports outdated costs on the statement of financial position, (**c**) is contrary to normal physical flow, (**d**) creates involuntary liquidation problems, and (**e**) invites poor buying habit.

Selection of Inventory Method

23.   (L.O. 11) LIFO is generally preferable to FIFO when: **(a)** selling prices and revenues have been increasing faster than costs, and **(b)** LIFO has been traditional, such as department stores and industries where a farily constant "base stock" is present. LIFO would not be preferable when: **(a)** prices tend to lag behind costs, **(b)** specific identification is traditional, and **(c)** unit costs tend to decrease as production increases, thereby nullyifying the tax benefit that LIFO might provide.

GLOSSARY

Average cost method.	An inventory costing method that assumes that the goods available for sale are homogeneous.
Consigned goods.	Goods shipped by a consignor who retains ownership to another party called the consignee.
Dollar-value LIFO method.	An inventory costing method whereby increases and decreases in a pool are determined and measured in terms of total dollar value, not the physical quantity of the goods in the inventory pool.
Finished goods inventory.	The costs identified with the completed but unsold units on hand at the end of the fiscal period.
First-In, First-Out method.	An inventory costing method that assumes that the costs of the earliest goods acquired are the first to be recognized as cost of goods sold.
F.O.B. destination.	The terms for shipping goods which state that title does not pass until the buyer receives the goods from the common carrier.
F.O.B. shipping point.	The terms for shipping goods which state that title passes to the buyer when the seller delivers the goods to the common carrier who acts as an agent for the buyer.
Last-In, First-Out method.	An inventory costing method that assumes that the costs of the latest units purchased are the first to be allocated to cost of goods sold.
LIFO liquidation.	The erosion of LIFO inventory, which can lead to distortions of net income and substantial tax payments.
Moving-average method.	An inventory costing method that uses the average cost method for perpetual inventory records.
Period costs.	Costs that are not considered to be directly related to the acquisition or production of goods including selling expenses and general administrative expenses.
Periodic inventory system.	An inventory system in which the quantity of inventory on hand is determined periodically.

Perpetual inventory system.	An inventory system in which the quantity and cost of each inventory item is maintained and the records continuously show the inventory that should be on hand at any time.
Product costs.	Costs that are directly connected with the bringing of goods to the place of business of the buyer and converting such goods to a salable condition.
Purchase discounts.	A reduction in the purchase price when the payment of goods is made within a stated period of time.
Raw materials inventory.	The cost of goods and materials on hand but not yet placed into production.
Specific identification method.	An actual physical flow costing method in which items still in inventory are specifically costed to arrive at the total cost of the ending inventory.
Work in process inventory.	The cost of the raw material on which production has been started but not completed, plus the direct labor cost applied specifically to this material and a ratable share of manufacturing overhead costs.

CHAPTER OUTLINE

Fill in the outline presented below.

(L.O. 1) Major Classifications of Inventory

Raw Materials

Work in Process

Finished Goods

(L.O. 2) Perpetual Inventory

Periodic Inventory

Basic Issues in Inventory Valuation

Goods in Transit

Consigned Goods

Special Sales Agreements

Sales with Buyback Agreements

Chapter Outline *(continued)*

          Sales with High Rates of Return

          Sales on Installment

(L.O. 3) Effect of Inventory Errors

(L.O. 4) Costs Included in Inventory

          Product Costs

          Period Costs

          Purchase Discounts

(L.O. 5) Methods Used to Price Inventories

          Specific Identification

          Average Cost

          First-In, First-Out (FIFO)

*(L.O. 6) LIFO Cost Flow Assumption

Chapter Outline *(continued)*

    *(L.O. 7) LIFO Reserve

    *(L.O. 8) LIFO Liquidation

    *(L.O. 9) Dollar-Value LIFO

    *(L.O. 10) Major Advantages of LIFO

        Major Disadvantages of LIFO

    *(L.O. 11) Basis for Selection of Inventory Method

REVIEW QUESTIONS AND EXERCISES

TRUE-FALSE

Indicate whether each of the following is true (T) or false (F) in the space provided.

_____ 1. (L.O. 1) In the determination of cost of goods sold, cost of goods manufactured is to a manufacturing concern what cost of goods purchased is to a merchandising concern.

_____ 2. (L.O. 2) A physical inventory should be taken at least annually, even when a perpetual inventory system is used.

_____ 3. (L.O. 2) The perpetual inventory system provides a continuous record of the balances in both the inventory account and the cost of goods sold account.

_____ 4. (L.O. 2) The cost of goods sold is the cost of goods available for sale during the period less the cost of the goods on hand at the end of the period.

_____ 5. (L.O. 2) When goods are shipped f.o.b. shipping point, title passes only when the seller receives full payment for the merchandise.

_____ 6. (L.O. 2) Goods held on consignment should be included in the consignee's inventory reported on the statement of financial position.

_____   7. (L.O. 2) Interest costs associated with getting inventories ready for sale usually are included in the cost of the inventory.

_____   8. (L.O. 3) An understatement of the ending inventory will cause cost of goods sold to be understated and net income to be overstated for that period.

_____   9. (L.O. 4) Period costs and product costs are both inventoriable costs that relate to manufactured rather than purchased inventory.

_____   10. (L.O. 4) If the gross method is employed, purchase discounts should be reported as a deduction from purchases on the income statement.

_____   11. (L.O. 4) The use of a Purchase Discounts Lost account indicates that purchases are being recorded net of purchase discounts.

_____   12. (L.O. 5) When a company selects a cost flow assumption (FIFO, average cost, etc.), it must be consistent with the actual physical movement of goods through the company.

_____   13. (L.O. 5) Under the average cost method, beginning inventory should be included in the total units available but not in the total cost of goods available in computing the average cost per unit.

_____   14. (L.O. 5) A major argument in favor of the FIFO method of inventory costing is that current costs are matched against current revenues.

_____   15. (L.O. 5) The ending inventory under a FIFO periodic inventory system will be the same as under a FIFO perpetual inventory system.

_____   16. (L.O. 6) The IASB prohibits the use of LIFO.

_____   17. (L.O. 6) LIFO comes closer than FIFO to stating inventory on the statement of financial position at current costs.

_____   18. (L.O. 7) A LIFO reserve account is generally used when a company uses LIFO for tax and external reporting purposes but uses another method for internal purposes.

_____   19. (L.O. 8) To alleviate LIFO liquidation problems and to simplify the accounting, goods can be combined into pools.

_____   20. (L.O. 9) Under dollar-value LIFO, there will never be a layer for a particular year unless the quantity of inventory increased during that year.

_____   21. (L.O. 9) All companies using the dollar-value LIFO method are required to use the same price index.

_____   22. (L.O. 10) In a period of rising prices, LIFO yields a larger cost of goods sold than does FIFO.

_____   23. (L.O. 10) Tax benefits are a significant advantage of the LIFO method.

_____   24. (L.O. 11) A change in inventory methods requires that the change be explained and its effect be disclosed in the financial statements.

_____   25. (L.O. 11) LIFO would probably be preferable where prices tend to lag behind costs.

MULTIPLE CHOICE

Select the best answer for each of the following items and enter the corresponding letter in the space provided.

_____ 1. (L.O. 2) The amount of inventory purchased during a particular year is accumulated in a Purchases account under a:

	Periodic Inventory System	Perpetual Inventory System
A.	Yes	No
B.	Yes	Yes
C.	No	Yes
D.	No	No

_____ 2. (L.O. 2) Valuation of inventories requires the determination of all of the following except:

A.   The costs to be included in inventory.
B.   The physical goods to be included in inventory.
C.   The cost of goods held on consignment from other companies.
D.   The cost flow assumption to be adopted.

_____ 3. (L.O. 2) Goods in transit at the statement of financial position date should be included in the purchaser's inventory if they are shipped:

	F.O.B. Destination	F.O.B. Shipping Point
A.	No	No
B .	No	Yes
C.	Yes	No
D.	Yes	Yes

_____ 4. (L.O. 2) The following items were included in Voigt Corporation's inventory account at December 31, 2012:

Goods held on consignment by Voigt	$ 7,000
Merchandise out on consignment, at sales price, including 30% mark-up on selling price	12,000
Goods purchased, in transit, shipped f.o.b. shipping point	9,000

Voigt's inventory account at December 31, 2012, should be reduced by:

A. $10,600
B. $12,600
C. $16,000
D. $28,000

_____ 5. (L.O. 3) The ending inventory of the Bonie Company is understated in year one by $20,000. This error is not corrected in year one or in year two. What impact will this error have on total net income for years one and two combined?

A.   No effect on total net income for the two years.
B.   Overstate total income by $20,000.
C.   Understate total income by $20,000.
D.   Overstate net income for year one by $20,000 and year two by $20,000 for a total overstatement of $40,000.

_____ 6. (L.O. 3) The failure to record a purchase of merchandise on account even though the goods are properly included in the physical inventory results in:

      A.   an overstatement of assets and net income.

      B.   an understatement of assets and net income.

      C.   an understatement of cost of goods sold and liabilities and an overstatement of assets.

      D.   an understatement of liabilities and an overstatement of owners' equity.

_____ 7. (L.O. 4) Costs which are inventoriable include all of the following except:

      A.   costs that are directly connected with the bringing of goods to the place of business of the buyer.

      B.   costs that are directly connected with the converting of goods to a salable condition.

      C.   buying costs of a purchasing department.

      D.   selling costs of a sales department.

_____ 8. (L.O. 4) Which of the following interest costs should be capitalized?

	Assets Constructed for Internal Use	Assets Produced as Discrete Projects for Sale or Lease
A.	Yes	Yes
B.	Yes	No
C.	No	Yes
D.	No	No

_____ 9. (L.O. 4) The use of a Purchase Discounts Lost account implies that the recorded cost of a purchased inventory item is its:

      A.   invoice price.

      B.   invoice price plus the purchase discount price.

      C.   invoice price less the purchase discount allowable, when taken.

      D.   invoice price less the purchase discount allowable, whether or not taken.

_____ 10. (L.O. 5) Which of the following inventory methods comes closest to stating ending inventory at replacement costs?

      A.   FIFO.

      B.   Specific identification.

      C.   Weighted-average.

      D.   Base stock.

_____ 11. (L.O. 6) The use of LIFO under a perpetual inventory system (units and costs):

      A.   may yield a higher inventory valuation than LIFO under a periodic inventory system when prices are steadily falling.

      B.   may yield a higher inventory valuation than LIFO under a periodic inventory system when prices are steadily rising.

      C.   always yields the same inventory valuation as LIFO under a periodic inventory system.

      D.   can never yield the same inventory valuation as LIFO under a periodic inventory system.

_____ 12. (L.O. 5) One argument against the use of the specific identification inventory method is:

      A.   actual costs are matched against actual revenues.

      B.   estimated costs are matched against actual revenues.

      C.   the potential for the manipulation of net income by selecting costs to match against revenues.

      D.   that it is difficult to understand.

_____ 13. (L.O. 5) Which of the following is false with regard to FIFO?

     A.   FIFO tends to approximate the physical flow of goods.

     B.   FIFO tends to prevent manipulation of income.

     C.   FIFO tends to match current costs against current revenues on the income statement.

     D.   FIFO tends to approximate replacement cost on the statement of financial position.

_____ 14. (L.O. 6) The Slowe Company has been using the LIFO cost method of inventory valuation for 8 years. Its 2012 ending inventory was $135,000 but it would have been $180,000 if FIFO had been used. Thus, if FIFO had been used, Slowe's net income before income taxes would have been:

     A. $45,000 less in 2012.

     B. $45,000 more in 2012.

     C. $45,000 greater over the 8-year period.

     D. $45,000 less over the 8-year period.

_____ 15. (L.O. 3) The purchase of inventory items on account using the perpetual inventory method:

     A.   changes working capital and the current ratio.

     B.   has no effect on working capital but probably changes the current ratio.

     C.   has no effect on the current ratio but probably changes working capital.

     D.   has no effect on working capital or the current ratio.

_____ 16. (L.O. 6) In periods of rising prices, use of LIFO rather than the FIFO inventory method will most likely have what effect on the following items?

	Net Income	Cost of Goods Sold	Working Capital
A.	Higher	Lower	Lower
B.	Lower	Higher	Lower
C.	Higher	Higher	Higher
D.	Lower	Higher	Higher

_____ 17. (L.O. 6) Just prior to a period of rising prices, Brooks Company changed its inventory measurement method from FIFO to LIFO. What would be the effect in the next period?

     A.   Decrease the current ratio and increase inventory turnover.

     B.   Increase both the current ratio and inventory turnover.

     C.   Decrease both the current ratio and inventory turnover.

     D.   Increase the current ratio and decrease inventory turnover.

_____ 18. (L.O. 8) The traditional LIFO approach which tends to emphasize specific goods in costing LIFO inventories is often unrealistic because:

     A.   it does not result in a proper matching of costs and revenues in a particular period.

     B.   cash flows are often distorted and can be delayed for one or two subsequent periods.

     C.   future price declines will adversely affect the ability to accurately report future earnings.

     D.   erosion of the LIFO inventory can easily occur which often leads to distortions of net income and large tax payments.

_____ 19. (L.O. 6) Assuming no beginning inventory, what can be said about the trend of inventory prices if cost of goods sold computed when inventory is valued using the FIFO method exceeds cost of goods sold when inventory is valued using the LIFO method?

     A.   Prices increased.

     B.   Prices decreased.

     C.   Prices remained unchanged.

     D.   Price trend cannot be determined from the information given.

_____ 20. (L.O. 9) The dollar-value inventory method is an improvement over the traditional LIFO pool approach because:

      A.   the mathematical computations are greatly simplified.

      B.   it is easier to apply where few inventory items are employed and little change in product mix is anticipated.

      C.   increases and decreases in a pool are determined and measured in terms of total dollar value rather than the physical quantity of the goods in the inventory pool.

      D.   dissimilar items of inventory can be grouped to form pools under the dollar-value LIFO method.

_____ 21. (L.O. 9) Which of the following statements is not true as it relates to the dollar-value LIFO inventory method?

      A.   It is easier to erode LIFO layers using dollar-value LIFO techniques than it is with specific goods pooled LIFO.

      B.   Under the dollar-value LIFO method, it is possible to have the entire inventory in only one pool.

      C.   Several pools are commonly employed in using the dollar-value LIFO inventory method.

      D.   Under dollar-value LIFO, increases and decreases in a pool are determined and measured in terms of total dollar value, not physical quantity.

_____ 22. (L.O. 9) Amidei Company adopts dollar-value LIFO inventory on 12/31/12 when its inventory at current price is $45,000. The inventory value on 12/31/13 at current prices is $65,000. If prices increased by 30% during 2013, what is the dollar-value LIFO inventory at 12/31/13

      A. $65,000.

      B. $58,000.

      C. $51,500.

      D. $48,700.

_____ 23. (L.O. 9) Estimates of price-level changes for specific inventories are required for which of the following inventory methods?

      A.   Weighted-average cost.

      B.   FIFO.

      C.   LIFO.

      D.   Dollar-value LIFO.

_____ 24. (L.O. 10) Which of the following is not considered an advantage of LIFO when prices are rising?

      A.   The inventory will be overstated.

      B.   The more recent costs are matched against current revenues.

      C.   There will be a deferral of income tax.

      D.   A company's future reported earnings will not be affected substantially by future price declines.

_____ 25. (L.O. 11) The acquisition cost of a heavily used raw material changes frequently. The inventory amount of this material at year end will be the same if perpetual records (units and costs) are kept as it would be under a periodic inventory method only if the inventory amount is computed under the:

      A.   weighted-average method.

      B.   first-in, first-out method.

      C.   last-in, first-out method.

      D.   direct costing method.

REVIEW EXERCISES

1.   (L.O.3) An examination of the records of Moran Company revealed that goods costing $1,000 were received on December 31, 2012. The purchase invoice for these goods was not received until January 4, 2013, at which time the purchase and related liability were recorded. Indicate whether the following financial statement items were understated (U), overstated (O), or not misstated (N) for the years 2012 and 2013.

	2012	2013
Purchases	_____	_____
Inventory, December 31	_____	_____
Cost of goods sold	_____	_____
Net income	_____	_____
Assets	_____	_____
Liabilities	_____	_____
Retained earnings	_____	_____

2.   (L.O.4) Garth purchased merchandise inventory costing $24,000 with credit terms of 2/10, net 30. Eight days after the purchase, Garth paid one-half of the outstanding obligation. The remaining amount was paid 30 days after the date of purchase.

Instructions:
Assuming Garth uses the periodic inventory system, prepare the journal entries Garth would make for the purchase and the two subsequent payments using:

a.   the gross method.
b.   the net method.

a.

General Journal J1			
Date	**Account Title**	**Debit**	**Credit**

b.

	General Journal		
			J1
Date	**Account Title**	**Debit**	**Credit**

3. (L.O.6) Doherty Company's records show the following information related to one of its products:

May 1	Balance on hand	300 units @ $5
May 12	Purchased	600 units @ $6
May 30	Purchased	100 units @ $7

Doherty Company uses a periodic inventory system. Assuming that 600 units were sold during May.

Instructions:
Compute the May 31 inventory and the cost of goods sold during May under each of the following methods:

a. FIFO
b. LIFO
c. Weighted-average

a.

b.

_____

_____

_____

_____

_____

_____

_____

c.

_____

_____

_____

_____

_____

_____

_____

4.   (L.O. 6) Spelling Company had the following transactions in connection with their inventory account during the month of August.

Purchases					**Sales**			
Aug. 1	(Goods on hand)	650	@	$8.40	Aug. 4	280	@	$12.60
Aug. 3		770	@	8.20	Aug. 10	350	@	12.60
Aug. 7		1,250	@	8.00	Aug. 12	900	@	13.00
Aug. 11		650	@	8.50	Aug. 17	650	@	13.00
Aug. 16		500	@	8.70	Aug. 20	860	@	13.50
Aug. 23		750	@	8.60	Aug. 25	700	@	13.50
		4,570				3,740		

Instructions:

a.   Assuming that the company keeps perpetual records in units only; compute the inventory at August 31, using (1) LIFO; and (2) average cost.

b.   Assuming that perpetual records are kept in dollars, compute the inventory at August 31, using (1) FIFO; and (2) LIFO.

c.   Calculate the cost of goods sold and gross profit Spelling Company should record for the month of August assuming FIFO and periodic inventory procedures.

a.

b.

c.

_____
_____
_____
_____
_____
_____
_____
_____
_____
_____
_____
_____
_____

5.   (L.O.8) Perry Company manufactures a single product. On December 31, 2012, Perry adopted the dollar-value LIFO inventory method. The inventory on that date using the dollar-value LIFO inventory method was $50,000. Inventory data are as follows:

Year	Inventory at Respective Year-End Cost Prices	Price Index at Year End
2012	$50,000	100
2013	73,500	105
2014	71,500	110

Instructions:
Compute the inventory at December 31, 2013 and 2014 using the dollar-value LIFO method.

_____
_____
_____
_____
_____
_____
_____
_____
_____
_____
_____
_____
_____
_____
_____
_____
_____
_____
_____
_____
_____
_____

5. *(continued)*

_____

_____

_____

_____

_____

_____

_____

_____

_____

_____

SOLUTIONS TO REVIEW QUESTIONS

TRUE-FALSE

1.   (T)

2.   (T)

3.   (T)

4.   (T)

5.   (F)   When goods are shipped f.o.b. shipping point, title passes to the buyer when the seller delivers the goods to the common carrier who acts as an agent for the buyer.

6.   (F)   Goods held on consignment by a consignee remain the property of the consignor until the goods are sold. Thus, goods on consignment are properly included in the consignor's inventory rather than the inventory of the consignee.

7.   (F)   Interest costs associated with getting inventories ready for sale usually are expensed as incurred.

8.   (F)   An understatement in ending inventory results in an overstatement of cost of good sold and a corresponding understatement of net income.

9.   (F)   Product costs are those costs that "attach" to the inventory (whether purchased or manufactured) and are considered to be a part of the total inventory valuation. Period costs are not considered to be directly related to the acquisition or production of goods and therefore are not considered to be a part of the inventories.

10. (T)

11. (T)

12. (F)   A company can select any cost flow assumption regardless of the physical flow of its goods.

13. (F)   Under the average cost method, beginning inventory is included in both the total units available and in the total cost of goods available in computing the average cost per unit.

14. (F) Under the FIFO method of inventory costing, the first costs into the inventory account which are the oldest costs are the costs matched against the current revenue. Thus, current costs are not matched against current revenue under the FIFO inventory method.

15. (T)

16. (T)

17. (F) LIFO is an inventory valuation method that emphasizes the recording of current costs on the income statement. Under LIFO the most recent inventory costs are charged against revenue; thus the older inventory costs are shown on the statement of financial position.

18. (T)

19. (T)

20. (T)

21. (F) Many companies use a general price-level index such as the Consumers Price Index for Urban Consumers (CPI-U) and when a specific index is not readily available, companies use an index computed using the following formula:

$$\frac{\text{Ending inventory for the period at current cost}}{\text{Ending inventory for the period at base - year cost}} = \text{Price index for current year}$$

22. (T)

23. (T)

24. (T)

25. (F) LIFO would probably not be preferable where prices tend to lag behind costs.

MULTIPLE CHOICE

1. (A)   Purchases of inventory are debited to the inventory account under a perpetual inventory system. The only time the purchases account is used is when a periodic inventory system is in place.

2. (C)   The costs, physical goods, and flow assumption are necessary elements in determining inventory valuation. Goods on consignment from other companies do not belong to the consignee and as such are not a part of the consignee's inventory valuation.

3. (B)   Goods shipped f.o.b. (free on board) shipping point in transit at the end of the year belong to the buyer and should be shown in the buyer's records.

4. (A)   The following reductions should be made in Voigt's inventory:

Goods held on consignment	$ 7,000*
Gross profit included in merchandise out	
on consignment (.30 × $12,000)	3,600**
	$10,600

   *   Goods held on consignment should be included in the consignor's inventory, not the inventory of Voigt, the consignee.
   ** Inventory should be valued at the lower of cost or market. Therefore, the gross profit on merchandise out on consignment should not be included in Voigt's inventory.
   Note: The $9,000 of goods purchased f.o.b. shipping point and which were in transit at December 31, 2012, should be included in Voigt's inventory since title to these goods had passed to Voigt at the time of shipment.

5. (A)   This is an example of a counterbalancing error. The income in year one will be understated by $20,000 because of the ending inventory error. However, in the second year the beginning inventory will be understated by $20,000 which will cause an overstatement of net income by the same amount. Thus, the effect of the error on total income over the two year period is zero.

6. (D)   The failure to record the purchases understates liabilities because the payable was not recorded. The fact that the amount of the purchase was properly included in the physical inventory but omitted from goods available for sale causes cost of goods sold to be understated. This understatement of cost of goods sold causes net income to be overstated resulting in an overstatement of owner's equity.

7. (D)   Inventoriable costs include costs that are directly connected with the bringing of goods to the place of business and converting such goods to a salable condition. The buying costs or expenses of a purchasing department are also included in the inventoriable costs. Selling costs of a sales department are considered period costs and are not inventoriable.

8. (A)   The IASB has ruled that interest costs related to assets constructed for internal use or assets produced as discrete projects (such as ships or real estate projects) for sale or lease should be capitalized.

9. (D)   The Purchase Discounts Lost account is used when the purchase of inventory is recorded net of the allowable discount and the purchaser does not pay within the discount period.

10. (A)   Because the oldest costs in inventory are charged against income under the FIFO inventory method, the inventory valuation shown on the statement of financial position represents the most recent inventory costs. Thus, FIFO comes closest to stating inventory at replacement costs when compared to the other three methods listed.

11. (D)   In a period of steadily rising prices, LIFO under a periodic inventory system will find the highest inventory cost being charged against revenue. Under the same set of circumstances, the use of LIFO under a perpetual inventory system (units and costs) might find inventory purchases made subsequent to the final sale. If such is the case, the perpetual method would yield a higher ending inventory valuation.

12. (C)   Use of the specific identification method allows for the potential manipulation of net income when similar items that have different costs can be selected for sale. Thus, if two identical inventory items have different costs, selecting the item with the lower cost will increase net income. Alternative "A" is an advantage of the specific identification method. Alternatives "B" and "D" are not relevant alternatives.

13. (C)   One of the disadvantages of FIFO is that the FIFO method fails to match current costs against current revenues; FIFO tends to report the most current costs on the statement of financial position.

14. (C)   The effect on net income of differences in ending inventory amounts wash out over two years. The reason for this is that the ending inventory for one year is the beginning inventory for the next year. For example, an overstatement of ending inventory at December 31, 2012, will result in an overstatement of 2012's income but an understatement of 2011's income. Therefore, the only difference in the net income before taxes for the 8 year period ending December 31, 2012, would be that net income before taxes computed under FIFO would be $45,000 greater than that computed under LIFO.

15. (B)   The purchase of inventory on account increases both current assets (inventory) and current liabilities (accounts payable) by the same amount. This results in no change in working capital. However, if current assets and current liabilities are both increased by the same amount, the current ratio will decrease if the current ratio was greater than one, increase if the current ratio was less than one, and remain the same if the current ratio was exactly one.

16. (B)   In periods of rising prices, the LIFO method will find the higher costs being charged to income resulting in a higher cost of goods sold and a lower net income. Also, with the higher costs being charged to net income, the ending inventory will be lower under LIFO than under FIFO. Thus, other things being equal, the working capital (current assets minus current liabilities) should be lower.

17. (A)   If prices are increasing, the inventory value determined using LIFO would be less than that determined by using FIFO. This is so because the oldest prices, in this case, would be used to value inventory. A smaller inventory value would result in decreasing the current ratio (current assets/current liabilities) and increasing the inventory turnover ratio (cost of goods sold/average inventory).

18. (D)   Alternatives A, B, and C are either advantages of using the LIFO inventory method or are indications of things that can be avoided by its use. However, the traditional LIFO approach does result in the potential for LIFO liquidation which takes away some of the advantages of LIFO and can result in poor earnings results. Using the specific goods pooled LIFO method can help alleviate the liquidation problem and its attendant negative affect on earnings.

19. (B)   LIFO charges the most recent purchases to cost of goods sold. Therefore, if cost of goods sold is less under LIFO than FIFO, prices must be decreasing.

20.   (C)   The dollar-value LIFO method not only allows increases and decreases in a pool to be determined and measured in terms of total dollar value, but also two additional advantages are noted. First, a broader range of goods may be included in a dollar-value LIFO pool than in a regular pool. Second, in a dollar-value LIFO pool, replacement is permitted if it is similar as to type of material, or similarity in use, or interchangeability.

21.   (A)   A major reason for the use of dollar-value LIFO concerns the difficulty in eroding the LIFO layers. The entire inventory under dollar-value LIFO can be in one pool or in numerous pools. Also, as the name implies, inventory pools are determined and measured in terms of total dollar value.

22.   (C)   Ending inventory at beginning of the year prices:
$65,000 \div 130\% = \$50,000$
Inventory increase in beginning of year prices:
$50,000 - \$45,000 = \$5,000$
Real dollar quantity increase:
$5,000 \times 130\% = \$6,500$
12/31/13 inventory valuation:

First layer (Base price 100%)	$45,000
Second layer (2013 increase @ 130%)	6,500
Dollar-value LIFO Inventory 12/31/13	$51,500

23.   (D)   Under dollar-value LIFO inventories are maintained at current prices. Estimates of price-level changes (index numbers) are used to convert the ending inventory from year-end prices to LIFO prices.

24.   (A)   The major advantages of LIFO are (1) the more recent costs are matched against current revenues to provide a better measure of current earnings; (2) as long as the price level increases and inventory quantities do not decrease, a deferral of income tax occurs in LIFO; (3) because of the deferral of income tax, there is improvement of cash; and (4) a company's future reported earnings will not be affected substantially by future price declines. A major disadvantage of LIFO when prices are rising is that inventories will be understated because the older (lower) costs are reflected in inventory.

25.   (B)   Whether inventory is priced under the periodic or perpetual method, the ending inventory valuation and cost of goods sold will be the same as long as the FIFO cost flow assumption is used.

REVIEW EXERCISES

1.

	2012	2013
Purchases	U	O
Inventory, December 31	N	N
Cost of goods sold	U	O
Net income	O	U
Assets	N	N
Liabilities	U	N
Retained earnings	O	N

2a. PURCHASE:

	2012	2013
Purchases	24,000	
Accounts Payable		24,000
PAYMENTS:		
(1) Accounts Payable	12,000	
Purchase Discounts		240
Cash		11,760
(2) Accounts Payable	12,000	
Cash		12,000

b. PURCHASE:

	2012	2013
Purchases	23,520	
Accounts Payable		23,520
PAYMENTS:		
(1) Accounts Payable	11,760	
Cash		11,760
(2) Accounts Payable	11,760	
Purchase Discounts Lost	240	
Cash		12,000

3.

		May 31 Inventory	Cost of Goods Sold
a.	FIFO	$2,500	$3,300
b.	LIFO	2,100	3,700
c.	Weighted-average	2,320	3,480

4a.　LIFO:

Beginning Inventory & Purchases	4,570
Sales for the Period (units)	3,740
Ending Inventory (units)	830

LIFO Costs:　　650　@　$8.40　=　$5,460
　　　　　　　　180　@　　8.20　=　　1,476
Ending Inventory　　　　　　　　　　$6,936

Average Cost:

$$\frac{\text{Total Cost}}{\text{Total Units}} \quad \frac{\$38,099}{4,570} \times 830 = \$6,920$$

b.　FIFO:

　　　　　　750　@　$8.60　=　$6,450.00
　　　　　　　80　@　　8.70　=　　　696.00
Total　　　　　　　　　　　　　　$7,146.00

LIFO:

Cost of Sales:

Aug. 4	280	@	$8.20	=	$ 2,296.00
Aug. 10	350	@	8.00	=	2,800.00
Aug. 12　(900)	650	@	8.50	=	5,525.00
	250	@	8.00	=	2,000.00
Aug. 17　(650)	500	@	8.70	=	4,350.00
	150	@	8.00	=	1,200.00
Aug. 20　(860)	500	@	8.00	=	4,000.00
	360	@	8.20	=	2,952.00
Aug. 25	700	@	8.60	=	6,020.00
Cost of Goods Sold					$31,143.00

Ending Inventory:

　　　　　　　50　@　$8.60　=　$ 430.00
　　　　　　130　@　　8.20　=　1,066.00
　　　　　　650　@　　8.40　=　5,460.00
Ending Inventory　　　　　　　　$6,956.00

c.
Total Sales		$49,148.00
Goods available for sale	$38,099.00	
Less Ending Inventory	7,146.00	
Cost of Goods Sold		30,953.00
Gross Profit		$18,195.00

5.

December 31, 2013 inventory at 2013 prices	$73,500
December 31, 2013, inventory at base-year prices ($73,500 ÷ 1.05)	70,000
January 1, 2013 inventory at base-year prices	50,000
2013 inventory increase at base-year prices	20,000
2013 inventory increase at 2013 prices ($20,000 × 1.05)	21,000

December 31, 2013 inventory:

Layer	Base-Year Prices	Price Index	Dollar-Value LIFO
2012	$50,000	100	$50,000
2013	20,000	105	21,000
	$70,000		$71,000

December 31, 2014 inventory at 2014 prices	$71,500
December 31, 2014 inventory at base-year prices ($71,500 ÷ 1.10)	65,000
January 1, 2014 inventory at base-year prices	70,000
2014 inventory decrease at base-year prices	5,000
2014 inventory decreases at prices in existence when most recent layer was added (2013) $5,000 × 1.05	5,250

December 31, 2014 inventory:

Layer	Base-Year Prices	Price Index	Dollar-Value LIFO
2012	$50,000	100	$50,000
2013	15,000	105	15,750
	$65,000		$65,750

9

Inventories: Additional Valuation Issues

CHAPTER LEARNING OBJECTIVES

1. Describe and apply the lower-of-cost-or-net realizable value rule.
2. Explain when companies value inventories at net realizable value.
3. Explain when companies use the relative sales value method to value inventories.
4. Discuss accounting issues related to purchase commitments.
5. Determine ending inventory by applying the gross profit method.
6. Determine ending inventory by applying the retail inventory method.
7. Explain how to report and analyze inventory.

CHAPTER REVIEW

1. Chapter 9 concludes the discussion of inventories by addressing certain unique valuation problems not covered in Chapter 8. Chapter 9 also includes a description of the development and use of various estimation techniques used to value ending inventory without a physical count.

Lower-of-Cost-or-Net Realizable Value (LCNRV)

2. (L.O. 1) When the **future revenue-producing ability** associated with inventory is below its **original cost,** the inventory should be written down to reflect this loss. Thus, the historical cost principle is abandoned when the future utility of the asset is no longer as great as its original cost. When this occurs, companies report their inventories at the lower-of-cost-or-net realizable value (LCNRV). The loss of utility in inventory should be charged against revenue in the period in which the loss occurs (not in the period of sale).

3. A company may apply the LCNRV (**a**) directly to each item, (**b**) to a group of similar or related items, or (**c**) to the total inventory. The individual-item approach is preferred by many companies because tax rules require its use when practical, and it produces the most conservative inventory valuation on the statement of financial position. Whichever method a company selects, it should apply the method consistently from period to period.

Recording Net Realizable Value Instead of Cost

4. Two methods are used to record inventory at net realizable value. The cost-of-goods-sold method records the write-down of inventory to NRV as part of cost of goods sold. Thus, the loss is buried in the cost of goods sold and no individual loss account is reported in the income statement. Under the second method, referred to as the loss method, the write-down of inventory to NRV is recorded as a debit to a separate loss account. IFRS does not specify a method to use, but recording the loss separately does not distort the cost of goods sold and clearly displays the loss that results from a market decline. To

reduce the inventory to NRV on the statement of financial position, companies generally credit an allowance account, rather than crediting the inventory account directly.

5. If economic conditions change and the net realizable value of inventory previously written down has now recovered to the point that it's above cost, the amount of the original write-down is reversed (limited to the amount of the original write-down).

Valuation Bases

6. (L.O. 2) Generally, inventory is recorded at the LCNRV. However, there are two common situations where net realizable value is the general rule for valuing inventory: agricultural assets and commodities held by broker-dealers.

7. Agricultural assets consist of biological assets and agricultural produce. Biological assets are noncurrent assets that are living animals or plants such as sheep or fruit trees. Agricultural produce is the product harvested from a biological asset, such as wool or apples. Biological assets are valued at fair value less costs to sell (NRV), with gains and losses in value reported in income in the period they arise. Agricultural produce is measured at the point of harvest at fair value less costs to sell (NRV). Subsequent to harvest, this value becomes the cost of the agricultural produce and it is accounted for similar to other inventory held for sale in the ordinary course of business.

8. Commodity broker-dealers buy and sell commodities (such as harvested corn or gold) for others or for themselves. Their main objective is to sell the commodities in the near future to profit from price fluctuations. These inventories are valued at fair value less costs to sell (NRV).

9. (L.O. 3) When a group of varying inventory items is purchased for a lump sum price, a problem exists relative to the cost per item. The **relative sales value method** apportions the total cost to individual items on the basis of the selling price of each item.

Purchase Commitments

10. (L.O. 4) **Purchase commitments** represent contracts for the purchase of inventory at a specified price in a future period. If material, the details of the contract should be disclosed in a note of the buyer's statement of financial position. If the contract price is in excess of the market price and it is expected that losses will occur when the purchase is effected, the loss should be recognized in the period during which the market decline took place.

The Gross Profit Method

11. (L.O. 5) The **gross profit method** is used to estimate the amount of ending inventory. Its use is **not** appropriate for financial reporting purposes; however, it can serve a useful purpose when an approximation of ending inventory is needed. Such approximations are sometimes required by auditors or when inventory and inventory records are destroyed by fire or some other catastrophe. The gross profit method should never be used as a substitute for a yearly physical inventory unless the inventory has been destroyed. The gross profit method is based on the assumptions that (**a**) the beginning inventory plus purchases equal total goods to be accounted for; (**b**) goods not sold must be on hand; and (**c**) if sales, reduced to cost, are deducted from the sum of the opening inventory plus purchases, the result is the ending inventory.

The Retail Inventory Method

12.   (L.O. 6) The **retail inventory method** is an inventory estimation technique based upon an observable pattern between cost and sales price that exists in most retail concerns. This method requires that a record be kept of (**a**) the total cost and retail of goods purchased, (**b**) the total cost and retail value of the goods available for sale, and (**c**) the sales for the period.

13.   Basically, the retail method requires the computation of the **cost-to-retail ratio** of inventory available for sale. This ratio is computed by dividing the **cost** of the goods available for sale by the **retail value** (selling price) of goods available for sale. Once the ratio is determined, total sales for the period are deducted from the retail value of inventory available for sale. The resulting amount represents ending inventory priced at retail. When this amount is multiplied by the cost to retail ratio, an approximation of the cost of ending inventory results. Use of this method eliminates the need for a physical count of inventory each time an income statement is prepared. However, physical counts are made at least yearly to determine the accuracy of the records and to avoid overstatements due to theft, loss, and breakage.

14.   To obtain the appropriate inventory figures under the retail inventory method, proper treatment must be given to markups, markup cancellations, markdowns, and markdown cancellations.

15.   When the cost to retail ratio is computed after net markups (markups less markup cancellations) have been added, the retail inventory method approximates lower of cost or net realizable value. This is known as the **conventional retail inventory method**. If both net markups and net markdowns are included before the cost to retail ratio is computed, the retail inventory method approximates cost.

16.   The retail inventory method becomes more complicated when such items as **freight-in, purchase returns and allowances**, and **purchase discounts** are involved. In essence, the treatment of the items affecting the cost column of the retail inventory approach follows the computation of cost of goods available for sale. Freight costs are treated as a part of the purchase cost; purchase returns and allowances are ordinarily considered a reduction of the price at both cost and retail; and purchase discounts usually are considered as a reduction of the cost of purchases.

17.   Other items that require careful consideration include **transfers-in, normal shortages, abnormal shortages,** and **employee discounts**. Transfers-in from another department should be reported in the same way as purchases from an outside enterprise. Normal shortages should reduce the retail column because these goods are no longer available for sale. Abnormal shortages should be deducted from both the cost and retail columns and reported as a special inventory amount or as a loss. Employee discounts should be deducted from the retail column in the same way as sales.

18.   The retail inventory method is widely used (**a**) to permit the computation of net income without a physical count of inventory, (**b**) as a control measure in determining inventory shortages, (**c**) in regulating quantities of inventory on hand, and (**d**) for insurance information.

Presentation and Analysis

19.   Inventories normally represent one of the most significant assets held by a business entity. Therefore, the accounting profession has mandated certain disclosure requirements related to inventories. Some of the disclosure requirements include: the composition of the inventory, the inventory financing, the inventory costing methods employed, and whether costing methods have been consistently applied. Two common financial ratios used to analyze inventory are (1) the inventory turnover ratio and (2) the average days to sell inventory.

GLOSSARY

Agricultural assets.	Include both biological assets (living animals and plants) and agricultural produce (harvested from the biological asset).
Cost-to-retail ratio.	Total goods available for sale at cost divided by the total goods available at retail.
Gross profit method.	A method for estimating the ending inventory by applying a gross profit rate to net sales.
Lower of cost or net realizable value (LCNRV).	A basis whereby inventory is stated at the lower of cost or net realizable value.
Markdown.	A decrease below the original retail price.
Markdown cancellation.	An increase in the selling price that follows a markdown. A markdown cancellation will never increase the selling price above the original retail price.
Markup.	An increase above the original retail price.
Markup cancellation.	A decrease in the selling price of an item that had been previously marked up above the original retail price. A markup cancellation will never reduce the selling price below the original retail price.
Net realizable value.	The estimated selling price in the ordinary course of business less reasonably predictable costs of completion and disposal.
Original retail price.	The price at which the item was originally marked for sale.
Purchase commitments.	Agreements to buy inventory weeks, months, or even years in advance.
Retail inventory method.	A method used to estimate the cost of the ending inventory by applying a cost to retail ratio to the ending inventory at retail.

CHAPTER OUTLINE

Fill in the outline presented below.

(L.O. 1) Lower of Cost or Net Realizable Value

(L.O. 3) Valuation Using Relative Sales Value

(L.O. 4) Purchase Commitments

(L.O. 5) The Gross Profit Method of Estimating Inventory

Computation of Gross Profit Percentage

(L.O. 6) The Retail Inventory Method

Conventional Method—With Markups and Markdowns

(L.O. 7) Presentation and Analysis of Inventories

DEMONSTRATION PROBLEMS

1.   (L.O.2) Stock Farms has 1,000 sheep that are being raised for their wool production. The company began operating on January 1, 2011 by purchasing the sheep for $275,400. The following information is available at December 31, 2011:

Sheep

Carrying value 1/1/11	$275,400
Change in fair value due to growth	14,300
Decrease in value due to shearing	8,600
Value of wool from shearing	33,600

What is the value of the sheep as reported in Stock Farms' statement of financial position at December 31, 2011?

Solution:

Sheep

Carrying value, 1/1/11	$275,400
Change in value due to growth	14,300
Decrease in value due to shearing	(8,600)
Carrying value, 12/31/11	$281,100

2.   (L.O.5) Compute the approximate ending inventory for the Fox Department Store assuming: beginning inventory (cost), $85,000; purchases (cost), $226,000; sales at selling price, $345,000; average gross profit rate on selling prices is 38%.

Solution:

Beginning inventory		$ 85,000
Purchases		226,000
Goods available		311,000
Sales	$345,000	
Less gross profit	131,100*	
Sales at cost		213,900
Approximate ending inventory		$ 97,100

*(38% × $345,000)

REVIEW QUESTIONS AND EXERCISES

TRUE-FALSE

Indicate whether each of the following is true (T) or false (F) in the space provided.

_____ 1. (L.O. 1) Inventory should be written down to net realizable value when its revenue-producing ability is no longer as great as its cost.

_____ 2. (L.O. 1) In most cases, companies apply lower-of-cost-or-net-realizable value on an item-by-item basis.

_____ 3. (L.O. 1) Net realizable value is the estimated selling price in the normal course of business less the normal profit margin.

_____ 4. (L.O. 1) It is acceptable practice to write down inventory to net realizable value when net realizable value is lower than cost, but it is not acceptable to write up inventory to net realizable value when net realizable value is higher than cost.

_____ 5. (L.O. 1) The loss resulting from the write-down of inventory to net realizable value normally should be shown in the income statement following net income, net of tax.

_____ 6. (L.O. 1) If inventory is written down to net realizable value in one period, it may be written back up to its original cost in a subsequent period.

_____ 7. (L.O. 2) Under the lower-of-cost-or-net-realizable-value rule, the income statement may show a larger net income in future periods than would be justified if the inventory were carried forward at cost.

_____ 8. (L.O. 2) Under the lower-of-cost-or-net-realizable-value rule, an item of inventory should not be valued at an amount in excess of net realizable value.

_____ 9. (L.O. 2) The application of the lower of cost or net-realizable-value rule to the inventory as a whole would yield a lower inventory value than would application of the rule to each individual item.

_____ 10. (L.O. 2) The recognition of inventories at selling price less cost of disposal means that income is usually recognized before the goods are transferred to an outside party.

_____ 11. (L.O. 3) The allocation of a lump sum cost among the individual units on the basis of relative sales value assumes that each individual unit should show the same dollar amount of profit.

_____ 12. (L.O. 4) No asset or liability is recognized at the inception of a purchase commitment because the contract is "executory" in nature.

_____ 13. (L.O. 4) The account Accrued Loss on Purchase Commitments should be included in the stockholders' equity section of the statement of financial position.

_____ 14. (L.O. 4) If the contracted price under a purchase commitment is less than market and it is expected that gains will occur when the purchase is effected, gains should be recognized in the period during which such increases in market prices take place.

_____ 15. (L.O. 5) Gross margin is the excess of selling price over cost.

_____ 16. (L.O. 5) The gross margin expressed as a percentage of cost is normally less than the gross margin expressed as a percentage of sales.

_____ 17. (L.O. 5) The use of the gross profit method for interim reports does not preclude the need for a physical inventory to be taken at least annually.

_____ 18. (L.O. 6) Regardless of which version is used, the retail inventory method is permitted under IFRS.

_____ 19. (L.O. 6) The retail inventory method is not useful for interim reports.

_____ 20. (L.O. 6) The conventional retail method includes net markdowns but excludes net markups in the computation of the cost to retail percentage.

_____ 21. (L.O. 6) The inclusion of both net markups and net markdowns in the computation of the cost to retail percentage yields an inventory valuation that approximates cost.

_____ 22. (L.O. 6) The retail method assumes that the mix of the ending inventory is the same as the mix of the total goods available for sale.

_____ 23. (L.O. 6) The conventional retail inventory method is designed to approximate the lower of average cost or net realizable value.

_____ 24. (L.O. 7) The basis upon which inventory amounts are stated (lower of cost or net realizable value) and the method used in determining cost (FIFO, average cost, etc.) should be disclosed in the notes of the financial statements.

_____ 25. (L.O. 8) The inventory turnover ratio measures the number of times, on average, a company sells its inventory during a period.

MULTIPLE CHOICE

Select the best answer for each of the following items and enter the corresponding letter in the space provided.

_____ 1. (L.O. 1) Which of the following represents the best justification for the departure from the historical cost principle that results when lower of cost or net realizable value is used?

    A.   It is easier to keep track of net realizable value than it is to keep track of cost.

    B.   Cost loses its relevance for the determination of cost of goods sold if the cost of inventory has been incurred in an earlier accounting period.

    C.   The statement of financial position valuation of inventory is the most important consideration in the preparation of financial statements.

    D.   The loss in utility that results from a decline in the net realizable value of inventory should be charged against revenues in the period in which it occurs.

_____ 2. (L.O. 1) The lower of cost or net realizable value rule suffers from some conceptual deficiencies including

    A.   Inconsistent treatment of decreases in the value of inventory compared to increases in value of inventory.

    B.   Inconsistency in valuation on the statement of financial position in that inventory may be at cost one year and at net realizable value the following year.

    C.   Using lower of cost or net realizable value may result in income being higher than expected in a subsequent period.

    D.   All of the choices are correct.

_____ 3. (L.O. 1) When using the lower-of-cost-or-net-realizable-value rule, what is the meaning of "net realizable value"?

      A.   Discounted present value.
      B.   Selling price less costs of completion and disposal.
      C.   Current replacement cost.
      D.   Selling price less a normal profit margin.

_____ 4. (L.O.1) A dudad has an original cost of $15 and a replacement cost of $12. The cost of completion and disposal is $2. If the dudad has a sales value of $16 and a normal profit margin of $5, its inventory value should be:

      A. $15
      B. $12
      C. $16
      D. $14

_____ 5. (L.O. 1) During Year 1 a unit of inventory has declined in value below original cost, and is reported on the statement of financial position at its net realizable value. In Year 2 the inventory item's value recovers such that its net realizable value is now above its cost. The reported value of the inventory item on the Year 2 statement of financial position is:

      A.   Original cost.
      B.   Year 1 net realizable value.
      C.   Year 2 net realizable value.
      D.   Any of these values may be used.

_____ 6. (L.O. 1) Let A equal the reported inventory value if the lower-of-cost-or-net-realizable-value (LCNRV) rule is applied to individual items of inventory; B equals the reported inventory value if the LCNRV rule is applied to the inventory as a whole. Which of the following best describes the relationship between A and B?

      A.   A will always be equal to B.
      B.   A will always be equal to or less than B.
      C.   A will always be equal to or greater than B.
      D.   A can never be equal to B.

_____ 7. (L.O. 1) In 2011, Martinez Corporation experienced a decline in the value of its inventory resulting in a write-down of its inventory from $550,000 to $430,000. The company used the loss method in 2011 to record the necessary adjustment and uses an allowance account to reduce inventory to NRV. In 2012, market conditions have improved dramatically and Martinez Corporation's inventory increases to $616,000. Which of the following will Martinez record in 2012?

      A.   A debit to recovery of inventory loss, $186,000.
      B.   A debit to recovery of inventory loss, $120,000.
      C.   A credit to recovery of inventory loss $120,000.
      D.   A credit to recovery of inventory loss, $66,000.

_____   8. (L.O. 2) Agricultural produce is:

      A.   a living animal or plant such as a cow or a tree.
      B.   reported at net realizable value at each statement of financial position date.
      C.   harvested product from a biological asset.
      D.   All of the choices are correct.

_____   9. (L.O. 1) When the cost-of-goods-sold method is used to record inventory at net realizable value:

      A.   there is a direct reduction in the selling price of the product that results in a loss being recorded on the income statement prior to the sale.
      B.   a loss is recorded directly in the inventory account by crediting inventory and debiting loss on inventory decline.
      C.   only the portion of the loss attributable to inventory sold during the period is recorded in the financial statements.
      D.   the net realizable value figure for ending inventory is substituted for cost and the loss is buried in cost of goods sold.

_____   10. (L.O. 2) Commodity broker-traders record inventory at

      A.   Lower of cost or net realizable value
      B.   Historical cost
      C.   Net realizable value, with changes in NRV recorded in net income
      D.   Any of the choices is acceptable.

_____   11. (L.O. 2) Biological assets:

      A.   Include harvested products such as wool, milk, and cotton.
      B.   Are recorded in the statement of financial position at lower of cost or net realizable value.
      C.   Have changes in value recorded as part of comprehensive income.
      D.   None of the above.

_____   12. (L.O. 3) Tract Homes purchases 105 home lots for a lump sum of $1,000,000. The 105 lots include 5 type "A" lots valued at $150,000 each; 50 type "B" lots valued at $10,000 each; and 50 type "C" lots valued at $5,000 each. Using the relative sales value method, the value assigned to each type "A" lot is (round to the nearest dollar)

      A. $9,524
      B. $150,000
      C. $100,000
      D. $66,667

_____   13. (L.O. 4) Maricel Company has a noncancelable purchase commitment to buy 10,000 units of a particular product during the next three years. The contract was signed one year prior to the first year in which the purchase commitment must be honored. At the end of the year in which the contract was signed Maricel Company should formally recognize in its statement of financial position:

	An Asset	**A Liability**
A.	Yes	Yes
B.	No	No
C.	Yes	No
D.	No	Yes

_____ 14. (L.O. 5) Which of the following is **not** a basic assumption of the gross profit method?

A. The beginning inventory plus the purchases equal total goods to be accounted for.
B. Goods not sold must be on hand.
C. If the sales, reduced to the cost basis, are deducted from the sum of the opening inventory plus purchases, the result is the amount of inventory on hand.
D. The total amount of purchases and the total amount of sales remain relatively unchanged from the comparable previous period.

_____ 15. (L.O. 5) On January 31, fire destroyed the entire inventory of Mojares Company. The following data are available:

Sales for January	$60,000
Inventory, January 1	10,000
Purchases for January	55,000
Markup on cost	25%

The amount of the loss is estimated to be:

A. $17,000
B. $20,000
C. $15,000
D. $16,250

_____ 16. (L.O. 5) Devers Company sells its product for $25.00 per unit. This price is set to yield a gross margin on selling price of 25%. What is the cost of the product and what is the markup on cost for the product?

	Cost of Product	Markup on Cost
A.	$ 6.25	40%
B.	$ 9.75	75%
C.	$12.50	20%
D.	$18.75	33%

_____ 17. (L.O. 6) Which of the following is **not** required when using the retail inventory method?

A. All inventory items must be categorized according to the retail markup percentage which reflects the item's selling price.
B. A record of the total cost and retail value of goods purchased.
C. A record of the total cost and retail value of the goods available for sale.
D. Total sales for the period.

_____ 18. (L.O. 6) To determine an inventory valuation that approximates lower of average cost or net realizable value using the retail method, the computation of the cost to retail percentage should:

A. include markups but not markdowns.
B. include markups and markdowns.
C. include markdowns but not markups.
D. exclude markups but not markdowns.

_____ 19. (L.O. 6) The retail method has been used by a retail department store during its first year of operations. As of the end of the year, compare (A) the markdowns with (B) the markdown cancellations:

A. A will be equal to B.
B. A will be less than or equal to B.
C. A will be greater than or equal to B.
D. A cannot be equal to B.

_____ 20. (L.O. 6) Phair Co., a specialty clothing store, uses the retail inventory method. The following relates to 2010 operations:

Inventory, January 1, 2012, at cost	$14,200
Inventory, January 1, 2012 at sales price	20,100
Purchases in 2012 at cost	32,600
Purchases in 2012 at sales price	50,000
Additional markups on normal sales price	1,900
Sales (including $4,200 of items that were marked down from $6,400)	60,000

The cost of the December 31, 2012 inventory determined by the conventional retail method is:

    A. $9,800
    B. $6,370
    C. $6,743
    D. $6,543

_____ 21. (L.O. 6) One of the basic assumptions of the conventional retail method is that:

    A.   net markups apply to the goods sold.
    B.   net markdowns apply to the total goods available for sale.
    C.   net markdowns apply only to the goods sold.
    D.   the cost to retail percentage is unchanged from that of prior years.

_____ 22. (L.O. 6) Under the retail inventory method, purchase returns and allowances are normally considered a reduction of price at:

	Cost	**Retail**
A.	No	No
B.	No	Yes
C.	Yes	No
D.	Yes	Yes

Items 23 and 24 are based on the following information:

The Stipes Company uses the retail-inventory method to value its merchandise inventory. The following information is available:

	Cost	**Retail**
Beginning inventory	$ 30,000	$ 60,000
Purchases	190,000	300,000
Freight-in	1,000	-
Markups (net)	-	2,000
Markdowns (net)		4,000
Employee discounts		1,000
Sales		290,000

_____ 23. (L.O. 6) What is the ending inventory at retail?

      A. $66,000
      B. $67,000
      C. $69,000
      D. $71,000

_____ 24. (L.O. 6) If the ending inventory is to be valued at the lower of cost or net realizable value, what is the cost-to-retail ratio?

      A. $221,000/$362,000
      B. $221,000/$360,000
      C. $221,000/$358,000
      D. $221,000/$357,000

_____ 25. (L.O. 6) Which of the following is **not** a reason the retail inventory method is used widely:

      A.   as a control measure in determining inventory shortages.
      B.   for insurance information.
      C.   to permit the computation of net income without a physical count of inventory.
      D.   to defer income tax liability.

REVIEW EXERCISES

1.   (L.O.1) Josie Bisset Company determines its inventory using the lower of cost or net realizable value inventory valuation. For the years ended 12/31/011 and 12/31/12 the data for inventory values at cost and net realizable value are as follows:

	Cost	Net Realizable Value
12/31/11	$296,000	$272,000
12/31/12	$321,000	$306,000

Instructions:

a.   Prepare the journal entries required at 12/31/011 and 12/31/12, assuming that the cost-of-goods-sold method is used and that rather than adjusting the inventory account directly, an allowance account is used.

b.   Prepare the journal entries required at 12/31/011 and 12/31/12, assuming that the loss method is used and that rather than adjusting the inventory account directly, an allowance account is used.

a.

General Journal			J1
Date	**Account Title**	**Debit**	**Credit**

b.

	General Journal		
			J1
Date	Account Title	Debit	Credit

2. (L.O.5) Scholl Company uses the gross profit method to estimate monthly inventory balances. During recent months, gross profit has averaged 30% of net sales. The following data for January are obtained from the ledger:

Inventory, January 1	$ 30,000
Purchases	100,000
Purchase returns	2,000
Freight-in	3,000
Sales	120,000
Sales returns	4,000

Instructions:
Compute the January 31 inventory.

3.   (L.O.5) Calabro Inc. had a majority of its inventory destroyed by a fire just prior to year-end. The company controller had kept the accounting records current and provided you with the following account balances.

Beginning inventory	$ 67,500
Purchases for the year	235,700
Purchase returns	17,500
Sales	326,800
Sales returns	16,200
Gross profit rate on sales	36%

Inventory with a selling price of $18,000 was undamaged by the fire. Damaged inventory with an original selling price of $10,000 had a net realizable value of $4,800.

Instructions:
Compute the amount of the loss caused by the fire, assuming no insurance coverage is carried by the company.

4.   (L.O. 6) The following information for the month of April is available from the records of Ireland Department Store:

	At Cost	At Retail
Inventory, April 1	$ 8,400	$12,000
Purchases	48,810	80,000
Freight-in	2,000	
Additional markups		4,300
Markup cancellations		800
Markdowns		6,600
Markdowns cancellations		200
Sales		72,600

Instructions:

Compute the April 30 inventory at the lower of cost or net realizable value using the conventional retail method.

_____

_____

_____

_____

_____

_____

_____

_____

_____

_____

_____

_____

_____

_____

_____

_____

_____

_____

_____

_____

SOLUTIONS TO REVIEW QUESTIONS AND EXERCISES

TRUE-FALSE

1. (T)

2. (T)

3. (F)   Net realizable value is defined as selling price less the estimated cost of completion and disposal.

4. (T)

5. (F)   The loss resulting from the write-down of inventory to market is shown as a separate item in the income statement but not net of tax and not following net income.

6. (T)

7. (T)

8. (T)

9. (F)   The lower-of-cost-or-net-realizable-value (LCNRV) rule may be applied directly to each item or to the total of the inventory. When the LCNRV rule is applied to the inventory as a whole, increases in the net realizable value of some items offset decreases in the net realizable value in other items to some extent. Thus, the application of the LCNRV rule to individual inventory items gives the lowest valuation for statement of financial position purposes.

10. (T)

11. (F)   When the relative sales value method is used, it is used because the items being valued vary in terms of such characteristics as shape, size, attractiveness, and so on. Because of these types of differences, the amount of gross profit generated by each item will be different.

12. (T)

13. (F)   If the contracted price of a purchase commitment is in excess of market price and it is expected that losses will occur when the purchase is effected, a loss should be recognized and an Accrued Loss on Purchase Commitments should be credited. The loss is reported on the income statement under other expenses and losses, and the Accrued Loss is reported in the liability section of the statement of financial position.

14. (F)   If the contracted price is in excess of market and it is expected that losses will occur when the purchase is effected, losses should be recognized in the period during which such declines in market prices take place. Gains are not recognized until they are realized.

15. (T)

16. (F)   Because selling price is greater than cost and the gross margin amount is the same for both, gross margin on selling price will always be less than the related percentage based on cost.

17. (T)

18. (T)

19. (F)   Because a fairly quick and reliable measure of inventory value is usually needed, the retail inventory method is particularly useful for any type of interim report.

20. (F)   The conventional retail inventory method is designed to approximate the lower of average cost or net realizable value. Thus, the cost percentage computation includes markups but not markdowns. When a company has an additional markup, it normally indicates that the market value of that item had increased. If the company has a net markdown, it means that a decline in the utility of that item has occurred. Therefore, if the attempt is to approximate lower of cost or net realizable value, markdowns are considered a current loss and are not involved in the calculation of the cost to retail ratio.

21. (T)

22. (T)

23. (T)

24. (T)

25. (T)

MULTIPLE CHOICE

1. (D)   The general rule is that the historical cost principle is abandoned when the future utility (revenue producing ability) of the inventory is no longer as great as its original cost. It is no easier to keep track of net value than it is to keep track of cost, and cost does not lose its relevance if net realizable value remains in excess. The statement of financial position valuation is not the most significant reason for lower of cost or net realizable value.

2. (D)   All of the choices describe conceptual deficiencies of the LCNRV rule.

3. (B)   "Net realizable value" as used in the lower-of-cost-or-net-realizable-value rule is the selling price less cost to complete and sell the inventory item.

4. (D)   Net Realizable Value $16 – 2 = $14
          Original Cost $15

          Application of the LCNRV rule would result in the dudad being recorded at its NRV of $14.

5. (A)   If economic conditions change and the net realizable value of inventory previously written down has now recovered to the point that it's above cost, the amount of the original write-down is reversed (limited to the amount of the original write-down) and the inventory item is reported on the statement of financial position at its original cost.

6. (B)   Increases in the net realizable value of some inventory items tend to offset decreases in other inventory items when the LCNRV rule is applied to the inventory as a whole. Thus, the inventory valuation that results from applying the LCNRV method to individual items in inventory (alternative A) will always be equal to or less than the inventory valuation that results from applying the LCNRV rule to the inventory as a whole (alternative B).

7. (C)   The value of the inventory has recovered above its original cost. In this case, Martinez should report the recovery of an inventory loss with a credit of $120,000 (difference between the inventory's old NRV of $430,000 and the cost of the inventory, $550,000). This amount represents the recovery of the previously reported loss of $120,000.

8.   (C)   Agricultural produce is harvested product from a biological asset such as a cow or a tree. It is valued at net realizable value at the point of harvest; subsequent to harvest it is accounted for similar to other inventories.

9.   (D)   Under the cost-of-goods-sold method, no entry for the decline in the value of the inventory is recorded. Merely, the ending inventory value used in computing cost of goods sold is valued at net realizable value (which is lower than cost) and the cost of goods sold that results is larger. This results in a lower net income so the loss is technically buried in the cost of goods sold computation.

10. (C)   Commodity broker-traders measure inventories at net realizable value, with changes in NRV recognized in net income in the period of change.

11. (D)   Biological assets include living animals or plants, are reported at net realizable value, and changes in net realizable value are reported in income as they arise.

12. (C)   Using the relative sales value method, the value assigned to each type "A" lot is $100,000 determined as follows:

Type "A" 5 × $150,000 = $ 750,000
Type "B" 50 × $10,000 =   500,000
Type "C" 50 × $5,000 =   250,000
Total sales value $1,500,000

Cost allocated to type "A" lots $750,000/$1,500,000 = 50% = $1,000,000 × 50% = $500,000/5 = $100,000

13. (B)   Even with formal, noncancelable purchase contracts, no asset or liability is recognized at the date of inception, because the contract is "executory" in nature; neither party has fulfilled its part of the contract. However, if material, such commitment details should be disclosed in the buyer's statement of financial position in a footnote.

14. (D)   The gross profit method assumes a constant gross profit percentage, but makes no assumptions about the total amount of sales or purchases. Alternatively (A), (B), and (C) are basic assumptions of the gross profit method.

15. (A)   A 25% markup on cost is equivalent to a 20% markup on selling price:

$$\text{GP on selling price} = \frac{\%\text{ markup on cost}}{100\% + \%\text{ markup on cost}}$$

$$\text{GP on selling price} = \frac{.25}{1.25}$$

$$\text{GP on selling price} = .20$$

Sales	$60,000
GP ($60,000 × .20)	12,000
Cost of goods sold	$48,000
Goods available for sale	65,000
Inventory loss	$17,000

16.(D)   C + .25SP = SP
          C = (1 − .25)SP
          C = .75SP
          C = .75($25)
          C = $18.75
          SP $25.00
          C   18.75
          GP $ 6.25

          Markup on Cost = $6.25 ÷ $18.75 = 33%

17. (A) Inventory items need not be categorized in any manner. The major benefit of the retail inventory method is that inventory items are accumulated without the need to separate them into distinct classifications. Alternatives B, C and D reflect the requirements for use of the retail inventory method.

18. (A) See explanation of True-False question No. 20.

19. (C) Markdown cancellations represent the cancellation of previous markdowns applied to a product. Therefore, markdown cancellations are limited to the total amount of markdowns previously recorded. Thus, for any entity, markdowns will be greater than or equal to markdown cancellations.

20. (B)

	Cost	Retail
Inventory 1/1/12	$14,200	$20,100
Purchase	32,600	50,000
	$46,800	$70,100
Additional Markups		1,900
Totals	$46,800	$72,000

          (Cost-to-retail ratio: $46,800 ÷ 72,000 = 65%)

Deduct Markdowns		2,200
Sales Price of Goods Available		$69,800
Deduct Sales		60,000
Ending Inventory at Retail		$ 9,800

          Ending Inventory at LCM: $9,800 × .65 = $6,370

21. (C) When the attempt is to approximate lower of cost or net realizable value, under the retail inventory method, markdowns are considered a current loss and are not involved in the calculation of the cost to retail ratio.

22. (D) Purchase returns and allowances are ordinarily considered both as a reduction of the price at cost and retail.

23.   (B)   Stipes Company's ending inventory at retail can be calculated as follows:

			Retail
Beginning inventory			$ 60,000
Purchases			300,000
Available			$360,000
Add:			
Markups, net			2,000
			$362,000
Less:			
Markdowns, net		$4,000	
Employee discounts		1,000	
			5,000
			$357,000
Less: Sales			290,000
Ending inventory at retail			$ 67,000

24.   (A)   Stipes Company's cost-to-retail ratio approximating lower of cost or market can be determined as follows:

	Cost	**Retail**
Beginning inventory	$ 30,000	$ 60,000
Purchases	190,000	300,000
Freight-in	1,000	-
	$221,000	360,000
Add: Markups, net		2,000
		$362,000

The cost-to-retail ratio approximating lower of cost or market includes net markups but not net markdowns: $221,000/$362,000 = 61.05%.

25.   (D)   The retail inventory method is used widely (1) to permit the computation of net income without a physical count of inventory, (2) as a control measure in determining inventory shortages, (3) in regulating quantities of merchandise on hand, and (4) for insurance information. The retail inventory method does not necessarily cause a decrease in income taxes like LIFO during a period of rising prices.

REVIEW EXERCISES

1.   a.

| 12/31/11 | Cost of Goods Sold .... | 24,000 | |
| | Allowance to Reduce Inventory .... | | 24,000 |

| 12/31/12 | Allowance to Reduce Inventory .... | 9,000 | |
| | Cost of Goods Sold... | | 9,000 |

     b.

| 12/31/11 | Loss Due to Decline in Inventory to NRV .... | 24,000 | |
| | Allowance to Reduce Inventory .... | | 24,000 |

| 12/31/12 | Allowance to Reduce Inventory .... | 9,000 | |
| | Recovery of Loss Due to Decline in Inv. to NRV ...... | | 9,000 |

Inventory at cost, 12/31/11 ....$296,000
Inventory at LCNRV, 12/31/11 272,000
Allowance needed to reduce inventory to LCNRV $24,000

Inventory at cost, 12/31/12 ....$321,000
Inventory at LCNRV, 12/31/11 306,000
Allowance needed to reduce inventory to LCNRV $15,000
Recovery of previously recognized loss $24,000 – $15,000 = $9,000.

2.

Inventory, January	$ 30,000
Purchases	100,000
Freight-in	3,000
Purchase returns...	(2,000)
Goods available (at cost)...	$131,000
Sales..	$120,000
Sales returns..	4,000
Net sales..	$116,000
Less gross profit (30% of 116,000)	34,800
Cost of goods sold...	81,200
Inventory, January 31 (at cost) (131,000 – 81,200)	$ 49,800

3.

Sales..	$326,800	
Sales returns..	(16,200)	
Net sales..	310,600	
Gross profit rate..	.36	
Gross profit..	$111,816	

Cost of goods sold: $310,600 – $111,816 = $198,784

Beginning inventory		$ 67,500
Purchases	235,700	
Purchase returns...	17,500	
Net purchases..		218,200
Goods available for sale		$285,700

Estimated ending inventory: $285,700 – $198,784 = $86,916

Inventory loss due to fire:

Estimated ending inventory	$86,916
Undamaged inventory [$18,000 – ($18,000 × 36%)]	(11,520)
NRV of damaged goods	(4,800)
Loss due to fire	$70,596

4.

	Cost	Retail
Inventory, April 1	$ 8,400	$12,000
Purchases	48,810	80,000
Freight-in	2,000	
Net markups		3,500
Goods available	$59,210	$95,500

Cost to retail ratio 59,210/95,500 = 62.0%

Less:

Sales	72,600	
Net markdowns	6,400	
		79,000
Inventory, April 30, at retail		$16,500

Inventory, April 30, at lower of cost or market
(16,500 × .62) $10,230

10

Acquisition and Disposition of Property, Plant, and Equipment

CHAPTER LEARNING OBJECTIVES

1. Describe property, plant and equipment.
2. Identify the costs to include in initial valuation of property, plant and equipment.
3. Describe the accounting problems associated with self-constructed assets.
4. Describe the accounting problems associated with interest capitalization.
5. Understand accounting issues related to acquiring and valuing plant assets.
6. Describe the accounting treatment for costs subsequent to acquisition.
7. Describe the accounting treatment for the disposal of property, plant, and equipment.

CHAPTER REVIEW

1.   Chapter 10 presents a discussion of the basic accounting problems associated with the incurrence of costs related to property, plant, and equipment; and the accounting methods used to retire or dispose of these costs. These assets, also referred to as fixed assets or plant assets, are of a durable nature and include land, building structures, and equipment. Fixed assets are an important part of the operations of most business organizations. They provide the major means of support for the production and/or distribution of a company's product or service.

2.   (L.O. 1) **Property, plant, and equipment** possess certain characteristics that distinguish them from other assets owned by a business enterprise. These characteristics may be expressed as follows: **(a)** acquired for use in operations and not for resale, **(b)** long-term in nature and usually depreciated, and **(c)** possess physical substance. An asset must be used in the normal business operations to be classified as a fixed asset. These assets last for a number of years and, other than land, their costs must be allocated to the periods which benefit from their use.

Acquisition of Property, Plant, and Equipment

3.   (L.O. 2) Property, plant and equipment are valued in the accounts by most companies at their **historical cost**. Historical cost is measured by the cash or cash equivalent price of obtaining the asset and bringing it to the location and condition necessary for its intended use. Thus, charges associated with freight costs and installation are considered a part of the asset's cost. The process of allocating the historical cost of property, plant, and equipment to the periods benefited by those assets is known as **depreciation**. The topic of depreciation is presented in Chapter 11.

4.   Subsequent to acquisition, companies value fixed assets using either the cost method or fair value (revaluation) method. Most companies use the cost method because (a) the cost of hiring an appraiser, and (b) the resultant higher fair values mean that companies report higher depreciation expense and lower net income.

5.   The assets normally classified on the statement of financial position as property, plant, and equipment include land, buildings, and various kinds of machinery and equipment. The cost of each item includes the acquisition price plus those expenditures incurred in getting the asset ready for its intended use. In the case of **land**, cost typically includes **(a)** purchase price; **(b)** closing costs such as title, attorney, and recording fees; **(c)** cost of grading, filling, draining, and clearing the property; **(d)** assumption of any liens, mortgages, or encumbrances on the property; and **(e)** any additional land improvements that have an indefinite life. The cost of removing an old building from land purchased for the purpose of constructing a new building is properly charged to the land account. Also, when improvements that have a limited life (fences, driveways, etc.) are made to the land they should be set up in a separate Land Improvements account so they can be depreciated over their estimated useful life.

6.   **Building costs** include materials, labor, and overhead costs incurred during construction. Also, any fees such as those incurred for building permits or the services of an attorney are included in acquisition cost. In general, all costs incurred from excavation of the site to completion of the building are considered part of the building costs.

7.   With respect to **equipment**, cost includes purchase price plus all expenditures related to the purchase that occur subsequent to acquisition but prior to actual use. These related costs would include such items as freight charges, insurance charges on the asset while in transit, assembly and installation, special preparation of facilities, and asset testing costs.

Self-Constructed Assets

8.   (L.O. 3) When machinery and equipment to be used by an entity are constructed rather than purchased, a problem exists concerning the allocation of **overhead costs**. These costs may be handled in one of two ways: **(a)** assign no fixed overhead to the cost of the constructed asset, or **(b)** assign a portion of all overhead to the construction process. The second method called a **full-costing approach** appears preferable because of its consistency with the historical cost principle. It should be noted that the cost recorded for a constructed asset can never exceed the price charged by an outside producer.

Interest Costs

9.   (L.O. 4) Capitalization of interest cost incurred in connection with financing the construction or acquisition of property, plant, and equipment generally follows the rule of **capitalizing only the actual interest costs incurred during construction**. While some modification to this general rule occurs, its adoption is consistent with the concept that the historical cost of acquiring an asset includes all costs incurred to bring the asset to the condition and location necessary for its intended use.

10.   To qualify for interest capitalization, assets must require a period of time to get them ready for their intended use. Assets that qualify for interest cost capitalization include assets under construction for an enterprise's own use (such as buildings, plants, and machinery) and assets intended for sale or lease that are constructed or otherwise produced as discrete projects (like ships or real estate developments). The period during which interest must be capitalized begins when three conditions are present: **(a)** expenditures for the asset have been made; **(b)** activities that are necessary to get the asset ready for its intended use are in progress; and **(c)** interest cost is being incurred.

11.   The amount of interest to capitalize is limited to the **lower** of **(a)** actual interest cost incurred during the period or **(b)** the amount of interest cost incurred during the period that theoretically could have been avoided if the expenditure for the asset had not been made **(avoidable interest)**. The potential amount of interest that may be capitalized during an accounting period is determined by multiplying interest rate(s) by the **weighted-average amount of accumulated expenditures** for qualifying assets during the period.

12.   Examples which demonstrate computation of the weighted-average accumulated expenditures and selecting the appropriate interest rate are included in the chapter. Also, a comprehensive illustration of interest capitalization is shown in the text. This illustration includes both the computations and the related journal entries that should be made in a situation when an asset is constructed and capitalizable interest is a part of the transaction.

13.   Two special issues relate to interest capitalization. If a company purchases land as a site for a structure, interest costs capitalized during the period of construction are part of the cost of the plant, not the land. Companies often borrow money prior to actually needing it for construction activity. These funds are usually invested in interest-bearing securities. IFRS requires that interest revenue earned on specific borrowings should offset any interest costs capitalized. Interest revenue from general borrowings is not offset.

Acquisition and Valuation

14.   (L.O. 5) A number of accounting problems are involved in the acquisition and valuation of fixed assets. In general, an asset should be recorded at the fair market value of what is given up to acquire it or its own fair value, whichever is more clearly evident. This appears to be a rather straight forward approach that can be easily followed. However, determining fair value is not always as easy as it might appear. Some of the problems one encounters in determining proper valuation are discussed in the paragraphs that follow.

15.   The purchase of a plant asset is often accompanied by a **cash discount** for prompt payment. Two different approaches are possible regarding discounts not taken: (a) the discount, whether taken or not, is a reduction in the cost of the asset; (b) the discount not taken is included as part of the cost of the asset. Currently, both methods are employed in practice, although most companies prefer the first method described.

16.   Plant assets purchased on **long-term credit contracts** should be accounted for at the present value of the consideration exchanged on the date of purchase. When the obligation stipulates no interest rate, or the rate is unreasonable, an imputed rate of interest must be determined for use in calculating the present value. Factors to be considered in imputing an interest rate are the borrower's credit rating, the amount and maturity date of the note, and prevailing interest rates. If determinable, the cash exchange price of the asset acquired should be used as the basis for recording the asset and measuring the interest element.

17.   In some instances a company may purchase a group of plant assets at a single **lump sum price.** The best way to allocate the purchase price of the assets to the individual items is the relative fair market values of the assets acquired. To determine fair value, an appraisal for insurance purposes, the assessed valuation for property taxes, or simply an independent appraisal by a qualified appraiser might be used. When assets are acquired for an entity's stock, the best measure of cost is the fair value of the stock issued.

Exchanges of Non-Monetary Assets

18.   **Nonmonetary assets** such as inventory or property, plant, and equipment are items whose price may change over time.   Controversy exists in regard to the accounting for these assets when one nonmonetary asset is exchanged for another nonmonetary asset

19.   As stated previously, ordinarily companies account for the exchange of nonmonetary assets on the basis of the fair value of the asset given up or the fair value of the asset received, whichever is more clearly evident. Thus, companies should recognize immediately any gains or losses on the exchange. The rationale for immediate recognition is that most transactions have **commercial substance** and therefore gains and losses should be recognized. An exchange has commercial substance if the future cash flows change as a result of the transaction. An exchange of trucks with different useful lives might have commercial substance while an exchange of trucks with no significant difference in useful lives would probably not.

20.   Companies immediately recognize losses they incur on all exchanges. The accounting for gains depends on whether the exchange has commercial substance. If the exchange has commercial substance, the company recognizes the gain immediately. However, the rule for immediate recognition of a gain when an exchange lacks commercial substance is treated differently. If the company receives no cash in such an exchange, it defers recognition of a gain. If the company receives cash in such an exchange, it recognizes part of the gain immediately. The portion to be recognized is equal to the ratio of the cash received to the total consideration received times the total gain indicated.

21.   To summarize these concepts, when a transaction involves an exchange of nonmonetary assets, losses are always recognized. Gains are recognized if the exchange has commercial substance. However, gains are deferred (not immediately recognized) if the exchange has no commercial substance, unless cash or some other form of monetary consideration is **received**, in which case a partial gain is recognized. Also, a gain or loss on the exchange on nonmonetary assets is computed by comparing the book value of the asset given up with the fair value of that same asset. The examples shown below are designed to demonstrate the various situations where exchanges of nonmonetary assets are included.

Exchange with Commercial Substance

Al Company exchanged a used machine with a book value of $26,000 (cost $54,000 less $28,000 accumulated depreciation) and cash of $8,000 for a delivery truck. The machine is estimated to have a fair market value of $36,000.

Cost of truck:		
Fair value of machine exchanged		$36,000
Cash paid		8,000
Cost of truck		$44,000

Journal entry:		
Truck	$44,000	
Accumulated Depreciation—Machine	28,000	
Machine		54,000
Gain on Machine Disposal		10,000
Cash		8,000

Exchange With No Commercial Substance

Al Company trades drill press A for drill press B from another company. Drill Press A has a book value of $11,000 (cost $32,000 less $21,000 accumulated depreciation) and a fair market value of $8,000. Drill press B has a list price of $38,000, and the seller has allowed a trade-in allowance of $15,000 on the press.

Cost of new machine:	
List price of drill press B	$38,000
Less trade-in allowance	15,000
Cash payment due	23,000
Fair value of drill press A	8,000
Cost of drill press B	$31,000

Journal entry:		
Equipment	31,000	
Accumulated depreciation	21,000	
Loss on disposal of equipment	3,000	
Equipment		32,000
Cash		23,000

Loss verification:	
Book value of drill press A	$11,000
Fair value of drill press A	8,000
Loss on disposal of drill press A	$ 3,000

Exchange with No Commercial Substance

Al Company contracts with Peg Company to exchange delivery vans. Al Company will trade four Dodge Caravans for four Ford Freestars owned by Peg Company. The fair value of the Caravans is $51,000 with a book value of $38,000 (cost $65,000 less $27,000 accumulated depreciation). The Freestars have a fair value of $66,000 and Al Company gives $15,000 in cash in addition to the Caravans.

Computation of Gain:	
Fair value of Caravans	$51,000
Book value of Caravans	38,000
Total gain (unrecognized)	$13,000

Basis of new vans to Al Company:	
Fair value of Freestars	$66,000
Less gain deferred	13,000
Basis of Freestar vans	$53,000

OR

Book value of Caravans	$38,000	
Cash paid	15,000	
Basis of Freestar vans	$53,000	

Al Company journal entry:

Freestar vans	53,000	
Accumulated depreciation	27,000	
Caravan vans		65,000
Cash		15,000

Exchange with No Commercial Substance-Gain Situation
(Some Cash Received)

From the previous example, assume the book value of the Freestar Vans exchanged by Peg Company was $52,000 (cost $75,000 less $23,000 of accumulated depreciation). Thus, the total gain on the exchange to Peg Company is as follows:

Fair value of vans exchanged	$66,000
Book value of vans exchanged	52,000
Total gain	$14,000

Recognized gain due to cash received:
$$\$15,000/(\$15,000 + \$51,000) \times \$14,000 = \$3,182$$

Deferred gain:
$$\$14,000 - \$3,182 = \$10,818$$

Basis of new vans to Peg Company:

Fair value of Caravans	$51,000
Less gain deferred	(10,818)
Basis of Caravans	$40,182

Peg Company journal entry:

Cash	15,000	
Caravan vans	40,182	
Accumulated depreciation	23,000	
Freestar vans		75,000
Gain on disposal of vans		3,182

22. Many companies receive assets through grants from the government. When an asset is received through a grant, the appraisal or fair market value of the asset should be used to establish its value on the books. In theory, the credit for this transaction could be made to (1) equity, or (2) income. IFRS requires that contributions received be recognized in income on a systematic basis that matches the benefit with the costs they are intended to compensate. This can be accomplished by either (a) recording the grant as deferred revenue and recognizing the revenue over the useful life of the assets, or (b) deducting the grant from the carrying amount of the assets received from the grant which causes the grant to be recognized in income as a reduction of depreciation expense.

23.   When a company contributes a non-monetary asset, it should record the donation as an expense at the fair value of the donated asset and recognize a gain or loss for the difference between the donated asset's book value and fair value.

Costs Subsequent to Acquisition

24.   (L.O. 6) Costs related to plant assets that are incurred after the asset is placed in use are either added to the asset account **(capitalized)** or charged against operations **(expensed)** when incurred. In general, costs incurred to achieve greater future benefits from the asset should be capitalized, whereas expenditures that simply maintain a given level of service should be expensed. For the costs to be capitalized, they must be measured reliably and it must be probable that the company will obtain future economic benefits as evidenced by increases in useful life, or increases in the quantity or quality of the product produced.

25.   Generally, expenditures related to plant assets being used in a productive capacity may be classified as: **(a)** additions, **(b)** improvements and replacements, **(c)** reinstallation and rearrangement, and **(d)** repairs. Because **additions** result in the creation of new assets, they should be capitalized.

26.   **Improvements** and **replacements** are substitutions of one asset for another. Improvements substitute a better asset for the one currently used, whereas a replacement substitutes a similar asset. The major problem in accounting for improvements and replacements concerns differentiating these expenditures from normal repairs. If an improvement or replacement increases the future service potential of the asset, it should be capitalized. Capitalization occurs by removing the old asset and its related depreciation and recognizing a loss. The cost of the new substituted asset is then recorded on the books.

27.   **Rearrangement and reinstallation** costs are expensed as incurred. IFRS indicates that once assets are in the location and condition necessary to begin operations as management intended costs are no longer capitalized. **Ordinary repairs** are expenditures made to maintain plant assets in operating condition. They are charged to an expense account in the period in which they are incurred.

Dispositions of Plant Assets

28.   (L.O. 7) When a plant asset is disposed of, the accounting records should be relieved of the cost and accumulated depreciation associated with the asset. Depreciation should be recorded on the asset up to the date of disposal, and any resulting gains or losses should be reported. Plant assets may be retired voluntarily or disposed of by **sale, exchange, involuntary conversion, or abandonment**.

GLOSSARY

Additions.	Expenditures on assets which increase or extend them.
Avoidable interest.	The amount of interest cost during the period that theoretically could have been avoided if expenditures for the asset had not been made.
Capital expenditure.	An expenditure on an asset whereby (1) the useful life of the asset is increased, (2) the quantity of units produced from the asset is increased, or (3) the quality of the units produced is enhanced.
Capitalization period.	The period of time during which interest must be capitalized. It begins when (1) expenditures for the asset have been made, (2) activities that are necessary to get the asset ready for its intended use are in progress, and (3) interest cost is being incurred. The time ends when the asset is substantially complete and ready for its intended use.
Commercial substance.	An exchange where future cash flows change as a result of the transaction.
Historical cost.	The value of an asset measured by the cash or cash equivalent price of obtaining the asset and bringing it to the location and condition necessary for its intended use.
Improvements (betterments).	Expenditures that substitute a better asset for an existing asset.
Involuntary conversion.	An asset's service is terminated through fire, flood, theft, condemnation or some other manner not intended by the owner of the asset.
Lump sum price.	The aggregate price at which a group of assets is acquired.
Major repairs.	Expenditures made to maintain plant assets whereby the expenditures benefit more than one year or one operating cycle, whichever is longer.
Nonmonetary assets.	Assets whose price in terms of the monetary unit may change over time, whereas monetary assets—cash and short- or long-term accounts and notes receivable—are fixed in terms of units of currency by contract or otherwise.
Ordinary repairs	Expenditures made to maintain plant assets in operating condition.
Property, plant and equipment.	Assets that (1) are acquired for use in operations and not for resale, (2) are long-term in nature and usually subject to depreciation, and (3) possess physical substance.

Rearrangement and reinstallation costs.	Expenditures that result from rearranging or reinstalling assets.
Replacements.	Expenditures that substitute a similar asset for an existing asset.
Self-constructed assets.	Assets constructed by a company rather than purchased.
Weighted-average accumulated expenditures.	The construction expenditures that are weighted by the amount of time that interest cost could be incurred on the expenditure.

CHAPTER OUTLINE

Fill in the outline presented below.

(L.O. 1) The three characteristics of property, plant and equipment

    1.

    2.

    3.

(L.O. 2) The acquisition of property, plant and equipment

    The cost of land

    The cost of buildings

    The cost of equipment

(L.O. 3) Self-constructed assets

(L.O. 4) Interest costs during construction

    Qualifying assets

    Capitalization period

Chapter Outline *(continued)*

>> Amount to Capitalize

>> Special issues related to interest capitalization

> (L.O. 5) Acquisition and valuation

>> Cash discount

>> Deferred payment contracts

>> Lump sum purchase

>> Issuance of stock

>> Exchanges of property, plant and equipment

>>> Exchange with commercial substance

>>> Exchange with no commercial substance—loss situation

>>> Exchange with no commercial substance—gain situation (no cash received)

>>> Exchange with no commercial substance—gain situation (some cash received)

Chapter Outline (continued)

Accounting for grants

Other asset valuation methods

(L.O. 6) Cost subsequent to acquisition

Additions

Improvements and replacements

Rearrangement and reinstallation

Repairs

(L.O. 7) Dispositions of plant assets

Sale of plant assets

Involuntary conversion

Miscellaneous problems

DEMONSTRATION PROBLEM (L.O. 5)

Rabillo Co. trades a used printing machine for a new model. The old machine has a book value of $12,000 (original cost $30,000 less $18,000 accumulated depreciation) and a fair value of $8,000. The new printing machine has a list price of $42,000, and Rabillo Co. receives a $14,000 trade-in allowance on the old machine. The transaction has commercial substance. Compute (a) the cost to be recorded in the books of Rabillo Co. for the new machine and (b) the amount of any gain or loss as a result of this transaction.

Solution:

(a)   Cost of new printing machine

List price of new machine	$42,000
Less trade-in allowance	14,000
Cash payment due	28,000
Fair value of old machine	8,000
Cost of new machine	$36,000*

*$36,000 represents the value given up by
Rabillo Co. to acquire the new machine.

(b)   Computation of loss

Book value of old machine	$12,000
Fair value of the old machine	8,000
Loss on trade of old machine	$ 4,000

REVIEW QUESTIONS AND EXERCISES

TRUE-FALSE

Indicate whether each of the following is true (T) or false (F) in the space provided.

_____   1. (L.O. 2) A building owned by a corporation is always classified as property, plant and equipment.

_____   2. (L.O. 2) The cash or cash equivalent price of items classified as property, plant and equipment best measures the value of the asset on the date of acquisition.

_____   3. (L.O. 2) Use of the current replacement cost method to account for property, plant and equipment would most likely result in the recognition of gains and losses prior to the time the asset is sold.

_____   4. (L.O. 2) The cost of items classified as property, plant, and equipment should include all expenditures related to the asset incurred during the first three months of the asset's useful life.

_____   5. (L.O. 2) When land has been purchased for the purpose of constructing a new building, all costs incurred in connection with preparing the land for excavation are considered building costs.

_____ 6. (L.O. 3) If the allocation of overhead to self-constructed assets results in an asset cost that is greater than the cost that would be charged by an independent producer, the excess overhead should be recorded as a period loss.

_____ 7. (L.O. 4) The interest costs on funds used to construct an asset should not be capitalized even if a significant period of time is required to bring the asset to a condition necessary for its intended use.

_____ 8. (L.O. 4) Land that is not being developed qualifies for interest capitalization.

_____ 9. (L.O. 4) The amount of interest to be capitalized is the higher of actual interest cost incurred during the period or avoidable interest.

_____ 10. (L.O. 4) The interest incurred on the specific borrowings is used for the portion of weighted-average accumulated expenditures that is less than or equal to any amounts borrowed specifically to finance construction of the assets.

_____ 11. (L.O. 5) An asset should be recorded at the fair value of the consideration given up to acquire it or at its fair market value, whichever is higher.

_____ 12. (L.O. 5) Equipment purchased through the use of deferred payment contracts should be accounted for at the present value of the contract.

_____ 13. (L.O. 5) The purpose of imputed interest is to approximate the interest rate of a deferred purchase contract when one is not expressly stated.

_____ 14. (L.O. 5) In general, because the exchange of nonmonetary assets does not constitute a sale by either party involved in the transaction, the accounting should be based on the book value of the assets involved.

_____ 15. (L.O. 5) If an exchange of nonmonetary assets occurs and the exchange has commercial substance, it is presumed that the earnings process related to these assets is complete.

_____ 16. (L.O. 5) If an exchange transaction involving no commercial substance of nonmonetary assets results in a loss, the loss is recognized immediately, even when cash is included as a part of the transaction.

_____ 17. (L.O. 5) Gains and losses on the exchange of nonmonetary assets are computed by comparing the book value of the asset given up with the fair value of the asset given up.

_____ 18. (L.O. 5) When an exchange of no commercial substance of nonmonetary assets results in a gain and insignificant cash is included as a part of the transaction, the gain to be recognized is limited to the amount of the cash received.

_____ 19. (L.O. 5) IFRS requires that grants be recognized using the income approach, with the grant being recognized in income on a systematic basis.

_____ 20. (L.O. 5) The recommended accounting treatment for donated property, plant, and equipment represents a departure from the cost principle.

_____ 21. (L.O. 6) Once an asset has been placed into productive use, the major criterion used to determine whether an expenditure should be capitalized or expensed is the significance of that expenditure in relation to the original cost.

_____ 22. (L.O. 6) By definition, any addition to a building or machine is capitalized because a new asset has been created.

_____ 23. (L.O. 6) IFRS requires each significant component of an asset be identified and depreciated separately.

_____ 24. (L.O. 7) Gains and losses on the retirement of property, plant, and equipment should be shown in the income statement below net income, net of tax.

_____ 25. (L.O. 6) The costs of reorganizing or rearranging existing plant assets are expensed as incurred.

MULTIPLE CHOICE

Select the best answer for each of the following items and enter the corresponding letter in the space provided.

_____ 1. (L.O. 2) Historical cost is the basis advocated for recording the acquisition of property, plant, and equipment for all of the following reasons except:

    A.   at the date of acquisition, cost reflects fair value.

    B.   property, plant, and equipment items are always acquired at their original historical cost.

    C.   historical cost involves actual transactions and, as such, is the most reliable basis.

    D.   gains and losses should not be anticipated but should be recognized when the asset is sold.

_____ 2. (L.O. 2) Which of the following is not a necessary characteristic for an item to be classified as property, plant, and equipment?

    A.   Usually subject to depreciation.

    B.   Characterized by physical substance.

    C.   Can be used in operations for at least 5 years.

    D.   Not acquired for resale.

_____ 3. (L.O. 2) Stacia Theater Corporation recently purchased the Robinson Theater and the land on which it is located. Stacia plans to raze the building immediately and build a new modern theater on the site. The cost to raze the Robinson Theater should be:

    A.   written off as a loss in the year the theater is razed.

    B.   capitalized as part of the cost of land.

    C.   depreciated over the period from the date of acquisition to the date the theater is to be razed.

    D.   capitalized as part of the cost of the new theater.

_____   4. (L.O. 2) On January 15, 2012, Thorne Corporation purchased a parcel of land as a factory site for $100,000. An old building on the property was demolished, and construction began on a new building which was completed on October 18, 2012. Costs incurred during this period are listed below:

Demolition of old building	$ 6,000
Architect's fees	15,000
Legal fees for title investigation and purchase contract	5,000
Construction costs	600,000

Salvaged materials resulting from demolition were sold for $3,000.

Thorne should record the cost of the land and new building respectively as:

A. $100,000 and $623,000
B. $105,000 and $618,000
C. $108,000 and $615,000
D. $111,000 and $615,000

_____   5. (L.O. 3) To be consistent with the historical cost principle, overhead costs incurred by an enterprise constructing its own building should be:
A.   allocated on the basis of lost production.
B.   eliminated completely from the cost of the asset.
C.   allocated on an opportunity cost basis.
D.   allocated on a pro rata basis between the asset and normal operations.

_____   6. (L.O. 4) Which of the following is the recommended approach to handling interest incurred in financing the construction of property, plant, and equipment?

A.   Capitalize only the actual interest costs incurred during construction.
B.   Charge construction with all costs of funds employed, whether identifiable or not.
C.   Capitalize no interest during construction.
D.   Capitalize interest costs equal to the prime interest rate times the estimated cost of the asset being constructed.

_____   7. (L.O. 4) Which of the following is not a condition that must be satisfied before interest capitalization can begin on a qualifying asset?

A.   Interest cost is being incurred.
B.   Expenditures for the assets have been made.
C.   The interest rate is equal to or greater than the company's cost of capital.
D.   Activities that are necessary to get the asset ready for its intended use are in progress.

_____   8. (L.O. 4) If land is purchased as a site for a structure (such as a plant site), interest costs capitalized during the period of construction are part of the cost of the:

	Plant	Land
A.	Yes	Yes
B .	Yes	No
C.	No	No
D.	No	Yes

_____   9. (L.O. 4) The capitalization of interest costs is justified as being necessary in order to fulfill the:

A.   Conservatism concept.
B.   Economic entity assumption.
C.   Revenue recognition principle.
D.   Historical cost principle.

_____ 10. (L.O. 4) On January 1, 2012, Probst, Inc. signed a contract to have MCL construct a major plant facility at a cost of $5,000,000. It was estimated that it would take two years to complete the project. In addition, Probst financed the construction costs on January 1, 2012 by borrowing $5,000,000 at an interest rate of 9%. During 2012 Probst made deposit and progress payments totaling $2,000,000 under the contract; the average amount of accumulated expenditures was $750,000 for the year. The excess borrowed funds were invested in short-term securities, from which Probst realized investment income of $30,000. What amount should Probst report as capitalized interest at December 31, 2012?

     A. $ 37,500
     B. $ 67,500
     C. $180,000
     D. $150,000

_____ 11. (L.O. 5) How should assets purchased on long-term credit contracts be accounted for?

     A.   At net realizable value, less an allowance for any potential increase in interest rates prior to the date of final payment.
     B.   Present value of the estimated valuation of the assets on the scheduled date of complete payment.
     C.   Present value of the consideration exchanged between the contracting parties or the future value of the asset when final payment is made, whichever is more readily determinable.
     D.   Present value of the consideration exchanged between the contracting parties at the date of the transaction.

_____ 12. (L.O. 5) When a group of plant assets are purchased for a lump sum purchase price, it would be appropriate to determine fair value using:

	An Insurance Appraisal	Assessed Valuation for Property Taxes	Independent Appraisal
A.	Yes	No	Yes
B.	No	Yes	Yes
C.	Yes	Yes	Yes
D.	Yes	Yes	No

_____ 13. (L.O. 5) When a property is acquired by a company by issuance of its actively traded ordinary shares, the cost of the property is properly measured by the:

     A.   par value of the shares.
     B.   stated value of the shares if it is in excess of the par value.
     C.   par value or stated value of the shares whichever is more readily determinable.
     D.   market value of the shares.

_____ 14. (L.O. 5) Which of the following nonmonetary exchange transactions represents a culmination of the earning process?

     A.   Exchange of assets with no difference in future cash flows.
     B.   Exchange of products by companies in the same line of business with no difference in future cash flows.
     C.   Exchange of assets with a difference in future cash flows.
     D.   Exchange of an equivalent interest in similar productive assets that causes the companies involved to remain in essentially the same economic position.

_____ 15. (L.O. 5) When cash is involved in an exchange having commercial substance:

      A.   gains or losses are recognized in their entirety.

      B.   gain or loss is computed by comparing the fair value of the asset received with the fair value of the asset given up.

      C.   only gains should be recognized.

      D.   only losses should be recognized.

_____ 16. (L.O. 5) The cost of a nonmonetary asset acquired in exchange for another nonmonetary asset when the exchange has commercial substance is usually recorded at:

      A.   the fair value of the asset given up, and a gain or loss is recognized.

      B.   the fair value of the asset given up, and a gain but not a loss may be recognized.

      C.   the fair value of the asset received if it is less reliable than the fair value of the asset given up.

      D.   either the fair value of the asset given up or the asset received, whichever one results in the largest gain (smallest loss) to the company.

_____ 17. (L.O. 5) In an exchange of no commercial substance of nonmonetary assets that results in a gain, the gain is totally deferred when

	Cash Is Received	No Cash Is Received
A.	Yes	Yes
B.	No	Yes
C.	Yes	No
D.	No	No

_____ 18. (L.O. 5)   The Chicago Cubs had a player contract with Ryan Dempster that was recorded in its accounting records at $7,450,000. The Chicago White Sox had a player contract with Mark Buehrle that was recorded in its accounting records at $7,600,000. The Cubs traded Dempster to the Sox for Buehrle by exchanging each player's contract. The fair value of each contract was $8,000,000 and the exchange is deemed to have no commercial substance.   What amount should be shown in the accounting records after the exchange of player contracts?

	Cubs	Sox
A.	$7,450,000	$7,450,000
B.	$7,450,000	$7,600,000
C.	$7,600,000	$7,600,000
D.	$8,000,000	$8,000,000

The following information relates to questions 19, 20, and 21:

Glen Inc. and Armstrong Co. have an exchange with no commercial substance. The asset given up by Glen Inc. has a book value of $12,000 and a fair market value of $15,000. The asset given up by Armstrong Co. has a book value of $20,000 and a fair market value of $19,000. Cash of $4,000 is received by Armstrong Co.

_____ 19. (L.O. 5) On the basis of the foregoing facts, what amount should Glen Inc. record for the asset received?

      A. $15,000

      B. $16,000

      C. $19,000

      D. $20,000

_____ 20. (L.O. 5) What amount should Armstrong Co. record for the asset received?

      A. $15,000
      B. $16,000
      C. $19,000
      D. $20,000

_____ 21. (L.O. 5) Would either company record a loss on the transaction?

      A.   Glen Inc. would record a loss.
      B.   Armstrong Co. would record a loss.
      C.   Both companies would record a loss.
      D.   Neither company would record a loss.

_____ 22. (L.O. 5) Hardin Company received $40,000 in cash and a used computer with a fair value of $120,000 from Page Corporation for Hardin Company's existing computer having a fair value of $160,000 and an undepreciated cost of $150,000 recorded on its books. The transaction has no commercial substance. How much gain should Hardin recognize on this exchange, and at what amount should the acquired computer be recorded, respectively?

      A. $0 and $110,000
      B. $769 and $110,769
      C. $2,500 and $112,500
      D. $40,000 and $150,000

_____ 23. (L.O. 5) Elizabeth Company recently accepted a donation of a building from the Glen City government. The land cost Glen City $200,000, but its current fair market value is $250,000. Which of the following is acceptable under IFRS to account for this donation?

      A.   Record the grant as deferred grant revenue and recognize it as income on a systematic basis of the asset's useful life.
      B.   Deduct the grant from the carrying amount of the assets received.
      C.   Neither A nor B is acceptable.
      D.   Both A and B are acceptable under IFRS.

_____ 24. (L.O. 6) An expenditure made in connection with a machine being used by an enterprise should be:

      A.   expensed immediately if it merely extends the useful life but does not improve the quality.
      B.   expensed immediately if it merely improves the quality but does not extend the useful life.
      C.   capitalized if it maintains the machine in normal operating condition.
      D.   capitalized if it increases the quantity of units produced by the machine.

_____ 25. (L.O. 7) When a company experiences an involuntary conversion, such as when forest land is condemned for a national park, which of the following is appropriate?

      A.   A gain or loss on condemnation is recorded, and any new assets purchased are recorded at their acquisition cost.
      B.   The book value of the condemned asset is transferred to the asset purchased to replace the condemned asset.
      C.   A loss may be recognized, but not a gain, on the condemnation, and the book value transferred to the asset purchased to replace the condemned asset.
      D.   All of the above are acceptable in accounting for condemned assets.

REVIEW EXERCISES

1.   (L.O.2 and 7) Stadnicki Corporation purchased a machine on January 1, 2006, for $25,000. Before the machine was utilized in a productive capacity, the following expenditures were made:

a.	Removal of a wall to accommodate the machine	$1,500
b.	Cost of training an operator	850
c.	Installation of a counting device	500
d.	Premium on a 3-year insurance policy	900

Depreciation on the machine was recorded at the end of each year. The depreciation rate is $3,000 per year. On October 1, 2012, the machine was sold for $8,000.

Instructions:
Prepare the journal entries Stadnicki Company should make for the purchase and sale of the machine.

General Journal			
			J1
Date	**Account Title**	**Debit**	**Credit**

2.   (L.O. 4) Ivaylo Company has been constructing an asset for its own use. In connection with the construction, Ivaylo Company has been capitalizing interest on expenditures for this asset since construction began. The following costs relate to the month of June:

Expenditures
Accumulated Expenditures (June 1) $2,500,000
Accumulated Expenditures (June 30)   3,000,000

Specific Construction Debt
16%, $1,200,000 note

Other Debt
10%, $750,000 short-term note payable
12%, mortgage payable of $1,500,000

Instructions:

a.   Compute the weighted-average accumulated expenditures, avoidable interest, and interest to be capitalized for the month of June.

b.   Determine the accumulated expenditure balance at the beginning of July.

a.

b.

3.   (L.O.5) Tamara Company acquired a group of plant assets at a cost of $150,000 from a company in financial difficulty. The fair market value of the assets acquired is estimated as follows:

Land	$ 36,000
Buildings..	108,000
Machinery	72,000

Instructions:

Prepare the journal entry for Tamara Company to record the purchase.

General Journal			
			J1
Date	**Account Title**	**Debit**	**Credit**

4.   (L.O.5) Becky and Bol Company enter into an agreement for the trade of certain nonmonetary assets (machinery). The assets involved perform the same function and are employed in the same line of business. The reason for the exchange involves the size of the product produced by the machines, and the transaction is deemed to not have any commercial substance. The machines exchanged by Becky Company have a book value of $245,000 (cost $325,000 less accumulated depreciation of $80,000) and a fair value of $275,000. The machines given up by Bol Company have a book value of $260,000 (cost $350,000 less accumulated depreciation of $90,000) and a fair value of $290,000. In addition to the exchange of the machines, Becky Company agrees to pay Bol Company $15,000 as part of the transaction.

Instructions:

Record the exchange transactions for

  a.   Becky Company, and
  b.   Bol Company

a.

General Journal			
			J1
Date	**Account Title**	**Debit**	**Credit**

b.

General Journal			J1
Date	Account Title	Debit	Credit

5.   (L.O.6) With respect to each of the following plant asset expenditures, indicate whether the item should be expensed or capitalized. Also, indicate whether the item is best classified as: (1) an addition, (2) an improvement, (3) a replacement, (4) a rearrangement and reinstallation, or (5) an ordinary repair.

	Expense	**Capitalize**	**Classification**
A. A new wing on a factory building.			
B. Steel beams in an old factory building substituted for wooden beams.			
C. New tires placed on a delivery truck.			
D. Fee of consulting firm for improvement of production flow by changing the placement of machinery in the factory.			
E. A new tile floor in the office building substituted for an old tile floor.			
F. Repainting the interior of the entire factory building.			
G. New device attached to machinery that automatically sorts production. Such a device has not previously been available.			
H. New motor installed in a machine. The old motor burned out unexpectedly.			

SOLUTIONS TO REVIEW QUESTIONS AND EXERCISES

TRUE-FALSE

1.   (F)   To be classified as property, plant, and equipment, the building (a) must be acquired for use in operations and not for resale, (b) be long-term in nature and generally subject to depreciation, and (c) possess physical substance. The second and third criteria would normally be met by any building owned by a company. However, a company could own a building that was not used in its operations and was held for sale. In this case the building would be classified as an other asset.

2.   (T)

3.   (T)

4.   (F)   Any costs related to an asset that are incurred after its acquisition such as additions, improvements, or replacements are added to the cost of the asset if they provide future service potential; otherwise, they are expensed in the period of incurrence.

5.   (F)   When land has been purchased for the purpose of constructing a building, all costs incurred up to the excavation for the new building are considered land costs. Removal of old buildings, clearing, grading, and filling are considered costs of the land because these costs are necessary to get the land in condition for its intended purpose.

6.   (T)

7.   (F)   To qualify for interest capitalization, assets must require a period of time to get them ready for their intended use. The amount of interest to be capitalized for qualifying assets is that portion of total interest cost incurred during the period that theoretically could have been avoided if expenditures for the asset had not been made.

8. (F)   Assets that are not undergoing the activities necessary to get them ready for use do not qualify for interest capitalization.

9. (F)   The amount of interest to be capitalized is limited to the lower of actual interest cost incurred during the period or avoidable interest.

10. (T)

11. (F)   An asset should be recorded at the fair value of what is given up to acquire it or at its own fair market value, whichever is more clearly evident.

12. (T)

13. (T)

14. (F)   The book value of assets can sometimes be misleading because of the variety of accounting methods that can be used to account for these items. Thus, when an exchange of nonmonetary assets is involved, the accounting should be based on the fair value of the asset given up or the fair value of the asset acquired, whichever is more clearly evident.

15. (T)

16. (T)

17. (T)

18. (F)   In this situation, part of the monetary asset is considered sold and part exchanged; therefore, only a portion of the gain is deferred. The formula to determine the amount of the gain recognized when cash is received is:

$$\frac{\text{Cash received}}{\text{Cash rec'd + fair value of asset rec'd}} \times \text{total gain} = \text{Gain recognized}$$

19. (T)

20. (T)

21. (F)   For an expenditure to be capitalized, it must measured reliably and it must be probable that the company will obtain future economic benefits as evidenced by increases in useful life, or increases in the quantity or quality of the product produced.

22. (T)

23. (T)

24. (F)   Gains or losses on the retirement of property, plant, and equipment should be shown in the income statement along with other items that arise from customary business activities.

25. (T)

MULTIPLE CHOICE

1. (B)   Property, plant, and equipment items are acquired at various times during their useful life. Thus, the original historical cost may be appropriate when the asset is originally acquired by a purchaser. However, if the asset is subsequently acquired by a different purchaser, the cost basis would most likely be something other than its original historical cost. The other alternatives represent reasons the historical cost basis is advocated for recording property, plant, and equipment purchases.

2. (C)   Items classified as property, plant, and equipment are characterized as items that are long-term in nature. The concept of long-term is generally considered to be in excess of one year, but no minimum number of years is required for this classification. Alternatives (A), (B), and (D) are appropriate characteristics for an item classified as property, plant, and equipment.

3. (B)   All expenditures made to acquire land and to ready it for use should be considered as part of the land cost. The purpose of the purchase was to acquire the land so a new theater could be constructed. The old theater has no economic use so that any portion of the purchase price attributable to the old theater is merely considered cost of the land acquired.

4. (C)   Thorne should allocate the costs to land and building as follows:

	Land	Building
Purchase price of land	$100,000	
Demolition of old building	6,000	
Architect's fees		$15,000
Legal fees for title investigation and purchase contract	5,000	
Construction costs		600,000
Cash received from salvaged materials resulting from demolition of old building	(3,000)	
	$108,000	$615,000

5. (D)   Based upon the historical cost principle, a portion of overhead cost should be assigned to a constructed asset to obtain that asset's total cost. The amount charged should be based upon a pro rata allocation between the asset and normal operations. The other allocation methods mentioned in alternatives A and C are difficult to measure and also are not consistent with the historical cost principle. Alternative B is not consistent with the historical cost principle.

6. (A)   This recommended approach is based on the historical cost concept stating that only actual transactions are recorded. It is argued that interest incurred is as much a cost of acquiring the asset as the cost of the materials, labor, and other resources used. The approaches referred to in alternatives B & C have some support but are not the recommended methods. Alternative D is not an approach to handling interest incurred during construction that has any support.

7. (C)   Alternatives A, B, and D reflect the conditions that must exist before the interest capitalization can begin on a qualifying asset.

8. (B)   When land is purchased with the intention of developing it for a particular use, interest costs associated with those expenditures qualify for interest capitalization. In the situation cited in the question the interest cost is capitalized as part of the plant, not the land. The purchase of the land was for the purpose of constructing a plant. If the land had been purchased for development in terms of lot sales then the interest would be capitalized as part of the land.

9. (D)   IFRS requires capitalizing actual interest (with modification). This method follows the concept that the historical cost of acquiring an asset includes all costs (including interest) incurred to bring the asset to the condition and location necessary for its intended use.

10. (A)   Probst should report $67,500 as its capitalized interest at December 31, 2012. Its capitalized interest can be calculated as follows:

Average amount of accumulated expenditures	$750,000
Interest rate on specific borrowing	× .09
Avoidable interest	$ 67,500
Less Interest revenue	(30,000)
Interest to be capitalized	$37,500

Note: IFRS requires that interest revenue earned on specific borrowings should offset interest costs capitalized.

11. (D)   To properly reflect cost, assets purchased on long-term credit contracts should be accounted for at the present value of the consideration exchanged between the contracting parties at the date of the transaction.

12. (C)   To determine fair value of the individual items in a lump sum purchase of plant assets, an appraisal for insurance purposes, the assessed valuation for property taxes, or simply an independent appraisal by an engineer or other appraiser might be used.

13. (D)   When property is acquired by the issuance of ordinary shares, the cost of the property is not properly measured by the par or stated value of such shares. If the shares are actively traded, the market value of the shares issued is a fair indication of the cost of the property acquired because shares are a good measure of the current cash equivalent price.

14. (C)   An exchange has commercial substance if the future cash flows change as a result of the transaction. If two entities exchange assets and the exchange has no commercial substance, the earnings process is not considered complete. Alternatives (A), (B), and (D) all represent exchanges having no commercial substance.

15. (A)   A nonmonetary asset acquired in an exchange having commercial substance is usually recorded at the fair value of the asset given up, and a gain or loss is recognized.

16. (A)   The cost of a nonmonetary asset acquired in an exchange having commercial substance is usually recorded at the fair value of the asset given up or the fair value of the asset received, whichever is more clearly evident. A gain or loss is usually recognized as the difference between the book value of the asset given up and its fair value.

17. (B)   If an exchange of assets having no commercial substance results in a gain, and the exchange does not include the receipt of cash, the gain should be totally deferred. In such a situation, it is assumed that the earnings process is not complete. When cash is received, part of the nonmonetary asset is considered sold and part exchanged; therefore, only a portion of the gain is deferred.

18. (B)   This is an exchange with gains having no commercial substance. The Cubs' and Sox's gains which will be deferred can be computed as follows:

	Cubs	Sox
Fair value of contract given up	$8,000,000	$8,000,000
Less: Book value of Dempster's contract	7,450,000	
Book value of Buehrle's contract		7,600,000
Gain on exchange to be deferred	$ 550,000	$ 400,000

The Cubs and Sox would determine the cost of their new player contracts as follows:

	Cubs	Sox
Cost (fair value) of new player's contract	$8,000,000	$8,000,000
Less: Deferred exchange gain	(550,000)	(400,000)
Cost to be recorded for new player's contract	$7,450,000	$7,600,000

19. (B)

Fair market value of Glen Inc. asset	$15,000
Book value of Glen Inc. asset	12,000
Total gain (unrecognized)	$ 3,000

Fair market value of Armstrong Co. asset	$19,000
Less gain deferred	3,000
Basis of acquired asset to Glen Inc.	$16,000

20. (A)   When nonmonetary assets are exchanged and a loss results, the loss should be recognized immediately.

Book value of Armstrong Co. asset	$20,000
Fair market value of Armstrong Co. asset	19,000
Loss on trade	$ 1,000

Armstrong Co.–Journal Entry

New asset	15,000	
Cash	4,000	
Loss on trade	1,000	
Old asset		20,000

21. (B)   See explanation in No. 20 above.

22. (C)   This is an exchange having no commercial substance of property at a gain with cash received. The gain to be recognized is computed as $40,000/$160,000 = 25\%$; $25\% \times \$10,000$ gain $= \$2,500$ gain recognized. The following entry would therefore be made:

Computer (new)	$112,500	
Cash	40,000	
Computer (old), net		150,000
Gain on disposal of computer		2,500

23. (D)   Under IFRS, grants are recognized in income on a systematic basis either by recording the grant as deferred grant revenue, which is recognized as income on a systematic basis over the useful life of the asset, or by deducting the grant from the carrying amount of the assets received from the grant, in which case the grant is recognized in income as a reduction of depreciation expense.

24. (D)   For an expenditure to be capitalized, it must measured reliably and it must be probable that the company will obtain future economic benefits as evidenced by increases in useful life, or increases in the quantity or quality of the product produced.

25. (A)   An involuntary conversion refers to events such as fire, flood, theft, or condemnation. The computation of the gain or loss that results from an involuntary conversion is the same as any computation of the gain or loss from any disposal. If the company purchases a replacement asset, that new asset is recorded at its acquisition cost.

REVIEW EXERCISES

1.   Purchase Price = $25,000 + $1,500 + $850 + $500 = $27,850
     Book Value at 10-1-12 = $27,850 – (6 × $3,000) = $9,850 (before 2012 depreciation)
     Journal entries:

1-1-06	Machine	27,850	
	Cash..		27,850
10-1-12	Depreciation Expense	2,250	
	Accumulated Depreciation.....................................		2,250
10-1-12	Cash	8,000	
	Accumulated Depreciation	20,250	
	Machine..		27,850
	Gain on Sale		400

2. a. Accumulated Expenditures (June 1) $2,500,000
      Accumulated Expenditures (June 30)   3,000,000
                                                         $5,500,000

   Weighted Average Accumulated Expenditures: $5,500,000/2 = $2,750,000

Weighted-Average Accumulated Expenditures	×	**Interest Rate**	=	**Avoidable Interest**
$1,200,000		16% × 1/12		$16,000
1,550,000		*11.33% × 1/12		14,635
$2,750,000				$30,635

   *Weighted-Average Interest Rate Computation:

	Principal	**Interest**
10%, note payable	$ 750,000	$ 75,000
12%, mortgage payable	1,500,000	180,000
	$2,250,000	$255,000

   Total Interest/Total Principal = Weighted Average Rate
   $255,000/$2,250,000 = 11.33%*

   Actual Interest:

$1,200,000 × 16% × 1/12 =	$16,000
750,000 × 10% × 1/12 =	6,250
1,500,000 × 12% × 1/12 =	15,000
	$37,250

   Interest to be Capitalized: $30,635

   b. Accumulated Expenditures (July 1) unadjusted $3,000,000
      Add: Capitalized Interest   30,635
                                                           $3,030,635

3.

	Fair Market Value	Percent of Fair Market Value	Apportionment of Cost
Land	$ 36,000	16-2/3%	$ 25,000
Building	108,000	50%	75,000
Machinery	72,000	33-1/3%	50,000
Total	$216,000		$150,000

Journal Entry:

Land..............................	25,000	
Building..........................	75,000	
Machinery........................	50,000	
Cash		150,000

4. a.   **Accounting by Becky Company**
   Computation of Gain:

Fair value of Becky machines	$275,000
Book value of Becky machines	245,000
Total gain (unrecognized)	$ 30,000

   Basis of New Machines to Becky:

Fair value of			Book value of Becky	
Bol machines	$290,000		machines	$245,000
Less gain deferred	(30,000)	OR	Cash paid	15,000
Basis of machines			Basis of machines	
received	$260,000		received	$260,000

   Journal Entry:

Machines (from Bol)	260,000	
Accumulated Depreciation	80,000	
Machines		325,000
Cash		15,000

   b.   **Accounting by Bol Company**
   Computation of Total Gain:

Fair value of Bol machines	$290,000
Book value of Bol machines	260,000
Total gain	$ 30,000

   Portion of Gain Recognized by Bol:

$$\frac{\$15,000}{\$15,000 \ + \ \$275,000} \times \$30,000 = \underline{\$1,552}$$

   Basis of New Machines to Bol:

Fair value of			Book value of	
Becky machines	$275,000		Bol machines	$260,000
Less gain deferred			Add gain recognized	1,552
(30,000 − $1,552)	(28,448)	OR	Less cash received	(15,000)
Basis of machines			Basis of machines	
received	$246,552		received	$246,552

   Journal Entry:

Cash	15,000	
Machines (from Becky)	246,552	
Accumulated Depreciation	90,000	
Machines		350,000
Gain on disposal of old machines		1,552

5.   A.   Capitalize—Addition   E.   Capitalize—Replacement
       B.   Capitalize—Improvement   F.   Expense—Repair
       C.   Expense—Repair   G.   Capitalize—Addition
       D.   Expense—Rearrangement   H.   Capitalize—Replacement

11

Depreciation, Impairments, and Depletion

CHAPTER LEARNING OBJECTIVES

1. Explain the concept of depreciation.

2. Identify the factors involved in the depreciation process.

3. Compare activity, straight-line, and diminishing-charge methods of depreciation.

4. Explain component depreciation.

5. Explain the accounting issues related to asset impairment.

6. Explain the accounting procedures for depletion of mineral resources.

7. Explain the accounting for revaluations.

8. Explain how to report and analyze property, plant, equipment, and mineral resources.

*9. Explain revaluation accounting procedures.

CHAPTER REVIEW

1. Chapter 11 presents a discussion of the factors involved in the accounting and recording of depreciation and depletion and the methods of writing off the cost of tangible assets and mineral resources. Depreciation refers to a cost allocation of tangible plant assets. Depletion is the term used to describe the cost allocation related to mineral resources such as oil, gas, or coal. Amortization is the term used to describe the expiration of intangible assets. In addition to a thorough discussion of the accounting problems involved, the chapter presents a detailed analysis and explanation of the various depreciation methods used in practice.

Depreciation Process

2. (L.O. 1) **Depreciation** is the accounting process of allocating the cost of tangible assets to expense in a systematic and rational manner to those periods expected to benefit from the use of the asset. The **cost allocation approach** is justified because it matches costs with revenues and because fluctuation in market values is difficult to determine.

3. (L.O. 2) To compute depreciation, an accountant must establish (a) the **depreciable base** to be used for the asset, (b) the asset's **useful life**, and (c) the **depreciation method** to be used. Determination of the first two factors requires the use of estimates.

4. The depreciable base is the difference between an asset's cost and its salvage value. **Salvage value** is the estimated amount that will be received at the time the asset is sold or removed from service.

---

* Note: All asterisked (*) items relate to material contained in the Appendix to the chapter.

5. The **useful life** (service life) of a plant asset refers to the number of years that asset is capable of economically providing the service it was purchased to perform. The service life of an asset should not be confused with its physical life. For example, a machine may no longer provide a useful service to an organization even though it remains physically functional. Thus, the estimate of an asset's service life is dependent upon both the economic factors and the physical factors related to its use. **Economic factors** are characterized by inadequacy, supersession, and obsolescence. **Physical factors** relate to wear and tear, decay, and casualties that prevent the asset from performing indefinitely.

Depreciation Methods

6. The depreciation method selected for a particular asset should be **systematic and rational**. Depreciation methods may be classified as:

      A.   Activity method.
      B.   Straight-line method.
      C.   Diminishing charge methods.
          a.   Sum-of-the-years'-digits.
          b.   Declining-balance method.

7. The following information for a piece of machinery will be used to illustrate some of the depreciation methods discussed in the following paragraphs.

Cost of machine	$260,000
Estimated useful life	10 years
Estimated salvage value	$20,000
Productive life in hours	60,000 hours

8. (L.O. 3) When the **activity method** (units of use or production) is used, depreciation is assumed to be a function of productivity rather than the passage of time. This method is most appropriate for assets such as machinery or automobiles where depreciation can be based on units produced or miles driven. One problem associated with the use of this method concerns a before-the-fact estimation of the total output the asset will achieve during its useful life.

Illustration

Assume the machine was used for 6,800 hours in the first year of its useful life.

$$\frac{(\text{Cost less salvage}) \times \text{hours this year}}{\text{Total estimated hours}} = \text{Depreciation Charge}$$

$$\frac{(\$260,000 - \$20,000) \times 6,800}{60,000} = \$27,200$$

9. Use of the **straight-line method** results in a uniform charge to depreciation expense during each year of an asset's service life. This method is based upon the assumption that the decline in an asset's usefulness is the same each year. Although the straight-line method is easy to use, it rests on an assumption that, in most situations, is not realistic.

Illustration

$$\frac{\text{Cost less salvage}}{\text{Estimated service life}} = \text{Depreciation Charge}$$

$$\frac{(\$260,000 - \$20,000)}{10} = \$24,000$$

10.   The **diminishing charge (accelerated depreciation) methods** result in a higher depreciation cost during the early years of an asset's service life and lower charges in later years. This approach is justified on the basis that assets lose a greater amount of service potential in earlier years and thus depreciation should be higher.

11.   The **sum-of-the-years'-digits** method and the **declining-balance** method are the two most often used diminishing charge methods. The sum-of-the-years' digits method requires multiplication of the **depreciable base** by a fraction that decreases during each year of an asset's service life. The declining-balance method requires use of a constant percentage applied to an **asset's book value (cost less accumulated depreciation).** Salvage value is initially ignored under the declining-balance method.

Illustration
Sum-of-Years' Digits

$$(\text{Cost} - \text{Salvage Value}) \times \text{Depreciation Fraction} = \text{Depreciation Charge}$$
$$(\$260,000 - \$20,000) \times 10/55^* = \$43,636$$

$*$ $\frac{n(n+1)}{2}$, where n = estimated useful life

Declining-Balance

The declining-balance method utilizes a depreciation rate that is some multiple of the straight-line method. One popular method is twice the straight-line rate. Thus, in our example the 10-year asset life would translate into a 20% declining rate.

	Beginning of the Year Book Value	×	Rate on Declining Balance	=	Depreciation Charge
Year 1	$260,000	×	20%	=	$52,000
Year 2	$208,000	×	20%	=	$41,600

It's important to note that when using the declining balance method of calculating depreciation, the cost less accumulated depreciation (book value) can never drop below the residual or salvage value. In this case, the total accumulated depreciation would be capped at $240,000 for the depreciable life of the asset.

12.   (L.O. 4) **Component depreciation** depreciates separately each part of an item of PPE that is significant to the total cost of the asset. It is required under IFRS and requires significant judgment to determine proper allocations to components. For example, assume that Carmel Company purchased a building for $4,000,000. The value of each component is as follows:

Component	Component Amount	Component Useful Life
Structure	$2,300,000	20 years
Roof	340,000	16 years
Heating/cooling system	560,000	10 years
Foundation	800,000	40 years

Using component depreciation, the total depreciation on the building would be (assuming straight-line depreciation):

Component	Component Amount/Useful life	Component Depreciation
Structure	$2,300,000/20	$115,000
Roof	340,000/16	21,250
Heating/cooling	560,000/10	56,000
Foundation	800,000/40	20,000
Total		$212,250

13. In general, depreciation should be based on the number of months an asset is used during an accounting period. If a diminishing charge depreciation method is used for assets purchased during an accounting period, a slight modification is appropriate. When this situation occurs, determine depreciation expense for the full year and prorate the expense between the two periods involved. This process continues throughout the service life of the asset. For example, assume an asset with a 5-year useful life and a depreciable cost of $45,000 is purchased on October 1. At the end of the first year the depreciation charge under sum-of-the-years'-digits method would be:

$$
\begin{array}{rl}
\text{1st Full Year:} & \$45,000 \times 5/15 = \$15,000 \\
\text{2nd Full Year:} & \$45,000 \times 4/15 = \$12,000 \\
\text{Year 1 (10/1 to 12/31):} & \$15,000 \times 1/4 = \textbf{3,750.} \\
\text{Year 2:} & (\$15,000 \times 3/4) + (\$12,000 \times 1/4) \\
& \$11,250 + \$3,000 = \textbf{\$14,250}
\end{array}
$$

14. Depreciation expense reduces net income for the accounting period in which it is recorded even though a current cash outflow is not involved. Depreciation should not be considered a source of cash. Cash is generated by revenues, not accounting procedures.

15. The estimates involved in the depreciation process are sometimes subject to revision as a result of unanticipated occurrences. Such revisions are classified as **changes in accounting estimates** and should be handled in the current and prospective periods.

Impairments

16. (L.O. 5) The process to determine an impairment loss is (a) review events for possible impairment, (b) if events suggest impairment, determine if the recoverable amount is less than the carrying amount, if so, then (c) the loss is the amount by which the carrying amount of the asset is greater than the recoverable amount. The recoverable amount is the higher of fair value less costs to sell or value-in-use (present value of cash flows expected from use and eventual sale).

17.   If an impairment loss is recorded, the recoverable amount becomes the new basis. If, in a subsequent period, a review indicates that the asset is no longer impaired, the impairment loss may be reversed. Generally, the amount of recovery of the loss is limited to the carrying amount that would have resulted if impairment had not occurred.

18.   Assets held for disposal are treated like inventory and are reported at the lower-of-cost-or-net realizable value, and are revalued each period. Therefore, assets can be written down due to impairments, and can be written-up for recovery of impairments, however, the write-up cannot exceed the carrying amount of the asset at the time of the original impairment.

Depletion

19.   (L.O. 6) **Depletion** refers to the process of recording the consumption of **mineral resources**. Mineral resources have two main features: (a) complete removal of the asset, and (b) replacement of the asset only by an act of nature. The depletion base for mineral resources includes pre-exploratory costs, exploratory and evaluation costs (E&E), and development costs.   Pre-exploratory costs are considered speculative and are expensed as incurred. E&E costs can be either expensed as incurred, or capitalized pending evaluation.   Once technological and commercial viability is demonstrated, E&E assets are reclassified as development costs.

20.   Once a company has determined that a reasonable level of mineral resources exist, the development phase begins. Development costs include tangible equipment costs (generally not included in the depletion base since equipment can be moved to other sites) and intangible development costs. Intangible development costs and restoration costs are considered part of the depletion base.

21.   Depletion is normally based on the number of units extracted during the period, which corresponds to the activity depreciation method discussed earlier. A major problem one faces when computing depletion is **estimating recoverable reserves.**
  When estimates of recoverable reserves change, it is accounted for as a change in estimate, similar to the accounting for changes in useful lives of equipment.

22.   A company may distribute a **liquidating dividend** when it owns property from which minerals are to be extracted and the company does not expect to purchase other properties. Liquidating dividends are those in excess of the amount of accumulated net income. Share Premium – Ordinary is debited for the portion of the original investment that is being returned to investors.

Revaluations

23.   (L.O. 7) Under IFRS companies may choose to revalue assets at fair value, or to record them at depreciated cost. Most companies do not choose revaluation accounting. When a company chooses to revalue its tangible assets to fair value, the unrealized gain is often referred to as revaluation surplus (reported as other comprehensive income in the year it arises), a revaluation decrease is reported as an expense.

Disclosures

24.   (L.O. 8) The basis for valuing property, plant, equipment, and mineral resources, which is normally historical cost, should be disclosed in the financial statements along with any pledges, liens, and other commitments related to these assets. Normally, assets not used in a productive capacity (held for future use or as an investment) should be segregated from assets used in operations and classified as "Other Assets."

25.   Analysis of property, plant, and equipment is often done using the asset turnover ratio (net sales/average total assets), the profit margin on sales ratio (net income/net sales), and rate of return on assets ratio (net income/average total assets).

Revaluation of Property, Plant, and Equipment

*26.   (L.O. 9) When companies choose to use revaluation accounting for PP&E they account for the change in fair value by adjusting the appropriate asset account and recording an unrealized gain, often referred to as revaluation surplus. The following table summarizes revaluation gains/losses:

Revaluation decrease that does not offset a previous revaluation increase	Expense/Income statement
Revaluation decrease that offsets a previous revaluation increase	Other comprehensive income/Equity
Revaluation increase that does not offset a previous revaluation decrease	Other comprehensive income/Equity
Revaluation increase that offsets a previous revaluation decrease	Income/Income statement

Most importantly, the Accumulated Other Comprehensive Income account related to revaluations can never have a negative (debit) balance.

GLOSSARY

Activity method (variable charge approach).	A depreciation method in which depreciation is a function of use or productivity instead of the passage of time.
Amortization.	The accounting process of allocating the cost of intangible assets (i.e., patents and goodwill) to expense.
Declining-balance method.	A depreciation method that applies a constant rate to the declining book value of the asset and produces a decreasing annual depreciation amount over the useful life of the asset.
Diminishing charge method (accelerated depreciation).	A depreciation method which provides for a higher depreciation cost in the earlier years and lower charges in later periods.
Depletion.	The accounting process of allocating the cost of mineral resources (i.e., timber, gravel, oil, and coal) to expense.
Depreciation.	The accounting process of allocating the cost of tangible assets to expense in a systematic and rational manner to those periods expected to benefit from the use of the asset.
Development costs.	The costs incurred to extract mineral resources and to get them ready for production or shipment.
Economic factors.	When an asset is retired because of inadequacy, supersession or obsolescence.
Exploration costs.	The costs incurred to find mineral resources.
Full cost concept.	Accounting for exploration costs where unsuccessful ventures are capitalized with successful ventures.
Impairment.	When the carrying amount of an asset is not recoverable and therefore a write-off is needed.
Inadequacy.	An economic factor for retiring an asset because the asset ceased to be useful to an enterprise due to the demands of the firm having increased.
Liquidating dividend.	A dividend which is a greater than the amount of accumulated net income, considered a return of capital to the shareholder.
Mineral resources.	Wasting assets such as petroleum, minerals, and timber.
Obsolescence.	An economic factor for retiring an asset that does not specifically relate to the factors of inadequacy or supersession.
Physical factors.	Wear, tear, decay, and casualties that make it difficult for an asset to perform indefinitely.

Restoration costs.	The costs incurred to restore property to its mineral state after extraction of mineral resources has occurred.
Salvage value.	The estimated amount that will be received at the time the asset is sold or removed from service.
Straight-line method.	A depreciation method in which periodic depreciation is the same throughout the service life of the asset.
Sum-of-the-years'-digits method.	A depreciation method that produces decreasing periodic depreciation by applying a decreasing fraction to the depreciable cost of the asset.
Supersession.	An economic factor for retiring an asset due to the replacement of one asset with another more efficient and economical asset.
Successful efforts concept.	Accounting for exploration costs where only successful ventures are capitalized.

CHAPTER OUTLINE

Fill in the outline presented below.

(L.O. 1) The Concept of Depreciation

(L.O. 2) Factors Involved in the Depreciation Process

Depreciable Base

Estimation of Service Lives

(L.O. 3) Methods of Depreciation
Activity method

Straight-line method

Sum-of-the-years'-digits method

Declining-balance method

(L.O. 4) Component depreciation

(L.O. 5) Impairments

Recoverable amount

Calculation of impairment loss

Restoration of impairment loss

Assets to be disposed of

Chapter Outline *(continued)*

(L.O. 6) Depletion

Establishing a depletion base

Pre-exploratory costs

Exploration and Evaluation costs (E&E)

Development costs

Restoration costs

(L.O. 7) Revaluation of Property, Plant, and Equipment

(L.O. 8) Presentation and Analysis of Property, Plant, and Equipment, and Mineral Resources

*(L.O. 9) Revaluation of Property, Plant, and Equipment

Revaluation Increases

Revaluation Decreases

REVIEW QUESTIONS AND EXERCISES

TRUE-FALSE

Indicate whether each of the following is true (T) or false (F) in the space provided.

_____ 1. (L.O. 1) The accounting concept of depreciation reflects the decline in value associated with a plant asset.

_____ 2. (L.O. 2) An asset's cost less its salvage value is referred to as the depreciable base.

_____ 3. (L.O. 2) Physical factors such as wear and tear set the outside limit for the service life of an asset.

_____ 4. (L.O. 2) Whenever the economic nature of the asset is the primary determinant of service life, maintenance plays an extremely vital role in prolonging service life.

_____ 5. (L.O. 2) Replacing a black and white monitor with a color monitor for a computer is an example of supersession.

_____ 6. (L.O. 2) Estimation and judgment are the primary means through which the service life of an asset is determined.

_____ 7. (L.O. 3) One problem associated with the activity method of depreciation concerns estimating the total units of output an asset will produce.

_____ 8. (L.O. 3) Companies that desire low depreciation during periods of low productivity and high depreciation during high productivity either adopt or switch to a declining-balance method.

_____ 9. (L.O. 3) The straight-line method considers depreciation a function of time rather than a function of usage.

_____ 10. (L.O. 3) The straight-line depreciation method is used most often in actual practice. This is because the assumptions upon which it is based apply to most plant assets.

_____ 11. (L.O. 3) Accelerated depreciation methods accomplish the objective of writing an asset off over a shorter period of time than its useful life.

_____ 12. (L.O. 3) Under the declining-balance depreciation method, salvage value is considered only in computing the amount of depreciation for the final year(s) of an asset's service life.

_____ 13. (L.O. 4) IFRS requires that each part of an item of property, plant, and equipment that is significant to the total cost of the asset must be depreciated separately.

_____ 14. (L.O. 4) When using component depreciation, the cost of individual components may be estimated based on reference to current market prices (if available), discussion with experts in valuation, or use of other reasonable approaches.

_____ 15. (L.O. 4) If one of the estimates used in computing depreciation is subsequently found to require adjustments, no change in prior years' financial statements is required.

_____ 16. (L.O. 5) An asset impairment test must be conducted on an annual basis by comparing the asset's recoverable amount with its carrying amount.

_____ 17. (L.O. 5) If the carrying amount is less than the recoverable amount, the difference is an impairment loss.

_____ 18. (L.O. 5) Losses or gains relating to impaired assets intended to be disposed of should be reported as part of other comprehensive income.

_____ 19. (L.O. 6) Depletion is the systematic allocation of the cost of mineral resources.

_____ 20. (L.O. 6) The depletion base includes development costs such as tangible equipment used for transportation and other heavy equipment necessary to extract a mineral resource and get it ready for production or shipment.

_____ 21. (L.O. 6) The full costing approach, related to accounting for exploratory and evaluation (E&E) costs, requires that the full cost of exploration be charged against income in the year it is incurred.

_____ 22. (L.O. 6) The computation of depletion is essentially the same as the activity method of depreciation.

_____ 23. (L.O. 6) Liquidating dividends are dividends greater than the amount of accumulated net income.

_____ *24. (L.O. 8) Companies account for a change in the fair value of property, plant, and equipment by adjusting the appropriate asset account and recording an unrealized gain on the revalued long-lived tangible asset..

_____ *25. (L.O. 8) If a company experiences a loss on impairment (decrease in value below historical cost), the loss reduces comprehensive income and is reported as part of accumulated other comprehensive income in the statement of financial position.

MULTIPLE CHOICE

Select the best answer for each of the following items and enter the corresponding letter in the space provided.

_____ 1. (L.O. 1) Which of the following most accurately reflects the concept of depreciation as used in accounting?

    A. The process of charging the decline in value of an economic resource to income in the period in which the benefit occurred.

    B. The process of allocating the cost of tangible assets to expense in a systematic and rational manner to those periods expected to benefit from the use of the asset.

    C. A method of allocating asset cost to an expense account in a manner which closely matches the physical deterioration of the tangible asset involved.

    D. An accounting concept that allocates the portion of an asset used up during the year to the contra asset account for the purpose of properly recording the fair market value of tangible assets.

_____ 2. (L.O. 2) The major difference between the service life of an asset and its physical life is that:

    A. service life refers to the time an asset will be used by a company and physical life refers to how long the asset will last.

    B. physical life is the life of an asset without consideration of salvage value and service life requires the use of salvage value.

    C. physical life is always longer than service life.

    D. service life refers to the length of time an asset is of use to its original owner, while physical life refers to how long the asset will be used by all owners.

_____ 3. (L.O. 2) The economic factors related to an asset's service life include:

    A. obsolescence.

    B. wear and tear.

    C. decay.

    D. unexpected casualties.

_____   4. (L.O. 2) The activity method of depreciation (often called the variable charge approach) assumes that depreciation is a function of:

	Productivity	**Passage of Time**
A.	Yes	Yes
B.	No	No
C.	Yes	No
D.	No	Yes

_____   5. (L.O. 3) Which of the following is a realistic assumption of the straight-line method of depreciation?

  A.   The asset's economic usefulness is the same each year.
  B.   The repair and maintenance expense is essentially the same each period.
  C.   The rate of return analysis is enhanced using the straight-line method.
  D.   Depreciation is a function of time rather than a function of usage.

_____   6. (L.O. 3) Which of the following statements is the assumption on which straight-line depreciation is based?

  A.   The operating efficiency of the asset decreases in later years.
  B.   Service value declines as a function of time rather than use.
  C.   Service value declines as a function of obsolescence rather than time.
  D.   Physical wear and tear are more important than economic obsolescence.

_____   7. (L.O. 3) A graph is set up with "depreciation expense" on the vertical axis and "time" on the horizontal axis. Assuming linear relationships, how would the graphs for declining-balance and straight-line, respectively, be drawn?

  A.   Sloping down to the right and vertically.
  B.   Sloping up to the right and vertically.
  C.   Sloping down to the right and horizontally.
  D.   Sloping up to the right and horizontally.

_____   8. (L.O. 3) Which of the following depreciation methods does not deduct the residual value in computing the depreciation base?

  A.   Straight-line.
  B.   Sum-of-years'-digits.
  C.   Declining-balance.
  D.   Activity or production.

_____   9. (L.O. 3) SL and YD Companies purchase identical equipment having an estimated service life of 5 years, with no residual value. SL Company uses the straight-line depreciation method; YD Company uses the sum-of-the-years' digits method. Assuming that the companies are identical in all other respects:

  A.   if both companies keep the asset for 5 years, YD Company's 5-year total for depreciation expense will be greater than SL Company's 5-year total.
  B.   if the asset is sold after 3 years, SL Company is more likely to report a gain on the transaction than YD Company.
  C.   SL Company's depreciation expense will be higher during the 1st year than YD's.
  D.   SL Company's net income will be lower during the 4th year than YD Company's.

_____   10. (L.O. 3) Each year Abner Corporation sets aside an amount of cash equal to depreciation expense on its only machine. When the asset is completely depreciated, the cash fund will allow the corporation to buy a new machine if:

  A.   prices rise throughout the life of the property.
  B.   an accelerated depreciation method was used.
  C.   prices remain reasonably constant during the life of the property.
  D.   the component depreciation method is used.

____ 11. (L.O. 3) When depreciation is computed for partial periods under a diminishing charge depreciation method, it is necessary to:

     A.   charge a full year's depreciation to the year of acquisition.

     B.   determine depreciation expense for the full year and then prorate the expense between the two periods involved.

     C.   use the straight-line method for the year in which the asset is sold or otherwise disposed of.

     D.   use a salvage value equal to the first year's partial depreciation charge.

____ 12. (L.O. 4) Component depreciation is a depreciation system whereby:

     A.   the residual value is not deducted in determining the depreciation base.

     B.   the cost of individual elements of a particular asset are depreciated individually over their respective useful lives.

     C.   an input measure, such as hours worked, is used to depreciate an asset used to produce the component parts for a company's product line.

     D.   the original cost of all items in a given group or class of assets is retained in the asset account and the cost of replacement components is charged to expense when they are acquired.

____ 13. (L.O. 4) Cannon Company purchased a building for $500,000 on January 2, 2010. Individual components of the building and their useful lives are as follows.

Component	Cost	Useful Lives
Roof	$250,000	10 years
Structure	180,000	5 years
Foundation	70,000	30 years

What amount of depreciation will Cannon Company record for 2010 assuming use of component depreciation and the straight-line method of depreciation?

     A. $33,333

     B. $63,333

     C. $100,000

     D. $16,667

____ 14. (L.O. 5) Thucydides Company purchased a new machine on May 1, 2002, for $25,000. At the time of acquisition, the machine was estimated to have a useful life of 10 years and an estimated salvage value of $1,000. The company has recorded monthly depreciation using the straight-line method. On March 1, 2011, the machine was sold for $800. What should be the loss recognized from the sale of the machine?

     A. $ 0

     B. $2,000

     C. $3,000

     D. $3,400

____ 15. (L.O. 4) Which of the following statements concerning depreciation is **incorrect?**

     A.   A change in the estimated life of a building is reported only in the current and prospective periods.

     B.   When assets are purchased in the middle of the year, companies normally compute depreciation on the basis of the nearest full month.

     C.   When assets are purchased in the middle of the year, companies may decide to take **no** depreciation in the year of acquisition and a full year's depreciation in the year of disposal.

     D.   Depreciation provides funds for the replacement of property, plant, and equipment.

_____ 16. (L.O. 4) The estimated life of a building that has been depreciated for 30 of its originally estimated life of 50 years has been revised to a remaining life of 10 years. On the basis of this information the accountant should:

      A.   continue to depreciate the building over the original 50-year life.

      B.   depreciate the remaining book value over the remaining life of the asset.

      C.   adjust accumulated depreciation to its appropriate balance, through net income, based on a 40-year life, and then depreciate the adjusted book value as though the estimated life had always been 40 years.

      D.   adjust accumulated depreciation to its appropriate balance, through retained earnings, based on a 40-year life, and then depreciate the adjusted book value as though the estimated life had always been 40 years.

_____ 17. (L.O. 4) Plato Corporation purchased a machine with a cost of $165,000 and a salvage value of $9,000 on April 1, 2011. The machine will be depreciated over a 12 year useful life using the sum-of-years'-digits method. The amount of depreciation Plato Corporation would record for the year ended 12/31/12 would be:

      A. $22,000

      B. $24,000

      C. $16,500

      D. $22,500

_____ 18. (L.O. 5) An impairment in the value of property, plant, and equipment is recorded by recognizing a:

	Loss	Reduction in Asset Book Value
A.	Yes	No
B.	Yes	Yes
C.	No	Yes
D.	No	No

_____ 19. (L.O. 5) Maimonides Inc. bought a machine on January 1, 2002 for $100,000. The machine had an expected life of 20 years and was expected to have a salvage value of $10,000. On July 1, 2012, the company reviewed the potential of the machine and determined that its recoverable amount is $50,000 and its discounted future net cash flows totaled $35,000. The company does not plan to dispose of the machine. What amount, if any, should Maimonides record as an impairment loss on July 1, 2012 assuming the straight-line method is used?

      A. $ 0

      B. $ 2,750

      C. $ 5,000

      D. $50,000

_____ 20. (L.O. 5) On December 31, 2011, Aquinas Company had land that had a carrying amount of $300,000 which the company wrote down to its $250,000 fair value. At the end of 2012 it was determined that the fair value of the land had risen to $320,000. At December 31, 2012, assuming Aquinas does not intend to dispose of the land, how should Aquinas record the change in fair value of the land?

      A.   The carrying amount of the land should not change.

      B.   The land should be recorded at $300,000.

      C.   The land should be recorded at $320,000.

      D.   The land should not be reported in the statement of financial position since an impairment loss was previously recorded on the land.

_____ 21. (L.O. 6) Of the following costs related to the development of mineral resources, which one is not a part of depletion cost?

     A. Acquisition cost of the mineral resource deposit.
     B. Restoration costs.
     C. Tangible equipment costs associated with machinery used to extract the mineral resource.
     D. Intangible development costs such as drilling costs, tunnels, and shafts.

_____ 22. (L.O. 6) The Xenophon Company acquired a tract of land containing an extractable mineral resource. Xenophon Company is required by its purchase contract to restore the land to a condition suitable for recreational use after it extracts the mineral resource. Geological surveys estimate that recoverable reserves will be 3 million tons and that the land will have a value of $600,000 after restoration. Relevant cost information follows:

Land...	$6,000,000
Restoration...	900,000
Geological surveys	300,000

If Xenophon Company maintains no inventories of extracted material, what should be the charge to depletion expense per ton of material extracted?

     A. $1.80
     B. $1.90
     C. $2.00
     D. $2.20

_____ 23. (L.O. 6) In January 2012, the Lucky Mine Corporation purchased a mineral mine for $3,400,000 with removable ore estimated by geological surveys at 4,000,000 tons. The property has an estimated value of $200,000 after the ore has been extracted. The company incurred $800,000 of development costs preparing the mine for production. During 2012, 400,000 tons were removed and 375,000 tons were sold. What is the amount of depletion cost that Lucky Mine should record for 2012?

     A. $375,000
     B. $393,750
     C. $400,000
     D. $420,000

_____ 24. (L.O. 7) Which of the following statements is true regarding revaluation accounting?

     A. The Accumulated Other Comprehensive Income account related to revaluations can have either a positive or a negative balance, depending upon whether revaluation have resulted in gains or losses.
     B. The unrealized gain that results from revaluation is referred to as revaluation surplus.
     C. The use of revaluation accounting is an "all or nothing" proposition, requiring companies who select revaluation to revalue all assets.
     D. All of the choices are correct.

_____ 25. (L.O. 8) Based on the following information for Lumber Company, compute the company's asset turnover ratio:

Net sales	€100,000
Total assets, 12/31/11	220,000
Total assets, 12/31/12	180,000
Net income	68,000

     A. 0.50
     B. 2.0
     C. 0.34
     D. 0.17

REVIEW EXERCISES

1.   (L.O.2 and 3) Augustine Corporation purchased two separate pieces of equipment in March 2005. Facts related to the two items are noted below. Augustine Corporation follows a policy of recording a full-year's depreciation in the year of acquisition and no depreciation in the year of disposition.

Item	Cost	Salvage Value	Useful Life	Depreciation Method	Annual Repair Cost
A	$113,000	$ 5,000	8 yrs.	Sum-of-year's-digits	$1,500
B	$140,000	$10,000	10 yrs.	Declining-balance (Double the SL rate)	$2,500

Because of a lack of experience, the bookkeeper for the corporation made the following entry for the repair cost each year after depreciation was recorded.

Dr. Accumulated Depreciation
Cr. Cash

As a result, when item A was sold in July 2010 for $25,000, the bookkeeper recorded a loss on the sale. Also, when item B was sold in September 2012 for $40,000, the bookkeeper also recorded a loss. (Assume the bookkeeper ignored the debits to Accumulated Depreciation in computing annual depreciation expense on each asset.)

Instructions:

a.   What journal entry did the bookkeeper record for each sale, assuming the only error was improperly charging the repair expense to accumulated depreciation?

b.   What entry should have been made for each sale?

a.

General Journal			
			J1
Date	**Account Title**	**Debit**	**Credit**

b.

General Journal			J1
Date	Account Title	Debit	Credit

2.   (L.O.3) Aristotle Company acquired a machine on July 1, 2012, at a cost of $32,000. The machine has an estimated salvage value of $2,000 at the end of its 4-year useful life. Aristotle Company uses the calendar year as its accounting period.

Instructions:
Using the depreciation methods indicated, compute the depreciation expense for years 2012 and 2013, and the book value of the machine at December 31, 2013.

Depreciation Method	Depreciation Expense 2012	Depreciation Expense 2013	Book Value December 31, 2013
Straight-line	_____	_____	_____
Sum-of-the-years'-digits	_____	_____	_____
Declining-balance (200%)	_____	_____	_____

3.   (L.O.8) Sand Dollar, Inc. has the following information at December 31:

	2011	2012
Total assets	$160,000	$190,000
Total liabilities	120,000	80,000
Net sales	600,000	480,000
Net income	46,000	58,000

Instructions:

Compute the following ratios for Sand Dollar, Inc. for the year ended December 31, 2012:

a. Asset turnover ratio.
b. Rate of return on assets.
c. Profit margin on sales.

4.   (L.O. 5) Alfarabi Company has an asset that had an original cost of $560,000 and depreciation taken to date of $240,000. On December 31, 2012, management of Alfarabi Company reviewed the asset for indicators of impairment and decided to perform an impairment test. The fair value less costs to sell is $80,000. Further, the asset has a remaining useful life of 3 years and a salvage value of $15,000 and its value-in-use is $61,000.

Instructions:

a.   Prepare the journal entry Alfarabi Company would make to record the impairment in the value of the asset.

b.   How is the gain or loss on this impairment reported in the income statement?

a.

General Journal			
			J1
Date	**Account Title**	**Debit**	**Credit**

b.

_____

_____

_____

_____

_____

_____

_____

_____

_____

_____

_____

_____

_____

_____

5.   (L.O. 6) Cicero Oil Company acquired the rights to explore for oil on a 2,000-acre plot of land in the Oklahoma Panhandle. The rights cost $80,000, and the exploration costs associated with the discovery of a major oil deposit amounted to $125,000. The company incurred $980,000 in developmental costs, of which $250,000 were for tangible equipment. This equipment has useful life of 10 years and should be of use in future exploration ventures. During the first year the company extracted 175,000 of the estimated 2.5 million barrels of oil related to the discovery.

Instructions:
Prepare the journal entry for the first year's depletion and show how the above-mentioned assets would be reported in the statement of financial position at the end of the first year.

General Journal

			J1
Date	**Account Title**	**Debit**	**Credit**

SOLUTIONS TO REVIEW QUESTIONS AND EXERCISES

TRUE-FALSE

1. (F) Depreciation is not a matter of valuation but a means of cost allocation in accounting. The concept is defined as the systematic allocation of the cost of an asset.

2. (T)

3. (T)

4. (F) When the economic nature of the asset is the primary determinant of service life, functional factors rather than physical factors (wear and tear) cause the asset to be retired. Functional factors (inadequacy, supersession, and obsolescence) cannot be reversed by repairs and maintenance.

5. (T)

6. (T)

7. (T)

8. (F) Companies that desire low depreciation during periods of low productivity and high depreciation during high productivity either adopt or switch to an activity method.

9. (T)

10. (F) The straight-line method is widely employed in practice because of its simplicity. The major objection to the straight-line method is that it rests on tenuous assumptions that in most situations are not realistic. The major assumptions are that (a) the asset's economic usefulness is the same each year and (b) the repair and maintenance expense is essentially the same each period.

11. (F) Accelerated depreciation methods provide for a higher depreciation cost in the earlier years and lower charges in later periods. The estimated useful life of an asset is unaffected by the depreciation method used.

12. (T)

13. (T)

14. (T)

15. (T)

16. (F) To determine if an asset is impaired, on an annual basis, companies review the asset for indicators of impairments—that is, a decline in the asset's cash-generating ability through use or sale. This review should consider internal sources (e.g., adverse changes in performance) and external sources (e.g., adverse changes in the business or regulatory environment) of information. If impairment indicators are present, then an impairment test must be conducted.

17. (F) If the carrying amount is higher than the recoverable amount, the difference is an impairment loss. If the recoverable amount is greater than the carrying amount, no impairment is recorded.

18. (F) Losses or gains relating to impaired assets intended to be disposed of should be reported as part of operating income in "Other income and expense."

19. (T)

20. (F)   Because companies can move the heavy equipment from one extracting site to another, companies do not normally include tangible equipment costs in the depletion base. Instead, they use separate depreciation charges to allocate the costs of such equipment.

21. (F)   Under the full costing approach, all costs, whether related to successful or unsuccessful projects, are capitalized and charged against future operations.

22. (T)

23. (T)

*24. (T)

*25. (F)   If a company experiences a loss on impairment (decrease of value below historical cost), the loss reduces income and retained earnings.

MULTIPLE CHOICE

1. (B)   Depreciation is a process of systematic and rational allocation of an asset's cost to the periods benefitted by the use of that asset. A decline in value is not a part of the depreciation process, and depreciation does not necessarily match the physical deterioration of the asset. Also, depreciation is a concept most concerned with allocating cost to expense rather than a focus on recording fair market value of an asset on the statement of financial position.

2. (A)   Service life is the period of time an asset will provide productive service to a company. Physical life indicates how long an asset may be physically capable of producing a product or being used. The major difference is that an asset with physical life may not be economical to use and, as such, would not be of service to an entity. Salvage value is not a relevant issue in this distinction. Also, while physical life may be longer than service life, it is not necessarily always longer. The distinction of original owner vs. future owners is not a major element of the difference.

3. (A)   The economic factors related to an asset's service life include: inadequacy, supersession, and obsolescence. The items listed in alternatives (B), (C), and (D) refer to the physical factors related to an asset's physical life.

4. (C)   The activity method assumes that depreciation is a function of productivity rather than the passage of time. The life of the asset is considered in terms of either the output it provides (units of production) or an input measure such as number of hours it works.

5. (D)   Alternatives A, B, and C reflect problems with use of the straight-line method of depreciation. An asset's economic usefulness is rarely the same each year, and with most assets, repair and maintenance costs increase as the asset gets older. Also, rate of return analysis is distorted under the straight-line method as well as other methods. The one true statement concerns the fact that the straight-line method is a function of time rather than a function of usage.

6. (B)   When the service value of an asset declines as a function of time rather than use, it is rational to allocate the asset's cost using the straight-line method. Answer (A) is incorrect because an accelerated-depreciation method gives a better allocation of an asset's cost when the operating efficiency of the asset decreases in later years. Answer (D) is incorrect because an activity depreciation method gives a better allocation of an asset's cost when physical wear and tear are more important than economic obsolescence. Answer (C) is incorrect because, although straight-line depreciation is commonly used in practice to depreciate assets when their service value declines as a function of obsolescence rather than time, this is done as a practical expedient. This practice does not provide the assumption on which straight-line depreciation is based.

7. (C)   Declining-balance depreciation results in the highest depreciation expense the first year of an asset's life and then decreases each year of the asset's life thereafter. Thus, the graph of the declining-balance depreciation would be sloping down to the right. Since straight-line depreciation is the same amount each year of an asset's life, the straight-line depreciation graph would be horizontal.

8. (C)   The declining-balance method does not deduct residual value in computing the depreciation base. The declining-balance rate is multiplied by the book value (cost less accumulated depreciation) at the beginning of each period. By applying the declining-balance rate to the book value each year, a decreasing charge is recorded each year. Depreciation on the asset continues until the asset's book value is equal to its residual value.

9. (D)   If both companies are identical in all respects other than depreciation, then the company using the straight-line depreciation method (SL) will have a higher depreciation expense in the 4th year of the asset's life than the company using the sum-of-the-year's-digits method (YD). Thus, SL company's net income will be lower during the 4th year.

10. (C)   Total depreciation on any asset is limited to the cost of that asset. If an amount of money equal to depreciation expense is set aside, the total accumulation will allow for the purchase of a new machine only if prices remain reasonably constant or decrease. The depreciation method employed has no impact on the total amount of depreciation.

11. (B)   Under diminishing charge depreciation methods, depreciation expense is computed for each complete year of an asset's life. If the asset being depreciated under the diminishing charge method is purchased during a year, the depreciation for the entire year is computed and then a portion is allocated to depreciation expense based on the percentage of the year that the asset was used.

12. (B)   Component depreciation takes each significant element of an asset (such as the roof of a building) and depreciates it individually over its useful life. Answer (A) describes declining-balance depreciation which does not consider residual value in computing the depreciation base. Answer (C) describes the activity method which uses an input measure, such as hours worked, to depreciate an asset. Answer (D) does not describe an acceptable method of depreciation.

13. (B)   Component depreciation is computed as $25,000($250,000/10) + 36,000($180,000/5) + 2,333 ($70,000/30) = $ 63,333.

14. (C)

Asset cost	$25,000
Depreciation 5/1/02 to 3/1/11 ($200/mo.)*	21,200
Book value at 3/1/11	$ 3,800
Sales price	800
Loss on sale	$ 3,000

*($25,000 – 1,000)/10 = $2,400 /year = $200/month

15. (D)   A common misconception about depreciation is that it provides funds for the replacement of property, plant, and equipment. Depreciation is like other expenses in that it reduces net income. It differs, though, in that it does not involve a current cash outflow. The funds for the replacement of assets come from revenues,.

16. (B)   Whenever the estimated useful life of an asset is changed, the undepreciated book value of the asset should be depreciated over the new estimated useful life. This change is merely a change in an estimate and does not require any special accounting treatment.

17. (D)   SYD Denominator = [12 × (12 + 1)] /2 = 78
            Depreciable Base: $165,000 – $9,000 = $156,000
            1st Full Year Depreciation: 12/78 × $156,000 = $24,000
            2nd Full Year Depreciation: 11/78 × $156,000 = $22,000
            2011 Depreciation (April 1 to December 31): $24,000 × 9/12 = $18,000
            2012 Depreciation (January 1 to December 31):
                    $24,000 – $18,000 = $ 6,000
                    $22,000 × 9/12 =   16,500
            2012 Depreciation $22,500

18. (B)   An impairment in the value of property, plant, and equipment is recorded by recognizing a loss
            and reducing the book value of the asset through a credit to accumulated depreciation.

19. (B)   Because the recoverable amount of $50,000 is less than the carrying value of $52,750 [$100,000 –
            (($100,000 – $10,000)/20) × 10.5] an impairment has occurred. The impairment loss is the
            amount by which the carrying amount of the asset exceeds the recoverable amount. Therefore, the
            impairment loss is equal to $2,750 ($52,750 – $50,000).

20. (B)   The amount of the recovery of the loss is limited to the carrying amount that would result if the
            impairment had not occurred. In this case, the land should be recorded at its original cost of
            $300,000.

21. (C)   Tangible equipment costs are normally not considered in the depletion base; instead, separate
            depreciation charges are employed because the asset can be moved from one drilling or mining
            site to another. Tangible assets that cannot be moved should be separately depreciated over their
            useful life or the life of the resource, whichever is shorter.

22. (D)   Land cost... $6,000,000
            Restoration   900,000
            Geological surveys..   300,000
            Total cost... $7,200,000
            Land residual value...   600,000
            Depletion base.. $6,600,000
            Depletion expense per ton $6,600,000 ÷ 3,000,000 = $2.20.

23. (C)   Lucky Mine's depletion rate per ton of mined ore can be calculated as follows:

            Depletable cost:
                Purchase price of mine $3,400,000
                Development cost   800,000
                                                                                $4,200,000
                Less: Estimated value of property after ore has
                       been extracted   200,000
            Total depletable cost $4,000,000

            $$\frac{\text{Depletable cost}}{\text{Estimated recoverable ore}} = \frac{\$4,000,000}{4,000,000 \text{ tons}} = \$1 \text{ depletion per ton of mined ore}$$

            Since Lucky Mine Corporation removed 400,000 tons of ore in 2012, it should record $400,000
            (400,000 tons × $1) as its depletion cost. This amount would be charged to the account Inventory
            of Mined Ore and credited to Accumulated Depletion.

            Answer (A) is incorrect because depletion cost would be recorded as the ore is mined, not as it is
            sold.

24. (B)   Answer (A) is incorrect because under no circumstances can the Accumulated Other Comprehensive Income account related to revaluations have a negative balance. Answer (C) is incorrect because the use of revaluation accounting is not an "all or nothing" proposition. That is, a company can select to value only one class of assets, say buildings, and not revalue other assets such as land or equipment. However, if a company selects only buildings, revaluation applies to all assets in that class of assets. Answer (D) is incorrect because answers (A) and (C) are not correct.

25. (A)   The asset turnover ratio is computed as Net sales/Average total assets. In this case €100,000/[(€220,000 + 180,000)/2] = €100,000/€200,000 = .50.

REVIEW EXERCISES

1. (a)   **Item A:**

Year	Computation	Depreciation Recorded
2005	$108,000 × 8/36	$24,000
2006	108,000 × 7/36	21,000
2007	108,000 × 6/36	18,000
2008	108,000 × 5/36	15,000
2009	108,000 × 4/36	12,000
	Total Depreciation	$90,000
	Repair Expense Charged to Accumulated Depreciation (1,500 × 5)	(7,500)
	Depreciation Balance (2009)	$82,500

Entry by bookkeeper for sale of item A:

Cash	25,000	
Accumulated depreciation	82,500	
Loss on sale	5,500	
Item A		113,000

Correct entry for sale of item A:

Cash	25,000	
Accumulated depreciation	90,000	
Gain on sale		2,000
Item A		113,000

(b) **Item B:**

Year	Computation	Depreciation Recorded
2005	$140,000 × .20	$ 28,000
2006	112,000 × .20	22,400
2007	89,600 × .20	17,920
2008	71,680 × .20	14,336
2009	57,344 × .20	11,469
	Total Depreciation	$94125
	Repair Expense Charged to Accumulated Depreciation (2,500 × 5)	(12,500)
	Depreciation Balance (2011)	$ 81,625

Entry by bookkeeper for sale of item B:

Cash	40,000	
Accumulated depreciation	81,625	
Loss on sale	18,375	
Item B		140,000

Correct entry for sale of item B:

Cash	40,000	
Accumulated Depreciation	94,125	
Loss on sale	5,875	
Item B		140,000

2.

Depreciation Method	Depreciation Expense 2012	Depreciation Expense 2013	Book Value December 31, 2013
Straight Line	$ 3,750 (a)	$ 7,500 (b)	$20,750 (c)
Sum-of-the-years'-digits	6,000 (d)	10,500 (e)	15,500 (f)
Declining-balance (200%)	8,000 (g)	12,000 (h)	12,000 (i)

(a) $30,000 × 1/4 × 1/2 = $3,750

(b) $30,000 × 1/4 = $7,500

(c) $32,000 – (a + b) = $20,750

(d) $30,000 × 4/10 × 1/2 = $6,000

(e) $6,000 + (9,000 × 1/2) = $10,500

(f) $32,000 – (d + e) = $15,500

(g) $32,000 × .5 × 1/2 = $8,000

(h) ($32,000 – 8,000) × 1/2 = $12,000

(i) 32,000 – (g + h) = $12,000

3.

a. Asset turnover = Net sales/Average total assets

$480,000/[($160,000 + 190,000)/2] = $480,000/$175,000 = 2.74

b. Rate of return on assets = Profit margin on sales × Asset turnover OR Net income/Average total assets

2.74 × .12 = .33

OR

$58,000//[($160,000 + 190,000)/2] = $58,000/$175,000 = .33

c. Profit margin on sales = Net income/Net sales

$58,000/$480,000 = .12

	2011	2012
Total assets	$160,000	$190,000
Total liabilities	120,000	80,000
Net sales	600,000	480,000
Net income	46,000	58,000

4. (a) Current Book Value: Cost $560,000
                              Accumulated Depreciation   240,000
                              Book Value $320,000

    After Impairment: Cost $560,000
                              Accumulated Depreciation   480,000
                              Book Value $ 80,000

Journal Entry:

Loss on Impairment   240,000
    Accumulated Depreciation   240,000

*($320,000 – $80,000)

(b) The loss of $240,000 is reported separately in the Other Expenses and Losses section of the income statement. .

5. Depletion base:
        Land rights... $ 80,000
        Exploration costs   125,000
        Intangible development costs ($980,000 – 250,000).....   730,000
            Depletion base................................. $935,000

Depletion rate per barrel: $935,000 ÷ 2,500,000 = $.374
First year's depletion: 175,000 × .374 = $65,450

Depletion expense   65,450
    Accumulated depletion of mineral resource..................   65,450

Statement of financial position presentation:
        Oil deposit (at cost) $935,000
        Less accumulated depletion.........................   65,450 $869,550

Tangible assets should be reported separately with a deduction for the related accumulated depreciation.

12

Intangible Assets

CHAPTER LEARNING OBJECTIVES

1. Describe the characteristics of intangible assets.
2. Identify the costs included in the initial valuation of intangible assets.
3. Explain the procedure for amortizing intangible assets.
4. Describe the types of intangible assets.
5. Explain the conceptual issues related to goodwill.
6. Describe the accounting procedures for recording goodwill.
7. Explain the accounting issues related to intangible asset impairments.
8. Identify the conceptual issues related to research and development costs.
9. Describe the accounting for research and development costs and similar costs.
10. Indicate the presentation of intangible assets and related items.

CHAPTER REVIEW

1. Chapter 12 discusses the basic conceptual and reporting issues related to intangible assets.

Valuing and Amortizing Intangibles

2. (L.O. 1) The characteristics of an intangible asset are: (1) they are identifiable, (2) they lack physical existence, and (3) they are not monetary assets. The most common types of intangibles reported are patents, copyrights, franchises, licenses, trademarks, trade names, and goodwill.

3. (L.O. 2) **Cost** is the appropriate basis for recording purchased intangible assets. Like tangible assets, cost includes acquisition price and all other expenditures necessary in making the asset ready for its intended use—for example, purchase price, legal fees, and other incidental expenses. When intangibles are acquired for consideration other than cash, the cost of the intangible is the fair market value of the consideration given or the intangible asset received, whichever is more clearly evident. Costs incurred to create **internally-created intangibles** are separated into research phase costs, which are expensed as incurred, and development phase costs, which are expensed until economic viability is met, after that point they are capitalized

Amortization of Intangibles

4. (L.O. 3) Intangibles have either a limited (finite) useful life or an indefinite useful life. An intangible asset with a limited life is amortized; an intangible asset with an indefinite life is not amortized.

Limited-Life Intangibles

5.   The expiration of intangible assets is called **amortization.** Limited-life intangibles should be amortized by systematic charges to expense over their useful life. IFRS requires that companies assess estimated residual values and useful lives at least annually. Additionally, annually companies must assess for an indication of impairment, if there's an indication of impairment, impairment testing is performed (discussed below).

6.   The amount of amortization expense for a limited-life intangible asset should reflect the pattern in which the asset is consumed or used up, if that pattern can be readily determined. If not, the straight-line method of amortization should be used. When intangible assets are amortized the charges should be shown as expenses, and the credits should be made either to the appropriate asset accounts or to separate accumulated amortization accounts. The amount of an intangible asset to be amortized should be its cost less residual value.

Indefinite-Life Intangibles

7.   If no legal, regulatory, contractual, competitive, or other factors limit the useful life of an intangible asset, the useful life is considered **indefinite.** An intangible with an indefinite life is not amortized, instead it is tested for impairment (discussed below).

Marketing-Related Intangible Assets

8.   (L.O. 4) **Marketing-related intangible assets** are those assets primarily used in the marketing or promotion of products or services. Examples are trademarks or trade names, newspaper masthead, Internet domain names, and noncompetition agreements.

9.   A **trademark** or **trade name** is a word, phrase, or symbol that distinguishes or identifies a particular enterprise or product. Under common law, the right to use a trademark or trade name, whether registered or not, rests exclusively with the original user as long as the original user continues to use it. When the total cost of a trademark or trade name is insignificant, it can be expensed rather than capitalized. In most cases, the life of a trademark or trade name is indefinite, and therefore its cost is not amortized.

Customer-Related Intangible Assets

10.   **Customer-related intangible assets** occur as a result of interactions with outside parties. Examples are customer lists, order or production backlogs, and both contractual and non-contractual customer relationships.

Artistic-Related Intangible Assets

11.   **Artistic-related intangible assets** involve ownership rights to plays, literary works, musical works, pictures, photographs, and video and audiovisual material. These ownership rights are protected by **copyrights.** A copyright is a government- granted right that all authors, painters, musicians, sculptors, and other artists have in their creations and expressions. A copyright is generally granted for the life of the creator plus 70 years. It gives the owner, or heirs, the exclusive right to reproduce and sell an artistic or published work. Copyrights are not renewable. Generally, the useful life of the copyright is less than its legal life (life in being plus 70 years). The costs of the copyright should be allocated to the years in which the benefits are expected to be received.

Contract-Related Intangible Assets

12. **Contract-related intangible assets** represent the value of rights that arise from contractual arrangements. Examples are franchise and licensing agreements, construction permits, broadcast rights, and service or supply contracts. A **franchise** is a contractual arrangement under which the franchisor grants the franchisee the right to sell certain products or services, to use certain trademarks or trade names, or to perform certain functions, usually within a designated geographical area. A **license or permit** is the arrangement commonly entered into by a governmental body and a business enterprise that uses public property. Franchises and licenses can have limited or indefinite lives. The cost of a franchise (or license) with a limited life should be amortized as operating expense over the life of the franchise; whereas those with an indefinite life should be carried at cost and not amortized.

Technology-Related Intangible Assets

13. Technology-related intangible assets relate to innovations or technological advances. Examples are patented technology and trade secrets. In many countries, a **patent** gives the holder exclusive right to use, manufacture, and sell a product or a process for a period of 20 years without interference or infringement by others. If a patent is purchased from an inventor (or other owner), the purchase price represents its cost. A company must expense all research costs and any development costs incurred before achieving economic viability related to the development of the product process. The costs of the patent should be amortized over its legal life or its useful life, whichever is shorter.

Goodwill

14. (L.O. 5 and 6) In a business combination, the cost (purchase price) is assigned where possible to the identifiable tangible and intangible net assets, and the remainder is recorded in an intangible asset account called **goodwill.** Goodwill generated internally should not be capitalized in the accounts—it is recorded only when an entire business is purchased. To record goodwill, the fair value of the net tangible and identifiable intangible assets are compared with the purchase price of the acquired business. The difference is goodwill. Goodwill is considered to have an indefinite life and therefore should not be amortized. When a purchaser in a business combination pays less than the fair value of the identifiable net assets, this is referred to as a **bargain purchase.** This excess amount is recorded as a gain by the purchaser.

Impairments

15. (L.O. 7) When the carrying amount of a long-lived asset (property, plant, and equipment or intangible assets) is above the recoverable amount, a write-off of the impairment is needed. The rules that apply to impairments of property, plant, and equipment also apply to limited-life intangibles. At each statement of financial position date, a company should review limited-life intangibles for impairment. If there is an indication that an intangible asset is impaired, the company performs an impairment test: compare the carrying value of the intangible asset to the recoverable amount. The impairment loss is reported as part of income from continuing operations, generally in the "Other expenses and losses" section. If, in a subsequent period, the recoverable amount is higher than the carrying amount, the impairment loss may be reversed.

16. Indefinite-life intangibles, including goodwill, should be tested for impairment at least annually. The impairment test for indefinite-life assets other than goodwill is the same as that for limited-life intangibles. That is, compare the recoverable amount of the intangible asset with the asset's carrying value. If the recoverable amount is less than the carrying amount, the company recognizes an impairment.

17.   The impairment rule for goodwill is conducted based on the cash-generating unit (CGU) to which goodwill is assigned. The CGU is the smallest identifiable group of assets that generate cash flows independently of the cash flows from other assets.   Under IFRS, the recoverable amount of the CGU is compared to its carrying amount.   If the recoverable amount is less than the carrying amount, an impairment is recorded. Goodwill impairment loss reversals are not permitted.

Research and Development Costs

18.   (L.O. 8) Planned research or critical investigation aimed at discovery of new knowledge are **research activities**. Translation of research findings or other knowledge into a plan or design for a new product or process or for a significant improvement to an existing product or process whether intended for sale or use are **development activities**. While R&D costs are not intangible assets, they often result in the development of an intangible asset (patent, formula, etc.).

19.   (L.O. 9) The costs associated with R & D activities and the accounting treatment accorded them are as follows:

     a.   **Materials, Equipment, and Facilities.** Expense the entire costs, unless the items have alternative future uses (in other R & D projects or otherwise) carry the items as inventory and allocate as consumed or capitalize and depreciate as used.

     b.   **Personnel.** Salaries, wages, and other related costs of personnel engaged in R & D should be expensed as incurred.

     c.   **Purchased Intangibles.** Recognize and measure at fair value. After initial recognition, account for in accordance with their nature (as either limited-life or indefinite intangibles).

     d.   **Contract Services.** The costs of services performed by others in connection with the reporting company's R & D should be expensed as incurred.

     e.   **Indirect Costs.** A reasonable allocation of indirect costs shall be included in R & D costs, except for general and administrative cost, which must be clearly related in order to be included and expensed.

20.   **Start-up costs, initial operating costs,** and **advertising costs** are also generally expensed as incurred.

Presentation of Intangibles and Related Items

21.   (L.O. 10) On the statement of financial position, all intangible assets other than goodwill should be reported as a separate item. If goodwill is present, it also should be reported as a separate item. On the income statement, amortization expense and impairment losses (and reversals) should be presented as part of continuing operations, usually as a separate line item.

GLOSSARY

Intangible assets.
Characteristics include: (1) identifiable, (2) lack of physical existence, and (3) not a monetary asset.

Limited-life intangibles.
Intangible assets with a foreseeable limit on the period of time over which the intangible assets are expected to provide cash flows.

Indefinite-life intangibles.
Intangible assets with no foreseeable limit on the period of time over which the intangible assets are expected to provide cash flows.

Marketing-related intangible assets.
Intangible assets used in the marketing or promotion of products or services.

Customer-related intangible assets.
Intangible assets that occur as a result of interactions with outside parties.

Artistic-related intangible assets.
Intangible assets that involve ownership rights to plays, literary works, musical works, pictures, photographs, and video and audiovisual material.

Contract-related intangible assets.
Intangible assets that represent the value of rights that arise from contractual arrangements.

Trademark or trade name.
A word, phrase, or symbol that distinguishes or identifies a particular enterprise or product. Under common law, the right to use a trademark or trade name, whether registered or not, rests exclusively with the original user as long as the original user continues to use it.

Copyright.
A government-granted right that all authors, painters, musicians, sculptors, and other artists have in their creations and expressions, which is generally granted for the life of the creator plus 70 years.

Franchise.
A contractual arrangement under which the franchisor grants the franchisee the right to sell certain products or services, to use certain trademarks or trade names, or to perform certain functions, usually within a designated geographical area.

License.
A right granted by a government body for the use of public property.

Technology-related intangible asset.
Intangible assets that relate to innovations or technological advances.

Patents.
Exclusive rights to the holder to use, manufacture, and sell a product or process for a period of 20 years without interference or infringement by others.

Goodwill.	The excess of cost over fair value of the identifiable net assets acquired in a business combination.
Bargain purchase	Occurs when the fair market value of the assets acquired is higher than the purchase price of the assets.
Impairment.	Occurs when the carrying amount of a long-lived asset (property, plant, and equipment or intangible assets) is not recoverable.
Research activities.	The planned search or critical investigation aimed at discovery of new knowledge.
Development activities.	The translation of research findings or other knowledge into a plan or design for a new product or process for a significant improvement to an existing product or process whether intended for sale or use.
Research and development costs.	The costs associated with research and development activities.
Start-up costs.	Costs incurred for one-time activities to start a new operation, such as opening a new plant, introducing a new product, or conducting business in a new territory.
Initial operating costs.	Losses in first year of operations.
Product patents.	Patents which cover actual physical products.
Process patents.	Patents which govern the process by which products are made.

CHAPTER OUTLINE

Fill in the outline presented below.

(L.O. 1) Characteristics of Intangible Assets

(L.O. 2) Valuation of Intangibles

(L.O. 3) Amortization of Intangibles

Limited-Life Intangibles

Indefinite-Life Intangibles

(L.O. 4) Categories of Intangibles

Marketing-Related Intangible Assets

Trademark and trade names

Customer-Related Intangible Assets

Chapter Outline *(continued)*

    Artistic-Related Intangible Assets

        Copyrights

    Contract-Related Intangible Assets

        Franchises

        Licenses

    Technology-Related Intangible Assets

        Patents

(L.O. 5) Goodwill

(L.O. 6) Recording Goodwill

    Internally created goodwill

    Purchased goodwill

    Goodwill write-off

    Bargain purchase

Chapter Outline *(continued)*

    (L.O. 7) Impairments

            Impairment of Property, Plant and Equipment

            Impairment of Limited-Life Intangibles

            Impairment of Indefinite-Life Intangibles Other Than Goodwill

            Impairment of Goodwill

            Restoration of Impairment Loss

    (L.O. 8) Research and Development Costs

    (L.O. 9) Recording Research and Development Costs

    (L.O. 10) Presentation of Intangibles and Related Items

REVIEW QUESTIONS AND EXERCISES

TRUE-FALSE

Indicate whether each of the following is true (T) or false (F) in the space provided.

_____   1. (L.O. 1) Lack of physical substance is the only characteristic of intangible assets that distinguishes them from all other assets reported on the statement of financial position.

_____   2. (L.O. 2) Cost is the basis for initially recording intangible assets, including acquisition price and all expenditures incurred to prepare the asset for its intended use.

_____   3. (L.O. 2) Costs incurred internally to create intangibles are generally the basis for recording intangible assets, which are then amortized over the estimated life of the intangible asset.

_____   4. (L.O. 3) Amortization is the systematic charge to income of the cost of an intangible asset.

_____   5. (L.O. 3) Intangible assets are amortized over their useful lives unless the intangible can remain in existence indefinitely.

_____   6. (L.O. 3) A trademark may properly be considered to have an indefinite life.

_____   7. (L.O. 4) A copyright is granted for the life of the creator or 70 years, whichever is longer.

_____   8. (L.O. 4) A copyright would generally not be amortized.

_____   9. (L.O. 4) Marsilius Company secured a copyright on a unique literary work. All conservative estimates indicate that the copyright will be useful for its maximum useful life; thus, this is the period over which the copyright should be amortized.

_____   10. (L.O. 4) Legal fees and other costs incurred in successfully defending a patent suit are expensed as incurred.

_____   11. (L.O. 6) Goodwill generated internally should be capitalized in the accounts.

_____   12. (L.O. 6) Goodwill is often identified on the statement of financial position as the excess of the fair value over the cost of the net assets acquired.

_____   13. (L.O. 6) Use of the master valuation approach to measure goodwill requires an estimate of a firm's excess earning power.

_____   14. (L.O. 6) Goodwill should be amortized over its useful life.

_____   15. (L.O. 6) A bargain purchase arises when the fair value of the assets acquired is higher than the purchase price of the assets.

_____   16. (L.O. 6) The general rules that apply to impairments of long-lived assets also apply to intangibles.

_____   17. (L.O. 7) For all indefinite-life intangibles the fair value test is used to determine whether an impairment has occurred.

_____   18. (L.O. 7) In a business combination, when the purchase price is less than the fair value of the identifiable net assets, a gain is recorded by the purchaser.

_____   19. (L.O. 7) Goodwill impairment loss reversals are not permitted.

_____ 20. (L.O. 7) Impairment testing for goodwill includes identifying the cash-generating unit to which the goodwill is assigned.

_____ 21. (L.O. 8) If a facility is built for research and development (R&D) activity, and if that facility has alternative future uses, the facility should be capitalized and depreciated as it is used.

_____ 22. (L.O. 9) The costs of services performed by others in connection with the reporting company's R&D should be expensed as incurred.

_____ 23. (L.O. 9) Start-up costs are usually charged to an account called Start-Up Costs and may be carried as an asset on the statement of financial position.

_____ 24. (L.O. 10) If goodwill is present, it should be reported as a separate item on the statement of financial position.

_____ 25. (L.O. 10) Acceptable accounting practice requires that disclosure be made in the financial statements (generally in the notes) of the total R&D costs charged to expense each period for which an income statement is presented.

MULTIPLE CHOICE

Select the best answer for each of the following items and enter the corresponding letter in the space provided.

_____ 1. (L.O. 1) Which of the following is not an intangible asset?

    A. Accounts receivable.
    B. Patents.
    C. Copyrights.
    D. Franchises.

_____ 2. (L.O. 2) When intangible assets are amortized, a journal entry may be made by debiting an expense account and crediting

	The Intangible Asset	Accumulated Amortization
A.	Yes	Yes
B.	Yes	No
C.	No	Yes
D.	No	No

_____ 3. (L.O. 3) In considering the useful life of a limited-life intangible, which of the following are considered? :

    A. Expected use by the company.
    B. Effects of competition or other economic factors.
    C. Legal or regulatory provisions.
    D. All of the choices are correct.

_____ 4. (L.O. 3) One factor that is not considered in determining the useful life of an intangible asset is:

    A. legal life.
    B. expected actions of competitors.
    C. salvage value.
    D. provisions for renewal or extension.

_____ 5. (L.O. 4) When a company develops a trademark or trade name the costs directly related to securing it should generally be capitalized. Which of the following costs associated with a trademark or trade name would not be allowed to be capitalized?

    A.   Attorney fees.
    B.   Consulting fees.
    C.   Research and development fees.
    D.   Design costs.

_____ 6. (L.O. 4) A large publicly held company has developed and registered a trademark during 2012. How should the cost of developing and registering the trademark be accounted for if it is considered to have a limited-life?

    A.   Charged to an asset account that should not be amortized.
    B.   Amortized over 10 years regardless of its useful life.
    C.   Expensed as incurred.
    D.   Amortized over its useful life.

_____ 7. (L.O. 3) Hooker Corporation acquired a franchise to operate a Good Pet Dog Kennel in January, 2009. The cost of the franchise was $125,000 and was estimated to have a limited life of 40 years. Early in the year 2015, the franchise was deemed worthless due to significant law suits that caused the franchisor to go out of business. What amount of cost or expense should be charged to the income statement of Hooker Corporation for the years noted below?

	2009	**2014**	**2015**
A.	$5,000	$5,000	$ 5,000
B.	$3,125	$3,125	$ 3,125
C.	0	0	$125,000
D.	$3,125	$3,125	$106,250

_____ 8. (L.O. 3) Smith Co. bought a window franchise from Paine, Inc., on January 2, 2012, for $100,000. It paid $30,000 in legal fees to secure the franchise. A highly regarded independent research company estimated that the remaining useful life of the franchise was 50 years.   Smith has decided to write off the franchise over the longest possible period. How much should be amortized by Smith Co. for the year ended December 31, 2012?

    A. $ 375
    B. $ 2,000
    C. $ 2,600
    D. $15,000

_____ 9. (L.O. 4) On January 15, 2003, Machiavelli Corporation was granted a patent on a product. On January 2, 2012, to protect its patent, Machiavelli purchased a patent on a competing product that originally was issued on January 10, 2005. Because of its unique plant, Machiavelli does not feel that the competing patent can be used in producing a product. The cost of acquiring the competing patent should be:

    A.   amortized over a maximum period of 11 years.
    B.   amortized over a maximum period of 16 years.
    C.   amortized over a maximum period of 20 years.
    D.   expensed in 2012.

_____ 10. (L.O. 5) Goodwill:

    A.   generated internally should not be capitalized unless it is measured by an individual independent of the enterprise involved.

    B.   is easily computed by assigning a value to the individual attributes that comprise its existence.

    C.   represents a unique asset in that its value can be identified only with the business as a whole.

    D.   exists in any company that has earnings that differ from those of a competitor.

_____ 11. (L.O. 6) The amortization of goodwill:

    A.   is dependent upon the number of years a company expects to use the benefits it provides.

    B.   does not happen as it is deemed to have an indefinite life.

    C.   represents as acceptable an accounting practice as does the immediate write-off method.

    D.   should be computed using the straight-line method unless another method is deemed more appropriate.

_____ 12. (L.O. 6) The reason goodwill is sometimes referred to as a master valuation account is because:

    A.   it represents the purchase price of a business that is about to be sold.

    B.   it is the difference between the fair market value of the net tangible and identifiable intangible assets as compared with the purchase price of the acquired business.

    C.   the value of a business is computed without consideration of goodwill and then goodwill is added to arrive at a master valuation.

    D.   it is the only account in the financial statements that is based on fair value, all other accounts are recorded at an amount other than their fair value.

_____ 13. (L.O. 6) The accounting profession does not allow the immediate write-off of goodwill. The best reason for this requirement seems to be that:

    A.   goodwill has a useful life like all assets and should be charged as an expense at a normal rate.

    B.   to write-off goodwill immediately would lead to the incorrect conclusion that goodwill has no future service potential.

    C.   the immediate write-off would cause net income to be much lower than it had been for the company in recent years and comparability would be distorted.

    D.   because the amortization of goodwill is tax deductible, an immediate write-off serves no useful purpose.

_____ 14. (L.O. 6) When the fair value of the assets acquired in a business purchase exceed the purchase price, a bargain purchase arises. When this happens, the difference is allocated:

    A.   to a gain.

    B.   to all periods benefited on an equitable basis.

    C.   to reduce proportionately the values assigned to certain noncurrent assets.

    D.   to reduce proportionately the values assigned to both current and noncurrent assets.

_____ 15. (L.O. 7) When conducting an impairment test, recoverable amount is defined as

    A.   The lower of fair value less costs to sell, or value-in-use.

    B.   The higher of fair value less costs to sell, or the cash-generating unit's cash flows.

    C.   The higher of fair value less costs to sell, or value-in-use.

    D.   The higher of fair value less costs to sell, or the cash-generating unit's cash flows.

_____ 16. Isa Company has a patent that, due to changes in the market, is reviewed for possible impairment. The asset's carrying amount is $400,000 ($500,000 cost less $100,000 accumulated amortization). The patent's value-in-use is determined to be $380,000 and it has a current market value of $350,000. What is the amount of the impairment, if any, that should be recorded by Isa Company?

    A. $0
    B. $ 20,000
    C. $ 50,000
    D. $400,000

_____ 17. (L.O. 7) Impairment loss reversals may be recorded on all of the following intangible assets except

    A.   Goodwill.
    B.   Patents.
    C.   Trademarks and trade names.
    D.   All of the choices are correct.

_____ 18. (L.O. 6) In 2009, Hume, Inc. purchased Rousseau Metals for $3 million. At December 31, 2012, the Rousseau division reported net assets of $3,300,000 (including $1,700,000 of goodwill). Hume reviewed the Rousseau division and determined that the recoverable amount based on a value-in-use estimate is $1,800,000. What entry should Hume record concerning the Rousseau division on December 31, 2012?

A.	No entry is needed.		
B.	Loss on impairment	1,500,000	
	Goodwill.		1,500,000
C.	Loss on impairment	1,200,000	
	Goodwill.		1,200,000
D.	Loss on impairment	1,500,000	
	Prorata deduction of all assets.		1,500,000

_____ 19. (L.O. 9) Which of the following is considered part of research and development costs?

    A.   Start-up costs for a new operation.
    B.   Initial operating losses.
    C.   The cost of services performed by others in connection with R&D (contract services).
    D.   Advertising costs.

_____ 20. (L.O. 9) In 2012, Descartes Corporation incurred R & D costs as follows:

Materials and facilities(no alternative use).............................	$ 80,000
Personnel	110,000
Indirect costs..	25,000
	$215,000

These costs relate to a product that will be marketed in 2012. It is estimated that these costs will be recovered by the end of 2015. What amount of R&D costs should be charged against 2012 income?

    A. $ 0
    B. $ 25,000
    C. $190,000
    D. $215,000

_____ 21. (L.O. 9) Which of the following would not be considered an R & D activity?

A.   Adaptation of an existing capability to a particular requirement or customer's need.
B.   Searching for applications of new research findings.
C.   Laboratory research aimed at discovery of new knowledge.
D.   Conceptual formulation and design of possible product or process alternatives.

_____ 22. (L.O. 7) Calvin Company incurred the following cost related to the start-up of the business:

Attorney's fee	$10,000
Underwriter's fee..	15,000
State incorporation fee..	7,000
	$32,000

The company wishes to amortize these costs over the maximum period allowed. Assuming that Calvin Company began operation on January 1, 2012, what amount of the start-up costs should be amortized in 2013?

A. $4,400
B. $2,200
C. $ 800
D. $ 0

REVIEW EXERCISES

1.   (L.O. 2, 3 and 4) A patent was acquired by Grotius Corporation on January 1, 2005, at a cost of $72,000. The useful life of the patent was estimated to be 10 years. At the beginning of 2009, Grotius spent $9,000 in successfully prosecuting an attempted infringement of the patent. At the beginning of 2010, Grotius purchased a patent for $25,000 that was expected to prolong the life of its original patent for 5 additional years. On July 1, 2013, a competitor obtained rights to a patent that made the company's patent obsolete. Grotius records amortization expense directly with a credit to the Patent account.

Instructions:
Calculate the following amounts for Grotius Corporation.

    a.   Amortization expense for 2005.
    b.   The balance in the Patent account at the beginning of 2009, immediately after the infringement suit.
    c.   Amortization expense for 2009.
    d.   The balance in the Patent account at the beginning of 2010, after purchase of the additional patent.
    e.   Amortization expense for 2010.
    f.   The amount of loss recorded at July 1, 2013.

Patent Account

2.   (L.O. 8 and 9) Montesquieu Pharmaceuticals Company has an extensive research and development effort designed to develop new products and new knowledge. The following costs were incurred during 2012 and are thought to be related to R & D activities; however, the accountant for Montesquieu Company is uncertain as to which costs are appropriately charged to research and development.

Machinery that will be used in R&D activities for the next six years, purchased on July 1, 2012	$240,000
Salaries for R&D personnel for 2012	126,000
Laboratory research costs	52,500
Costs associated with improving XR-33 (a high quality pain reliever)	34,000
Expenditures to support legal defense of lawsuits over Baldnomore (hair growth product)	116,000
Material and labor cost to design an oven to heat chemicals to a very high degree for testing purposes	87,000
Technical engineering support for production facility to move a new product to the manufacturing stage	23,000
Quality control efforts in the production of XR-33	28,500

Instructions:
Compute the amount of research and development expense Montesquieu Company should report for the year ending December 31, 2012.

_____

_____

_____

_____

_____

_____

_____

_____

_____

_____

_____

_____

_____

_____

SOLUTIONS TO REVIEW QUESTIONS AND EXERCISES

TRUE-FALSE

1. (F)   In addition to lack of physical existence, the characteristics of an intangible asset are that they also are (1) identifiable and (2) not a monetary asset.

2. (T)

3. (F)   Costs incurred internally to create intangibles are generally expensed as incurred.

4. (T)

5. (T)

6. (T)

7. (F)   A copyright is generally granted for the life of the creator plus 70 years.

8. (F)   Because a copyright has a limited life and the useful life is usually less than the legal life, a copyright is generally amortized.

9. (T)

10. (F)   Legal fees and other costs incurred in successfully defending a patent suit are debited to Patents, an asset account, because such a suit establishes the legal rights of the holder of the patent.

11. (F)   Goodwill generated internally should not be capitalized in the accounts.

12. (F)   Goodwill is often identified on the statement of financial position as the excess of the cost over the fair value of the net assets acquired.

13. (F)   When the master valuation approach is used to measure goodwill, it is considered to be the excess of the cost over the fair value of the identifiable net assets acquired.

14. (F)   Goodwill is considered to have an indefinite life and therefore should not be amortized.

15. (T)

16. (T)

17. (F)   The fair value test is only used for indefinite-life intangibles other than goodwill. For goodwill, a more complex fair value test is used.

18. (T)

19. (T)

20. (T)

21. (T)

22. (T)

23. (F) Start-up costs are to be expensed as incurred.

24. (T)

25. (T)

MULTIPLE CHOICE

1. (A) Accounts receivable would be considered a monetary asset and therefore would not be classified as an intangible asset. B, C, and D are all examples of intangible assets.

2. (A) When intangible assets are amortized, the charges should be shown as expenses, and the credits should be made either to the appropriate asset accounts or to separate accumulated amortization accounts.

3. (D) All of the choices are among the factors a company must consider when establishing the useful life of an intangible asset.

4. (C) The useful life of an intangible asset may be limited by its legal life. Actions of competitors as well as renewal or extension provisions affect the useful life of an intangible asset. Salvage value is a concept related to the computation of depreciation on tangible fixed assets. Salvage value is not a factor used in determining useful life of an intangible.

5. (C) When a trademark or trade name is developed by a company, the costs associated with that development should be capitalized. The only cost that is not appropriately capitalized are costs related to research and development.

6. (D) A trademark is no different than any other limited-life intangible asset. The costs associated with the acquisition of the trademark are to be amortized over its useful life.

7. (D) During the first six years of the franchise useful life the amortization would be the cost ($125,000) divided by the 40 year maximum life. This would result in an annual charge to expense of $3,125 ($125,000/40) for the first six years (2009 through 2014). Thus, at the beginning of 2015, when the franchise was considered worthless, the book value of the franchise account would be $106,250 [$125,000 – ($3,125 × 6)]. When the franchise is deemed worthless, it should be written off immediately.

8. (C) Smith Corporation should record franchise amortization expense of $2,600 in 2012 ($130,000/50 years = $2,600).

9. (A) The reason for acquiring the patent on the competing product is to protect the original patent acquired on 1/15/03. The original patent will expire during 2023. Thus, the cost of the patent on the competing product should be amortized over 11 years, the time between its acquisition (2012) and the expiration of the original patent's useful life (2023).

10. (C) Goodwill is recorded only when an entire business is purchased because goodwill is a going-concern valuation and cannot be separated from the business as a whole. Goodwill generated internally should not be capitalized in the accounts because measuring the components of goodwill is simply too complex and associating any costs with future benefits is too difficult.

11. (B) Goodwill is considered to have an indefinite life and therefore should not be amortized. Income statements are not charged unless goodwill has been impaired.

12. (B)   Goodwill is the difference between the fair value of the net tangible and identifiable intangible assets and the purchase price of a business organization. It does not represent the entire purchase price nor is it an amount added to the purchase price to arrive at a master valuation. Also, there are many accounts that appear in the financial statements at their fair market value, so alternative D is not correct.

13. (B)   The reason goodwill arises is because of the future economic benefits of a purchased business. Thus, goodwill reflects the future positive results that were purchased. To write this amount off immediately would be inconsistent with the reason for its initial recording.

14. (A)   The IASB requires that a bargain purchase be recognized as a gain.

15. (C)   The recoverable amount is defined as the higher of fair value less costs to sell or value-in-use. Fair v

16. (B)   The recoverable amount is defined as the higher of fair value less costs to sell or value-in-use. Therefore, in this case the recoverable amount is $380,000. Because the recoverable amount is less than carrying amount, an impairment has occurred. The difference between the carrying amount of Isa Company's asset and its recoverable amount is the impairment loss of $20,000 or ($400,000 – $380,000).

17. (A)   Goodwill impairment loss reversals are not permitted.

18. (B)   The recoverable amount of the unit is less than the carrying amount of the unit. Therefore, an impairment has occurred. The impairment loss is the amount by which the carrying amount of the assets exceeds the recoverable amount ($3,300,000 – $1,800,000 = $1,500,000).

19. (C)   R&D costs include contract services performed by others for the company. Start-up costs, initial operating losses, and advertising costs are not part of R&D costs.

20. (D)   Since the materials, equipment and facilities have no alternative use and they are expensed as incurred, as are the personnel costs and the indirect costs. Thus, the 2012 expenditures of $215,000 should be charged against 2012 income.

21. (A)   R & D costs are expenditures made to develop new products or processes, to improve present products, and to discover new knowledge that may be valuable at some future date. The only alternative that does not fit the general classification of R & D expenditures is alternative A. Adapting existing capabilities to a specific requirement or need does not involve R & D.

22. (D)   Start-up costs are to be expensed as incurred; therefore, there should be no costs associated with the organization in 2012 that will be amortized in 2013.

REVIEW EXERCISES

1.

PATENT ACCOUNT

	1-1-05	72,000	7,200	Amortization 12-31-05 (a)
			7,200	Amortization 12-31-06
			7,200	Amortization 12-31-07
			7,200	Amortization 12-31-08
Infringement Suit	1-09	9,000		
(b) Balance	1-09	$52,200	8,700	Amortization 12-31-09 (c)
Patent Purchased		25,000		
(d) Balance	1-10	$68,500	6,850	Amortization 12-31-10 (e)
			6,850	Amortization 12-31-11
			6,850	Amortization 12-31-12
			3,425	Amortization 7-1-13
		$44,525	44,525	Loss on 7-1-13 (f)

(a) $72,000 \div 10 = $7,200

(c) $52,200 \div 6 = $8,700

(e) $68,500 \div 10 = $6,850

2. Depreciation of equipment to be used for six years in R&D activities

($240,000/6) /2 = ...	$ 20,000
Salaries for R&D personnel..	126,000
Laboratory research costs	52,500
Materials & labor for oven design...	87,000
Engineering support for production facility	23,000
Total R&D expense for 2012..	$308,500

13

Current Liabilities, Provisions, and Contingencies

CHAPTER LEARNING OBJECTIVES

1. Describe the nature, type and valuation of current liabilities.
2. Explain the classification issues of short-term debt expected to be refinanced.
3. Identify types of employee-related liabilities.
4. Explain the accounting for different types of provisions.
5. Identify the criteria used to account for and disclose contingent liabilities and assets.
6. Indicate how to present and analyze liability-related information.

CHAPTER REVIEW

1. Chapter 13 presents a discussion of how convergence of IFRS with U.S. GAAP should lead to improved reporting of liabilities. Attention is focused on the similarity of IFRS disclosures to the FASB's disclosures and the challenges of developing accounting rules for liabilities that meet the needs of investors while avoiding harm to the companies reporting the information. Also included is a discussion concerning the basic issues related to accounting and reporting for current liabilities, provisions, and contingencies.

Current Liabilities

2. (L.O. 1) The IASB, as part of its conceptual framework, defines liabilities as a present obligation of a company arising from past events, the settlement of which is expected to result in an outflow from the company of resources, embodying economic benefits. In other words, a liability has three essential characteristics: (**a**) it is a present obligation; (**b**) it is an unavoidable obligation; and (**c**) it results from an outflow of resources (cash, goods, or services). A company must satisfy currently maturing obligations in the ordinary course of business to continue operating. Liabilities with a more distant due date do not, as a rule, represent a claim on the company's current resources. They are therefore in a slightly different category. This feature gives rise to the basic division of liabilities into (1) current liabilities and (2) noncurrent liabilities.

3. Current assets are cash or other assets that companies reasonably expect to convert into cash, sell, or consume in operations within a single operating cycle or within a year (if completing more than one cycle each year). Similarly, a **current liability** is reported if one of two conditions exists: (1) The liability is expected to be settled within its normal operating cycle; or (2) The liability is expected to be settled within 12 months after the reporting date. The IASB also indicates two other conditions that do not normally occur. The first is that if the liability is held primarily for trading purposes, it should be reported as a current liability. Trading means that the liability is subject to selling or repurchasing in the short-term. These liabilities are recorded at fair value, and gains or losses are reported in income. In addition, if a liability is not subject to an unconditional right of the company to defer settlement of the liability for at least 12 months after the reporting date, it is classified as current.

Accounts Payable

4. **Accounts payable** represents obligations owed to others for goods, supplies, and services purchased on open account. These obligations, commonly known as **trade accounts payable,** should be recorded to coincide with the receipt of the goods or at the time title passes to the purchaser. Attention must be paid to transactions occurring near the end of one accounting period and at the beginning of the next to ascertain that the record of goods received (inventory) is in agreement with the liability (accounts payable) and that both are recorded in the proper period.

Notes Payable

5. **Notes payable** are written promises to pay a certain sum of money on a specified future date and may arise from sales, financing, or other transactions. Notes may be classified as short-term or long-term, depending on the payment due date.

6. Short-term notes payable resulting from borrowing funds from a lending institution may be interest-bearing or zero-interest-bearing. Interest-bearing notes payable are reported as a liability at the face amount of the note along with any accrued interest payable. A zero-interest-bearing note is initially recorded at the amount of cash received (or the present value of the note). The present value of the note equals the face value of the note at maturity less the interest charged by the lender for the term of the note. As time passes, interest is accrued as an increase to the note payable. For example, Bush Co. issues a $138,000 four-month, zero-interest-bearing note on March 1, 2012, that has a present value amount of $135,000. The entry to record the issuance on Bush's books would be as follows:

Cash	135,000	
Notes Payable		135,000

Bush credits the Notes Payable account for the present value of the note, which is $135,000. If Bush prepares financial statements semiannually, it makes the following adjusting entry to recognize the interest expense and the increase in the note payable of $3,000 at June 30.

Interest Expense	3,000	
Notes Payable		3,000

At maturity (July 1), Bush must pay the face value of the note, as follows.

Notes Payable	138,000	
Cash		138,000

7. The currently maturing portion of long-term debts may be classified as a current liability. When a portion of long-term debt is so classified, it is assumed that the amount will be paid within the next 12 months out of funds classified as current assets.

Refinancing

8. (L.O. 2) Certain short-term obligations expected to be refinanced on a long-term basis should be **excluded** from current liabilities. A short-term obligation is excluded from current liabilities if both of the following conditions are met: (1) the company must intend to refinance the obligation on a long-term basis, *and* (2) it must have an unconditional right to defer settlement of the liability for at least 12 months after the reporting date. Both conditions must exist before the item can be excluded from current liabilities. Intention to refinance on a long-term basis means that the company intends to refinance the short-term obligation so that it will not require the use of working capital during the ensuing fiscal year (or operating cycle, if longer). Entering into a financing arrangement that clearly permits the company to refinance the debt on a long-term basis on terms that are readily determinable before the next reporting

date is one way to satisfy the second condition. In addition, the fact that a company has the right to refinance at any time and intends to do so permits the company to classify the liability as non-current.

Dividends Payable

9. **Cash dividends payable** are classified as current liabilities during the period subsequent to declaration and prior to payment. Once declared, a cash dividend is a binding obligation of a corporate entity payable to its stockholders. Share dividends distributable are reported in the equity section when declared.

Returnable Deposits

10. When **returnable deposits** are received from customers or employees, a liability corresponding to the asset received is recorded. The classification of these items as current or non-current liabilities depends on the time between the date of the deposit and the termination of the relationship that required the deposit.

Unearned Revenues

11. A company sometimes receives cash in advance of the performance of services or issuance of merchandise. Such transactions result in a credit to a deferred or unearned revenue account classified as a current liability on the statement of financial position. As claims of this nature are redeemed, the liability is reduced and a revenue account is credited. The statement of financial position should report obligations for any commitments that are redeemable in goods and services. The income statement should report revenues earned during the period.

Sales Taxes Payable

12. Current tax laws require most business enterprises to collect sales tax from customers during the year and periodically remit these collections to the appropriate governmental unit. In such instances the enterprise is acting as a collection agency for a third party. If tax amounts due to governmental units are on hand at the financial statement date, they are reported as current liabilities. Sometimes, the sales tax collections credited to the liability account are not equal to the liability as computed by the governmental formula. In such a case, an adjustment of the liability account is made by recognizing a gain or a loss on sales tax collections.

13. To illustrate the collection and remittance of sales tax by a company, assume that Bentham Company recorded sales for the period of $230,000. Further assume that Bentham is subject to a 7% sales tax collection that must be remitted to the government. If Bentham recorded the gross amount of sales and remits the required tax at the end of the period, then the $230,000 of sales includes the 7% sales tax. Thus, dividing the $230,000 by 1.07 will yield the amount of sales for the period or $214,953.27. If we subtract this amount from the recorded sales figure we arrive at the amount of sales tax due the taxing unit for the period ($230,000 – $214,953.27 = $15,046.73). The entry to record the sales tax liability is:

Sales	15,046.73	
Sales Tax Payable		15,046.73

When payment is made the Sales Tax Payable account would be debited and Cash would be credited.

Income Taxes Payable

14.   Differences between taxable income under the tax laws and accounting income under IFRS sometimes occur. Because of these differences, the amount of income tax payable to the government in any given year may differ substantially from income tax expense as reported on the financial statements. Chapter 19 is devoted solely to income tax matters and presents an extensive discussion of this complex topic.

Employee-Related Liabilities

15.   (L.O. 3) Amounts owed to employees for salaries or wages of an accounting period are reported as a current liability. The following items are related to employee compensation and often reported as current liabilities:

        a.   Payroll deductions.
        b.   Compensated absences.
        c.   Bonuses.

16.   **To the extent that a company has not remitted the amounts deducted to the proper authority at the end of the accounting period, it should recognize them as current liabilities.** The following illustrates the concept of accrued liabilities related to payroll deductions. Assume Mill Company has a weekly payroll of $25,000 that is entirely subject to Social Security taxes of 8%, with income tax withholding amounts of $3,300, and union dues of $975. Two entries are necessary to record the payroll, the first for the wages paid to employees and the second for the employer's payroll taxes. The two entries are as follows:

Wages and Salaries Expense	25,000	
Withholding Taxes Payable		3,300
Social Security Taxes Payable		2,000
Union Dues Payable		975
Cash		18,725
Payroll Tax Expense	2,000	
Social Security Taxes Payable		2,000

17.   **Compensated absences** are absences from employment—such as vacation, illness, and holidays—for which it is expected that employees will be paid anyway. In connection with compensated absences, **vested rights** exist when an employer has an obligation to make payment to an employee even if that employee terminates. **Accumulated rights** are those rights that can be carried forward to future periods if not used in the period in which earned. **Non-accumulating rights** do not carry forward; they lapse if not used. As a result, a company does not recognize a liability or expense until the time of absences (benefit).

18.   The accounting profession requires that a liability be accrued for the cost of compensation for future absences if **all** of the following conditions are met: (**a**) the employer's obligation relating to employees' rights to receive compensation for future absences is attributable to employees' services already rendered, (**b**) the obligation relates to rights that vest or accumulate, (**c**) payment of the compensation is probable, and (**d**) the amount can be reasonably estimated. A modification of the general rules relates to the issue of **sick pay**. If sick pay benefits vest, a company must accrue them. If sick pay benefits accumulate but do not vest, a company may choose whether to accrue them. If an employer fails to accrue a liability because of a failure to meet only condition (d), that fact should be disclosed. The expense and related liability for compensated absences should be recognized in the year earned by employees. Thus, if employees are entitled to a two week vacation after working one year, the vacation

pay is considered to be earned during the first year. The entry to accrue the accumulated vacation pay at the end of year one would include a debit to Wages Expense and a credit to Vacation Wages Payable.

Profit-Sharing and Bonus Plans

19.   Bonus agreements are common incentives established by companies for certain key executives or employees. In many cases, the bonus is dependent upon the amount of income earned by the company. A company may consider **bonus payments to employees** as additional wages and should include them as a deduction in determining the net income for the year. **The liability, Profit-Sharing Bonus Payable, is usually payable within a short period of time. Companies should include it as a current liability in the statement of financial position.** Similar to bonus agreements are contractual agreements for **conditional expenses**. Examples would be agreements covering rents or royalty payments conditional on the amount of revenues earned or the quantity of product produced or extracted. Conditional expenses based on revenues or units produced are usually less difficult to compute than bonus arrangements.

Provisions

20.   (L.O. 4) A **provision** is a liability of uncertain timing or amount (sometimes referred to as an *estimated liability*). Provisions are very common and may be reported either as current or non-current depending on the date of expected payment. Although companies generally report only one current and one non-current amount for provisions in the statement of financial position, IFRS also requires extensive disclosure related to provisions in the notes to the financial statements. Common types of provisions are obligations related to litigation, warranties or product guaranties, premiums, onerous contracts, business restructurings, and environmental damage. The difference between a provision and other liabilities (such as accounts or notes payable, salaries payable, and dividends payable) is that **a provision has greater uncertainty about the timing or amount of the future expenditure required to settle the obligation**.

Recognition of a Provision

21.   Companies accrue an expense and related liability for a provision only if the following three conditions are met:

1. A company has a present obligation (legal or constructive) as a result of a past event;
2. It is probable that an outflow of resources embodying economic benefits will be required to settle the obligation; (In applying the second condition, the term **probable** is defined as "more likely than not to occur." This phrase is interpreted to mean the probability of occurrence is greater than 50 percent.) and
3. A reliable estimate can be made of the amount of the obligation. If these three conditions are not met, no provision is recognized.

22.   A **constructive obligation** is an obligation that derives from a company's actions where:

1. By an established pattern of past practice, published policies, or a sufficiently specific current statement, the company has indicated to other parties that it will accept certain responsibilities; and
2. As a result, the company has created a valid expectation on the part of those other parties that it will discharge those responsibilities.

Under IFRS, the amount recognized should be the **best estimate of the expenditure required to settle the present obligation**. Best estimate represents the amount that a company would pay to settle the obligation at the statement of financial position date.

Litigation Provisions

23. Companies must consider the following factors, among others, in determining whether to record a liability with respect to **pending or threatened litigation** and actual or possible **claims** and **assessments**.

      1. The **time period** in which the underlying cause of action occurred.
      2. The **probability** of an unfavorable outcome.
      3. The ability to make a **reasonable estimate** of the amount of loss.

To report a loss and a liability in the financial statements, **the cause for litigation must have occurred on or before the date of the financial statements**. With respect to **unfiled suits** and **unasserted claims and assessments**, a company must determine (1) the degree of **probability** that a suit may be filed or a claim or assessment may be asserted, and (2) the **probability** of an unfavorable outcome.

Warranty Provisions

24. A **warranty** (product guarantee) represents a promise by a seller to a buyer to make good on any deficiency of quantity, quality or performance specifications in a product. Product warranty costs may be accounted for using the **cash basis method** or the **accrual basis method.** The cash basis method must be used when a company does not accrue a warranty liability in the year of sale either because (1) it is not probable that a liability has been incurred or (2) the amount of the liability cannot be reasonably estimated. Under the cash basis method, warranty costs are charged to expense as they are incurred (when they are paid by the seller). No liability is recorded under the cash basis method for future costs arising from warranties.

25. The accrual method includes two different accounting treatments: (a) the **expense warranty approach** and (b) the **sales warranty approach.** The expense warranty method is the generally accepted method for financial accounting purposes and should be used whenever the warranty is an integral and inseparable part of the sale and is viewed as a loss contingency. The sales warranty method defers a certain percentage of the original sales price until some future time when actual costs are incurred or the warranty expires. Under the expense warranty method the estimated warranty expense is recorded in the year in which the item subject to the warranty is sold. When the warranty is honored in a subsequent period, the liability is reduced by the amount of the expenditure to repair the item. For example, if 200 units are sold and the estimated warranty cost is $300 per unit, the following entry would be made for the warranty:

Warranty Expense	60,000	
Warranty Liability		60,000

Actual expenditures made to honor the warranty would debit the liability account and credit cash, parts or service required under the warranty contract.

Premiums and Coupons

26.   If a company offers premiums to customers in return for coupons, a liability should normally be recognized at year-end for outstanding premium offers expected to be redeemed. The liability should be recorded along with a charge to a premium expense account. Companies should charge the **costs of premiums and coupons to expense in the period of the sale** that benefits from the plan.

Environmental Provisions

27.   As with other provisions, a company must recognize an **environmental liability** when it has an existing legal obligation associated with the retirement of a long-lived asset and when it can reasonably estimate the amount of the liability.

Onerous Contract Provisions

28.   **Onerous contracts** are contracts in which "the unavoidable costs of meeting the obligations exceed the economic benefits expected to be received." For example, an onerous contract may be a loss recognized on an unfavorable non-cancelable purchase commitment related to inventory items. The expected costs should reflect the least net cost of exiting from the contract, which is the lower of (1) the cost of fulfilling the contract, or (2) the compensation or penalties arising from failure to fulfill the contract.

Restructuring Provisions

29.   IFRS is very restrictive regarding when a restructuring provision can be recorded and what types of costs may be included in a restructuring provision. Restructurings are defined as a "program that is planned and controlled by management and materially changes either (1) the scope of a business undertaken by the company; or (2) the manner in which that business is conducted." Examples of restructurings are the sale of a line of business, changes in management structures such as eliminating a layer of management, or closure of operations in a country.

Self-Insurance

30.   Self-insurance is **not** *insurance*, but risk assumption. The conditions for accrual stated in IFRS are not satisfied prior to the occurrence of the event. Until that time, there is no diminution in the value of the property. And unlike an insurance company, which has contractual obligations to reimburse policyholders for losses, a company can have no such obligation to itself and, hence, no liability either before or after the occurrence of damage.

Disclosures Related to Provisions

31.   The disclosures related to provisions are extensive. A company must provide a reconciliation of its beginning to ending balance for each major class of provisions, identifying what caused the change during the period. In addition, the provision must be described and the expected timing of any outflows disclosed. Also, disclosure about uncertainties related to expected outflows as well as expected reimbursements should be provided.

Contingencies: Contingent Liabilities

32.   (L.O. 5) In a general sense, all provisions are contingent because they are uncertain in timing or amount. However, IFRS uses the term "contingent" for liabilities and assets that are not recognized in the financial statements.

33.   **Contingent liabilities** are not recognized in the financial statements because they are (1) a possible obligation (not yet confirmed as a present obligation), (2) a present obligation for which it is not probable that payment will be made, or (3) a present obligation for which a reliable estimate of the obligation cannot be made. Examples of contingent liabilities are:

- A lawsuit in which it is only possible that the company might lose.
- A guarantee related to collectability of a receivable.

34.   Unless the possibility of any outflow in settlement is remote, companies should disclose the contingent liability at the end of the reporting period, providing a brief description of the nature of the contingent liability and, where practicable:

1. An estimate of its financial effect;
2. An indication of the uncertainties relating to the amount or timing of any outflow; and
3. The possibility of any reimbursement.

Contingent Assets

35.   A **contingent asset** is a possible asset that arises from past events and whose existence will be confirmed by the occurrence or non-occurrence of uncertain future events not wholly within the control of the company. Contingent assets are not recognized on the statement of financial position.

Presentation of Current Liabilities

36.   (L.O. 6) **In practice, current liabilities are usually recorded and reported in financial statements at their full maturity value.** The current liabilities accounts are commonly presented after non-current liabilities in the statement of financial position. Within the current liabilities section, companies may list the accounts in order of maturity, in descending order of amount, or in order of liquidation preference.

37.   Detail and supplemental information concerning current liabilities should be sufficient to meet the requirement of full disclosure. Companies should clearly identify secured liabilities, as well as indicate the related assets pledged as collateral. If the due date of any liability can be extended, a company should disclose the details. Companies should not offset current liabilities against assets that it will apply to their liquidation. Finally, current maturities of long-term debt are classified as current liabilities.

Analysis of Current Liabilities

38.   Two ratios often used to analyze current liabilities are the **current ratio** and the **acid-test ratio**. The **current ratio** is the ratio of total current assets to total current liabilities. The ratio is frequently expressed as a coverage of so many times. Sometimes it is called the **working capital ratio** because working capital is the excess of current assets over current liabilities. The **acid-test** or **quick ratio** relates total current liabilities to cash, short-term investments, and receivables.

GLOSSARY

Accumulated rights.
Obligations by an employer to an employee that can be carried forward to future period if not used in the period in which earned.

Acid-test (quick ratio).
The sum of Cash plus Short-term investments plus Net Receivables divided by current liabilities

Assessments.
Assessments deal with the degree of probability that may be asserted regarding a litigation provision.

Bonus.
Compensation to certain or all officers and employees in addition to their regular salary or wage.

Cash basis method of warranty costs.
Warranty costs are charged to expense as they are incurred.

Cash dividends payable.
An amount to be paid in cash owed by a corporation to its shareholders as a result of board of directors' authorization.

Claims.
Obligations asserted as part of litigation.

Compensated absences.
Absences from employment, such as vacation, illness, and holidays, for which employees are paid anyway.

Constructive obligation.
An obligation that derives from a company's established pattern of past, published or current actions and creation of a valid expectation to accept responsibility.

Contingency.
All provisions that are uncertain in timing or amount. They are not recognized in the financial statements.

Contingent liabilities.
(1) A possible obligation (not yet confirmed as a present obligation), (2) a present obligation for which it is not probable that payment will be made, or (3) a present obligation for which a reliable estimate of the obligation cannot be made.

Current liabilities.
Reported if one of two conditions exists: (1) the liability is expected to be settled within its normal operating cycle, or (2) the liability is expected to be settled within 12 months after the reporting date.

Current maturities of long-term debt.
The portion of bonds, mortgage notes, and other long-term indebtedness that matures within the next fiscal year.

Current ratio.
A liquidity ratio computed by dividing current assets by current liabilities.

Discount on notes payable.	The difference between the present value of a zero-interest-bearing note and the face value of the note at maturity.
Environmental liabilities.	Recognition is required when it has an existing legal obligation associated with the retirement of a long-lived asset and when it can reasonably estimate the amount of the liability.
Expense warranty approach (Accrual basis method of warranty costs).	Warranty costs are charged to operating expense in the year of sale.
Liabilities.	Probable future sacrifices of economic benefits arising from present obligations of a particular entity to transfer assets or provide services to other entities in the future as a result of past transactions or events.
Litigation, claims and assessments.	Companies must consider the time period of a cause, probability of an unfavorable outcome and the ability to make a reasonable estimate in determining whether to record a liability with respect to **pending or threatened litigation** and actual or possible **claims** and **assessments**.
Non-accumulating rights.	Benefit rights do not carry forward; they lapse if not used. As a result, a company does not recognize a liability or expense until the time of absences (benefit).
Notes payable (trade notes payable).	Written promises to pay a certain sum of money on a specified future date and may arise from sales, financing, or other transactions.
Onerous contract.	Contracts where the unavoidable costs of meeting the obligations exceed the economic benefits expected to be received.
Operating cycle.	The period of time elapsing between the acquisition of goods and services involved in the manufacturing process and the final cash realization resulting from sales and subsequent collections.
Preference dividends in arrears.	Accumulated but undeclared dividends on cumulative preferred stock.
Premiums.	Silverware, dishes, a small appliance, a toy, or other goods given to customers in exchange for boxtops, certificates, coupons, labels or wrappers.
Probable.	More likely than not to occur; this phrase is interpreted to mean the probability of occurrence is greater than 50 percent.
Provision.	A liability of uncertain timing or amount (sometimes referred to as an *estimated liability*).

Restructurings.	Programs that are planned and controlled by management and materially change either (1) the scope of a business undertaken by the company; or (2) the manner in which that business is conducted.
Returnable cash deposits.	Deposits received by a company from customers to guarantee performance of a contract or service or as guarantees to cover payment of expected future obligations.
Sales warranty approach.	The seller recognizes separately the sale of the product with the manufacturer's warranty and the sale of the extended warranty.
Self-insurance.	Not insurance but risk assumption that is not recognized as a provision.
Short-term obligations expected to be refinanced.	Replacing a short-term obligation with a long-term obligation or equity securities, or renewing, extending, or replacing it with short-term obligations for an uninterrupted period extending beyond one year (or the normal operating cycle) from the date of the company's statement of financial position.
Social security taxes.	The combination of Federal Insurance Contribution Act (FICA) tax and Hospital Insurance tax.
Trade accounts payable.	Balances owed to others for goods, supplies, or services purchased on open account.
Trade notes payable.	Written promises to pay a certain sum of money on a specified future date and may arise from sales, financing, or other transactions. Trade notes payable are required by some industries as part of the sales/purchases transaction in lieu of the normal extension of open account credit.
Unearned revenues.	Cash received by a company in exchange for future goods or services.
Vested rights.	The obligation by an employer to make payment to an employee even if his or her employment has been terminated.
Virtually certain.	At least a 90% probability for purposes of reporting a provision.
Warranty.	A promise made by a seller to a buyer to make good on a deficiency of quantity, quality, or performance in a product.
Working capital ratio.	The excess of current assets over current liabilities.

CHAPTER OUTLINE

Fill in the outline presented below.

(L.O. 1) Liability

    Current Liability

    Types of Current Liabilities

        Accounts payable

        Notes payable

            Interest-bearing note

            Zero-interest-bearing note

            Current maturities of long-term debt

(L.O. 2) Short-term obligations expected to be refinanced

    Dividends payable

    Customer Advances and Deposits

Chapter Outline *(continued)*

       Unearned revenues

       Sales taxes payable

       Income taxes payable

(L.O. 3) Employee-related liabilities

       Payroll deductions

          Social security taxes

          Income tax withholding

       Compensated absences

       Profit-sharing and Bonus Plans

(L.O. 4) Provisions

         Recognition of a Provision

         Measurement of Provisions

         Common Types of Provisions

            Litigation Provisions

            Warranty Provisions

Cash Basis

Accrual Basis

Expense Warranty Approach

Sales Warranty Approach

Premiums and Coupons

Environmental Provisions

Onerous Contract Provisions

Restructuring Provisions

Self-Insurance

Disclosures Related to Provisions

(L.O. 5) Contingencies

Contingent liabilities

Contingent assets

Chapter Outline *(continued)*

(L.O. 6) Presentation and Analysis

Presentation of Current liabilities

Analysis of Current liabilities

Current ratio

Acid-test ratio

REVIEW QUESTIONS AND EXERCISES

TRUE-FALSE

Indicate whether each of the following is true (T) or false (F) in the space provided.

_____ 1. (L.O. 1) The operating cycle is the period of time elapsing between the acquisition of goods and services involved in the manufacturing process and the final cash realization resulting from sales and subsequent collections.

_____ 2. (L.O. 1) Notes payable are only classified as short-term.

_____ 3. (L.O. 1) No interest is charged on a zero-interest-bearing note.

_____ 4. (L.O. 1) On a zero-interest-bearing note, the present value equals the face value of the note at maturity minus the interest or discount charged by the lender for the term of the note.

_____ 5. (L.O. 1) The currently maturing portion of a serial bond should not be classified as a current liability if it will be paid out of a long-term asset such as a sinking fund.

_____ 6. (L.O. 2) Companies can exclude long-term debts maturing currently as current liabilities if they are to be: (a) retired by assets accumulated for this purpose that properly have not been shown as current assets, (2) refinanced, or retired from the proceeds of a new debt issue, or (3) converted into ordinary shares.

_____ 7. (L.O. 2) When refinancing on a long-term basis is expected to be accomplished through the issuance of equity securities, it is not appropriate to include the short-term obligation in owners' equity.

_____ 8. (L.O. 2) If a short-term obligation is excluded from current liabilities because of refinancing, a footnote to the financial statements should be included disclosing the particulars of the refinancing arrangement.

_____ 9. (L.O. 2) Preferred dividends in arrears should be recognized as a liability in the statement of financial position.

_____ 10. (L.O. 2) Dividends payable in the form of additional shares are recognized as a liability.

_____ 11. (L.O. 2) A current liability results when a company collects sales taxes from customers.

_____ 12. (L.O. 3) The amount of unremitted employee and employer social security tax on gross wages paid should be reported by the employer as a current liability.

_____ 13. (L.O. 3) Maternity benefits are vesting rights.

_____ 14. (L.O. 3) Vested rights exist when an employer has an obligation to make payment to an employee but not if the employee is terminated.

_____ 15. (L.O. 3) If sick pay benefits accumulate but do not vest, accrual is permitted but not required.

_____ 16. (L.O. 4) Provisions are very common and must be reported as current liabilities.

_____ 17. (L.O. 5) Under IFRS, contingent liabilities are recognized in the financial statements but contingent assets are not.

_____ 18. (L.O. 4) To report a loss and a liability in the financial statements, the cause for litigation can occur after the date of the financial statements.

_____ 19. (L.O. 4) With respect to unfiled suits and unasserted claims and assessments, a company must determine (1) the degree of probability that a suit may be filed or a claim or assessment may be asserted, and (2) the probability of an unfavorable outcome.

_____ 20. (L.O. 4) Use of the cash basis method in accounting for product warranty costs is required when a company is unable to make a reasonable estimate of the amount of warranty obligations at the time of sale.

_____ 21. (L.O. 4) When a company offers premiums to its customers in return for coupons, the cost of the premiums should be charged to expense when the premiums are distributed to customers.

_____ 22. (L.O. 4) The number of outstanding premium offers that will be presented for redemption must be estimated in order to reflect the existing current liability and to match costs with revenues.

_____ 23. (L.O. 4) When there is an absence of insurance, a firm should estimate the amount of possible future losses and record a liability at the date of the financial statements.

_____ 24. (L.O. 6) Current liabilities are generally measured by the present value of the future outlay of cash required to liquidate them.

_____ 25. (L.O. 6) Because current liabilities tend to be liquidated within a short period of time, present value techniques are not normally applied.

MULTIPLE CHOICE

Select the best answer for each of the following items and enter the corresponding letter in the space provided.

_____ 1. (L.O. 1) A liability has three essential characteristics, which of the following is not one of them?

    A. It is a present obligation that entails settlement by probable future transfer or use of cash, goods, or services.

    B. The obligation must be liquidated using cash, goods, or services that were earned by the entity in the performance of their normal business operation.

    C. The liability must be an unavoidable obligation.

    D. The transaction or other event creating the obligation must have already occurred.

_____ 2. (L.O. 1) The IASB indicates all of the following conditions for classification of current liabilities except:

    A. Liabilities are expected to be settled within a normal operating cycle or within 12 months after the reporting date.

    B. If the liability is held primarily for trading purposes, it should be reported as a current liability.

    C. If a liability is not subject to an unconditional right of the company to defer settlement of the liability for at least 12 months after the reporting date, it is classified as current.

    D. Notes payable cannot be current liabilities, as notes are always long-term.

_____ 3. (L.O. 1) On October 1, 2011, a company borrowed cash and signed a one-year, interest-bearing note on which both the principal and interest are payable on October 1, 2012. How will the note payable and the related interest be classified in the December 31, 2011, the statement of financial position?

	Note Payable	Accrued Interest
A.	Current liability	Noncurrent liability
B.	Noncurrent liability	Current liability
C.	Current liability	Current liability
D.	Noncurrent liability	Noncurrent liability

_____ 4. (L.O. 1) The Hsu Co. issues a $208,000 6-month, zero-interest-bearing note to the Tang National Bank. The present value of the note is $200,000. The entry to record the maturity and payment of this note by Hsu Co. on Hsu's records would include:

      A.   a credit to Notes Payable of $200,000.
      B.   a debit to Interest Payable of $8,000.
      C.   a credit to Interest Payable of $8,000.
      D.   a debit to Cash of $200,000.

_____ 5. (L.O. 1,2) The currently maturing portion of long-term debt should be classified as a current liability in all of the following cases except:

      A.   when the debt is due on demand.
      B.   when there is a violation of a debt covenant.
      C.   when the company has the ability and intention to defer the payment for two years.
      D.   when the company can retires the debt through a series of annual installments.

_____ 6. (L.O. 2) An enterprise is required to exclude a short-term obligation from current liabilities if it intends to refinance the obligation on a long-term basis and:

      A.   the enterprise can demonstrate the ability to consummate the refinancing.
      B.   the obligation is not a part of normal operations.
      C.   it can demonstrate that a negative effect on working capital will result if it is not reclassified.
      D.   the interest rate on the long-term obligation is not above the prime rate.

_____ 7. (L.O. 2) Grice Corporation has $1,500,000 of short-term debt it expects to retire with proceeds from the sale of 50,000 shares of common stock. If the stock is sold for $20 per share subsequent to the date of the statement of financial position, but before the statement of financial position is issued, what amount of short-term debt could be excluded from current liabilities?

      A. $1,000,000
      B. $1,500,000
      C. $ 500,000
      D. $ 0

_____ 8. (L.O. 2) If a short-term obligation is excluded from current liabilities because of refinancing, the footnote to the financial statements describing this event should include all of the following information except:

      A.   a general description of the financing arrangement.
      B.   the terms of the new obligation incurred or to be incurred.
      C.   the terms of any equity security issued or to be issued.
      D.   the number of financing institutions that refused to refinance the debt, if any.

_____ 9. (L.O. 3) Which of the following are typically included in employer payroll taxes?

      A.   Social security taxes.
      B.   Union dues.
      C.   Income tax withholding.
      D.   Uniform fees.

_____ 10. (L.O. 3) In accounting for compensated absences, a company following IFRS would account for the liability using the:

	Cash Basis	**Accrual Basis**
A.	Yes	Yes
B.	Yes	No
C.	No	Yes
D.	No	No

_____ 11. (L.O. 3) In accounting for compensated absences, the difference between vested rights and accumulated rights is:

      A.   vested rights are normally for a longer period of employment than are accumulated rights.
      B.   vested rights are not contingent upon an employee's future service.
      C.   vested rights are a legal and binding obligation on the company, whereas accumulated rights expire at the end of the accounting period in which they arose.
      D.   vested rights carry a stipulated dollar amount that is owed to the employee; accumulated rights do not represent monetary compensation.

_____ 12. (L.O. 5) Under IFRS, contingent liabilities are not recognized in the financial statements for all of the following reasons except:

      A.   they are possible obligations and are not yet confirmed as present obligations.
      B.   they are present obligations for which it is not probable that payments will be made.
      C.   they are present obligations for which reliable estimates of the obligations cannot be made.
      D.   they present a virtually certain probability of settlement.

_____ 13. (L.O. 4) Which of the following would most likely be accrued as a provision?

      A.   Pending or threatened litigation.
      B.   General or unspecified business risk.
      C.   Obligations related to product warranties.
      D.   Risk of property loss due to fire.

_____ 14. (L.O. 4) With respect to the following which would most likely be accrued or not accrued?

	Loss Related to Receivable Collections	**Loss Related to Product Warranties**
A.	Accrued	Not Accrued
B.	Not Accrued	Accrued
C.	Not Accrued	Not Accrued
D.	Accrued	Accrued

_____ 15. (L.O. 4) All of the following could be characteristic of an onerous contract **except**:

      A.   A penalty is involved which exceeds the economic benefit expected to be received.
      B.   The excessive costs of meeting the contract are unavoidable and do not result in economic benefit for the company.
      C.   A noncancelable lease requires continued monthly rentals for nonuse, but will not allow subleasing of the property.
      D.   Gains result from noncancelable purchase commitments.

_____ 16. (L.O. 4) During 2011, Warren Co. introduced a new line of machines that carry a three-year warranty against manufacturer's defects. Based on industry experience, warranty costs are estimated at 2% of sales in the year of sale, 4% in the year after sale, and 6% in the second year after sale. Sales and actual warranty expenditures for the first three-year period were as follows:

	Sales	**Actual Warranty Expenditures**
2011	$ 200,000	$ 3,000
2012	500,000	15,000
2013	700,000	45,000
	$1,400,000	$63,000

What amount should Warren report as a liability at December 31, 2013?

- A. $ 0
- B. $ 5,000
- C. $ 68,000
- D. $105,000

_____ 17. (L.O. 4) Malcom Co. CornFlakes Company offers its customers a silver cereal spoon if they send in 5 boxtops from Malcom Co. CornFlakes boxes and $1.00. The Company estimates that 75% of the boxtops will be redeemed. In 2012 the Company sold 450,000 boxes of Corn Flakes and customers redeemed 220,000 boxtops receiving 44,000 spoons. If the spoons cost Malcom Company $2.50 each, how much liability for outstanding premiums should be recorded at the end of 2012?

- A. $23,500
- B. $35,250
- C. $58,750
- D. $82,250

_____ 18. (L.O. 4) Use of the accrual method in accounting for product warranty costs:

- A. is required for federal income tax purposes.
- B. is frequently justified on the basis of expediency when warranty costs are immaterial.
- C. finds the expense account being charged when the seller performs in compliance with the warranty.
- D. represents accepted practice and should be used whenever the warranty is an integral and inseparable part of the sale.

_____ 19. (L.O. 4) Vargas Company is involved in a litigation suit concerning the clean-up of old underground oil storage tanks on property it sold to a housing development company five years ago. The attorneys for Vargas Company cannot give a best estimate for the probable liability; however, the attorneys state that the liability to Vargas Company will probably fall within a range of $2 million to $10 million. According to IFRS, what should Vargas Company record with regards to this environmental liability?

- A. No entry is required.
- B. A loss and liability of $10 million.
- C. A loss and liability of $6 million.
- D. A loss and liability of $2 million.

REVIEW EXERCISES

1.   (L.O. 1) The following transactions were entered into by the Moore Appliance Company during the month of December.

A.   On December 6, Moore received a deposit from Rigger Company for a refrigerator to be used at a charity cookout. The deposit of $3,000 will be returned when the refrigerator is returned, most likely in early January.

B.   The Company recorded cash sales of $621,000 during December. This amount includes 8% sales tax that must be remitted to the state by the 15th of the following month.

C.   On December 10, the Company borrowed $100,000 from the Valient Company. The loan carries a 12% interest rate, is due in one year, and interest is due when the note is paid.

D.   On December 15, the Company purchased a delivery truck for $45,000, paying $10,000 in cash and signing a one-year, 15% note for the balance.

Instructions:

a.   Prepare journal entries for the transactions listed above.

b.   Assuming Moore's year-end is December 31, prepare adjusting journal entries for the transactions which require adjustment.

a.

General Journal J1			
Date	**Account Title**	**Debit**	**Credit**

b.

	General Journal		
			J1
Date	**Account Title**	**Debit**	**Credit**

2.   (L.O. 4) Hussein Company included a coupon in each box of its cereal. For every 10 coupons returned by a customer, Hussein offered a silver spoon. Each spoon costs Hussein 75 cents. During the first year of the offer, Hussein sold 500,000 boxes of cereal. The company estimated that 80% of the coupons would be redeemed. Hussein distributed 28,000 spoons during the year.

Instructions:

a.   Compute the premium expense for the first year.
b.   Compute the amount of estimated liability that Hussein should show on its year-end statement of financial position for unredeemed coupons.

a. and b.

3.   (L.O. 4) Crimson Corporation manufactures satellite phones. Each phone is sold with a two-year unconditional warranty against defects. During 2012, 280 phones were sold for $150 each. The company estimates that the warranty cost will average $20 per unit. The actual warranty costs incurred in 2012 amounted to $2,350.

Instructions:
Prepare the journal entries for the sale of phones, the estimated warranty cost, and the actual warranty cost incurred.

General Journal			
			J1
Date	**Account Title**	**Debit**	**Credit**

4.   (L.O. 4) Mega Petroleum purchased an oil rig platform on January 1, 2012 for $9,000,000. Mega expects to operate the platform for 15 years. At the conclusion of the platform's usual life, Mega is legally obligated to dismantle the platform and seal the underwater well-head. It is estimate that this will cost $1,100,000.

Required:
(a) Prepare journal entries to record the purchase of the platform and the environmental provision at January 1, 2011. Based on an effective interest rate of 5%, the fair value of the environmental provision on January 1, 2012 is $529,122.

(b) Prepare the required journal entries at December 31, 2012. Mega uses straight-line depreciation and the estimated residual value for the platform is zero.

(c) On December 31, 2026, Mega pays $1,500,000 for the removal of the platform and the capping of the well-head. Prepare the journal entry for the settlement of the environmental provision.

		General Journal		
				J1
Date		**Account Title**	**Debit**	**Credit**

SOLUTIONS TO REVIEW QUESTIONS AND EXERCISES

TRUE-FALSE

1. (T)

2. (F)   Notes payable may be classified as short-term or long-term, depending upon the payment due date.

3. (F)   A zero-interest-bearing note does not explicitly state an interest rate on the face of the note; however, interest is still charged.

4. (T)

5. (T)

6. (T)

7.   (T)
8.   (T)

9.   (F)   Preferred dividends in arrears are not an obligation until formal action is taken by the board of directors authorizing the distribution of earnings (although a disclosure may be involved).

10. (F)   Dividends payable in the form of additional shares are not recognized as a liability; the additional shares are reported as part of equity.

11. (T)

12. (T)

13. (F)   Maternity benefits are not vesting rights; they are non-accumulating rights.

14. (F)   Vested rights exist when an employer has an obligation to make payment to an employee even if his or her employment is terminated.

15. (T)

16. (F)   Provisions are very common and may be reported either as current or noncurrent, depending upon the date of expected payment.

17. (F)   Neither contingent liabilities or contingent assets are recognized on the financial statements.

18. (F)   To report a loss and a liability in the financial statements, the cause for litigation must have occurred on or before the date of the financial statements.
19. (T)

20. (T)
21. (F)   The cost of premiums should be charged to expense during the period in which the sale that gave rise to the premium is made. This method will find some of the premium cost being charged to expense when the premiums are distributed to customers. However, any portion of the estimated premium expense not charged to expense during the period of sale must be accrued at year-end so that a proper matching of revenues and expense takes place.

22. (T)

23. (F)   The absence of insurance does not mean that a liability has been incurred at the date of the financial statements.

24. (F)   Theoretically, current liabilities should be measured by the present value of the future outlay of cash required to liquidate them. But, in practice, current liabilities are usually recorded in accounting records and reported in financial statements at their full maturity value.

25. (T)

MULTIPLE CHOICE

1.   (B)   A liability must meet the three characteristics noted in alternatives A, C, and D. The indication in alternative B that the obligation be liquidated using assets earned in the normal course of operations is not an essential characteristic. The funds used to liquidate a liability could come from borrowing.

2.   (D)   It is possible for the currently due portion of notes payable to be classified as a current liability

3.   (C)   Since these liabilities will be paid within one year from the December 31, 2011 the date of the statement of financial position, both the note payable and the related accrued interest payable should be classified as current liabilities.

4.   (B)   The following entry would be made by Hsu Co.:

Notes Payable	200,000	
Interest Payable	8,000	
Cash		208,000

5.   (C)   In the case where the company has the ability and intention to defer the payment for two years, it cannot be classified as current.

6.   (A)   An enterprise is required to exclude a short-term obligation from current liabilities if it intends to refinance the obligation on a long-term basis and the enterprise can demonstrate the ability to consummate the refinancing. The effect on working capital and the interest rate on the long-term obligation have nothing to do with the specific requirements for reclassifying the debt from current to long-term.

7.   (A)   The maximum amount of short-term debt that can be excluded from current liabilities is limited to the amount secured through the refinancing arrangement. In this case the amount is $1,000,000 ($50,000 \times 20).

8.   (D)   Alternatives A, B, and C must be disclosed in the footnotes to the financial statements. There is no requirement to indicate failures to secure financing.

9.   (A)   The employer must remit to the government its share of Social Security tax along with the amount of Social Security tax deducted from each employee's gross compensation.

10.   (C)   The accounting profession requires that a liability be accrued for the cost of compensation for future absences if all of the following conditions are met:

1.   The employer's obligation relating to the employees' rights to receive compensation for future absences is attributable to employees' services already rendered.
2.   The obligation relates to rights that vest or accumulate.
3.   Payment of the compensation is probable.
4.   The amount can be reasonably estimated.

11.   (B)   Vested rights exist when an employer has an obligation to make payment to an employee even if his or her employment is terminated; thus, vested rights are not contingent on an employee's future service. Accumulated rights are those that can be carried forward to future periods if not used in the period in which they are earned. The length of time, the legality, or compensation involved are not characteristics which identify specific differences.

12. (D)   Contingent liabilities are not recognized in the financial statements because they are (1) a possible obligation (not yet confirmed as a present obligation), (2) a present obligation for which it is not probable that payment will be made, or (3) a present obligation for which a reliable estimate of the obligation cannot be made.

13. (C)   Obligations related to product warranties would most likely be accrued as provisions.

14. (D)   Both of these items represent would normally be accrued. In both cases the loss is probable and the amount can be reasonably estimated.

15. (D)   Onerous contracts are those where the unavoidable costs of meeting the obligations exceed the economic benefits expected to be received. Although a purchase commitment is noncancelable, the fact that it somehow resulted in a gain does not fit the definition of an onerous contract.

16. (D)   Warren's warranty liability at December 31, 2013, can be computed as follows:

Total credited to the warranty liability account in 2011, 2012, and 2013 (12%* × $1,400,000)	$168,000
Less: Total amount debited to the warranty liability account in 2011, 2012, and 2013	63,000
Warranty liability, 12/31/13	$105,000

*2% + 4% + 6% = 12%

17. (B)

Boxtops sold in 2012	450,000	
Estimated redemptions:		450,000 × .75 = 337,500
Boxtops redeemed in 2012		220,000
Estimated future redemptions		117,500
Liability for outstanding claims:		
117,500/5 = 23,500 × ($2.50 – $1.00) = $35,250		

18. (D)   Accounting for product warranty costs by accruing an expense is an accepted practice that should be used whenever the warranty is an integral and inseparable part of the sale.

19. (C)   According to IFRS, each point in the range has the same probability of occurrence, so it should be measured at the midpoint of the range.

REVIEW EXERCISES

l. a. A.   12/6   Cash   3,000
                      Returnable Deposits   3,000
       B.   Cash   621,000
                      Sales   621,000
       C.   12/10 Cash   100,000
                      Notes Payable   100,000
       D.   12/15 Delivery Truck   45,000
                      Cash   10,000
                      Notes Payable   35,000

   b.   Sales   46,000.00
                      Sales Tax Payable   46,000.0
                      ($621,000 – (621,000/1.08) = $46,000)
                   Interest Expense   666.67
                      Interest Payable   666.6
                      ($100,000 × .12 = $12,000)
                      ($12,000/12 = $1,000 × 2/3 = $666.67)
                   Interest Expense   218.75
                      Interest Payable   218.7
                      ($35,000 × .15 = $5,250)
                      ($5,520/12 = $437.50/2 = $218.75)

2. a.   Estimate of coupons to be redeemed (500,000 × .8)   400,000
        Coupons redeemed (28,000 × 10)   280,000
           Estimated coupons redeemable   120,000

        First year's premium expense:
           Coupons redeemed (28,000 × $0.75) .... $ 21,000
           Additional redemptions expected
              [(120,000 ÷ 10) × $0.75]   9,000
                 Total premium expense $30,000
   b.   Estimated year-end premium liability (12,000 × $0.75) .... $ 9,000

3.   Journal Entries:
           Sale of phones (280 × $150):
              Cash or Accounts Receivable   42,000
                 Sales   42,000
           Estimated warranty cost (280 × $20):
              Warranty expense   5,600
                 Estimated liability under warranties   5,600
           Actual warranty cost:
              Estimated liability under warranties   2,350
                 Cash   2,350

4.   Journal Entries:

(a)   January 1, 2012

Oil Platform..	9,000,000	
Cash		9,000,000

Oil Platform..	529,122	
Environmental Liability		529,122

(b)   December 31, 2012

Depreciation Expense...	600,000*	
Accumulated Depreciation..		600,000

Depreciation Expense...	35,275**	
Accumulated Depreciation..		35,275

Interest Expense...	26,456***	
Environmental Liability		26,456

        *$9,000,000 / 15 = $600,000
        ** $529,122/ 15 = $35,275
        ***$529,122 × .05 = $26,456

(c)   December 31, 2026

Environmental Liability	1,100,000	
Loss on Settlement of Environmental Liability	400,000	
Cash		1,500,000

14

Non-Current Liabilities

CHAPTER LEARNING OBJECTIVES

1. Describe the formal procedures associated with issuing non-current liabilities.
2. Identify various types of bond issues.
3. Describe the accounting valuation for bonds at date of issuance.
4. Apply the methods of bond discount and premium amortization.
5. Explain the accounting for long-term notes payable.
6. Describe the accounting for the extinguishment of non-current liabilities.
7. Describe the accounting for the fair value option.
8. Explain the reporting of off-balance-sheet financing arrangements.
9. Indicate how to present and analyze non-current liabilities.

CHAPTER REVIEW

1. Chapter 14 presents a discussion of the issues related to non-current liabilities. Non-current liabilities consist of probable future sacrifices of economic benefits. These sacrifices are payable in the future, normally beyond one year or operating cycle, whichever is longer. Coverage in this chapter includes bonds payable, long-term notes payable, mortgage notes payable, and issues related to extinguishment of debt. The accounting and disclosure issues related to non-current liabilities include a great deal of detail due to the potentially complicated nature of debt instruments.

Non-current Liabilities

2. (L.O. 1) Non-current liabilities consist of obligations that are **not** payable within the operating cycle or one year, whichever is longer. These obligations normally require a **formal agreement** between the parties involved that often includes certain **covenants and restrictions** for the protection of both lenders and borrowers. These covenants and restrictions are found in the **bond indenture** or **note agreement,** and include information related to amounts authorized to be issued, interest rates, due dates, call provisions, security for the debt, sinking fund requirements, etc. The important issues related to the non-current liabilities should always be disclosed in the financial statements or the notes thereto.

3. Long-term liabilities include **bonds payable, mortgage notes payable, long-term notes payable, lease obligations,** and **pension obligations.** Pension and lease obligations are discussed in later chapters.

Bonds Payable

4. (L.O. 2) **Bonds payable** represent an obligation of the issuing corporation to pay a sum of money at a designated maturity date plus periodic interest at a specified rate on the face value. See the glossary for terms commonly used in discussing the various aspects of corporate bond issues.

5. **Bonds** are debt instruments of the issuing corporation used by that corporation to borrow funds from the general public or institutional investors. The use of bonds provides the issuer an opportunity to divide a large amount of long-term indebtedness among many small investing units. Bonds may be sold through an **underwriter** who either (a) guarantees a certain sum to the corporation and assumes the risk of sale or (b) agrees to sell the bond issue on the basis of a commission. Alternatively, a corporation may sell the bonds directly to a large financial institution without the aid of an underwriter.

6. (L.O. 3) Bonds are issued with a **stated rate** of interest expressed as a percentage of the **face value** of the bonds. When bonds are sold for more than face value (at a **premium**) or less than face value (at a **discount**), the interest rate actually earned by the bondholder is different from the stated rate. This is known as the **effective yield** or **market rate** of interest and is set by economic conditions in the investment market. The effective rate exceeds the stated rate when the bonds sell at a discount, and the effective rate is less than the stated rate when the bonds sell at a premium.

7. To compute the effective interest rate of a bond issue, the present value of future cash flows from interest and principal must be computed. This often takes a financial calculator or computer to calculate.

Discounts and Premiums

8. (L.O. 4) Discounts and premiums resulting from a bond issue are recorded at the time the bonds are sold. The amounts recorded as discounts or premiums are amortized each time bond interest is paid. The time period over which discounts and premiums are amortized is equal to the period of time the bonds are outstanding (date of sale to maturity date). Amortization of bond premiums decreases the recorded amount of bond interest expense, whereas the amortization of bond discounts increases the recorded amount of bond interest expense.

9. To illustrate the recording of bonds sold at a discount or premium the following examples are presented. If Aretha Company issued $100,000 of bonds dated January 1, 2012 at 98, on January 1, 2012, the entry would be as follows:

Cash ($100,000 × .98)	98,000	
Bonds Payable		98,000

If the same bonds noted above were sold for 102 the entry to record the issuance would be as follows:

Cash ($100,000 × 1.02)	102,000	
Bonds Payable		102,000

10. Interest expense is computed as the book value of the bond payable times the market rate of interest, while the cash interest paid is computed as the face amount of the bonds times the stated rate. The difference between the interest expense and the cash payment is debited or credited to bonds payable.

11.   To illustrate amortization of a discount under the effective-interest method, Lumber Yard, Inc. issued $1,000,000 of 8 percent term bonds on January 1, 2012, due on January 1, 2017, with interest payable each July 1 and January 1. Because the investors required an effective-interest rate of 10 percent, they paid $922,779 for the $1,000,000 of bonds, creating a $77,221 discount. The first interest payment is made July 1, 2012 and is recorded as follows:

Bond Interest Expense ($922,779 × 5%)	46,139	
Bonds Payable		6,139
Cash ($1,000,000 × 4%)		40,000

The entry to accrue interest at December 31, 2012 would be recorded as follows:

Bond Interest Expense	46,446*	
Bonds Payable		6,446
Interest payable ($1,000,000 × 4%)		40,000

*($922,779 + 6,139) × 5%

Note that the amortization of the discount increases the bond interest expense for the period; the amortization of bond premium will reduce bond interest expense for the period.

12.   When bonds are issued between interest dates, the purchase price is increased by an amount equal to the interest earned on the bonds since the last interest payment date. On the next interest payment date, the bondholder receives the entire semiannual interest payment. However, the amount of interest expense to the issuing corporation is the difference between the semiannual interest payment and the amount of interest prepaid by the purchaser. For example, assume a 10-year bond issue in the amount of $300,000, bearing 9% interest payable semi-annually, dated January 1, 2012. If the entire bond issue is sold at par on March 1, 2012, the following journal entry would be made by the seller:

Cash	304,500	
Bonds Payable		300,000
Bond Interest Expense		4,500*
*($300,000 × .09 × 2/12)		

The entry for the semi-annual interest payment on July 1, 2012 would be as follows:

Bond Interest Expense	13,500	
Cash		13,500

The total bond interest expense for the six month period is $9,000 ($13,500 – $4,500), which represents the correct interest expense for the four-month period the bonds were outstanding. If the bonds are sold at a premium or a discount, the issuer must also account for the amount of effective amortization for the partial period.

13.   The effective interest method is best accomplished by preparing a **Schedule of Bond Interest Amortization.** This schedule provides the information necessary for each semiannual entry for interest and discount or premium amortization. The chapter includes an illustration of a Schedule of Bond Interest Amortization for both a discount and premium situation. Also, the demonstration problem at the end of the Chapter Review section illustrates the preparation of this schedule.

14.   If the interest payment date does not coincide with the financial statement's date, the amortized premium or discount should be prorated by the appropriate number of months to arrive at the proper interest expense.

15.   Some of the costs associated with issuing bonds include engraving and printing costs, legal and accounting fees, commissions, and promotion expenses. These costs are recorded as a reduction to the issue amount of the bond payable and are amortized over the life of the bond issue through an adjustment to the effective interest method.

Notes Payable

16.   (L.O. 5)   The difference between current notes payable and long-term notes payable is the maturity date. Accounting for notes and bonds is quite similar.

17.   Interest-bearing notes are treated the same as bonds—a discount or premium is amortized over the life of the note if the stated rate is different than the effective rate. Zero-interest-bearing notes represent a discount on the note and the discount is amortized similar to the manner as discounts on interest-bearing notes.

18.   When a debt instrument is exchanged for **noncash consideration** in a bargained transaction, the stated rate of interest is presumed fair unless: (**a**) no interest rate is stated, (**b**) the stated rate is unreasonable, or (**c**) the face amount of the debt instrument is materially different from the current cash price of the consideration or the current market value of the debt instrument. If the stated rate is determined to be inappropriate, an **imputed interest rate** must be used to establish the present value of the debt instrument. The imputed interest rate is used to establish the present value of the debt instrument by discounting, at that rate, all future payments on the debt instrument.

19.   When an imputed interest rate is used for valuation purposes it will normally be at least equal to the rate at which the debtor can obtain financing of a similar nature from other sources at the date of the transaction. The objective is to approximate the rate that would have resulted if an independent borrower and an independent lender had negotiated a similar transaction under comparable terms and conditions.

20.   **Mortgage notes** are a common means of financing the acquisition of property, plant, and equipment in a proprietorship or partnership form of business organization. Normally, the title to specific property is pledged as security for a mortgage note. Points (1% of the face amount of the note) raise the effective interest rate above the stated rate. If a mortgage note is paid on an installment basis, the current installment should be classified as a current liability.

21.   Because of unstable interest rates and a tight money supply, the traditional **fixed-rate mortgage** has been partially supplanted with new and unique mortgage arrangements. **Variable-rate mortgages** feature interest rates tied to changes in the fluctuating market rate of interest. Generally, variable-rate lenders adjust the interest rate at either one or three-year intervals.

Extinguishment of Non-Current Liabilities

22.   (L.O. 6)   The extinguishment, or payment, of non-current liabilities can be a relatively straightforward process which involves a debit to the liability account and a credit to cash. The process can also be a complicated one when the debt is extinguished prior to maturity.

23.   The reacquisition of debt can occur either by payment to the creditor or by reacquisition in the open market. At the time of reacquisition, any unamortized premium or discount, and any costs of issue related to the bonds, must be amortized up to the reacquisition date. If this is not done any resulting gain or loss on the extinguishment would be misstated. The difference between the reacquisition price and the net carrying amount of the debt is a gain (reacquisition price lower) or loss (reacquisition price greater).

24.   If a company uses non-cash assets to extinguish debt, the assets must first be valued at fair market value, which may result in a gain or loss on disposition of the assets. Then, the company will calculate a gain or loss on extinguishment of debt as the difference between the carrying value of the debt and the fair market value of the property given up in the transaction.

25.   If an extinguishment or settlement is done by modifying the terms of the debt, the creditor is granting favorable concessions to the debtor, and the debtor has an economic gains. These concessions can be a reduction in the interest rate or the face amount of the debt, extension of the maturity date of the debt, or reduction/deferral of accrued interest. In these cases, the original obligation is extinguished, the new payable is recorded at fair value, and a gain is recognized for the difference in the fair value of the new obligation and the carrying value of the old obligation.

Fair Value Option

26.   (L.O.7) Non-current liabilities are generally measured at amortized cost; however, companies have the option of using fair value to measure bonds and notes payable. If the fair value option is chosen, unrealized holding gains and losses (changes in fair value from one period to the next, excluding interest expense recognized but not recorded) are recognized in net income. The company must continue to use fair value in all subsequent periods.

Off-Balance-Sheet Financing

27.   (L.O. 8) A significant issue in accounting today is the question of off-balance-sheet financing. **Off-balance-sheet financing** is an attempt to borrow monies in such a way that the obligations are not recorded. Off-balance-sheet financing can take many different forms. Some examples include (1) non-consolidated subsidiary, (2) a special purpose entity, and (3) operating leases.

28.   The IASB response to off-balance-sheet financing arrangements has been increased disclosure (note) requirements.

Presentation of Non-Current Liabilities

29.   (L.O. 9) Companies that have large amounts and numerous issues of non-current liabilities frequently report only one amount in the statement of financial position and support this with comments and schedules in the accompanying notes to the financial statements. These footnote disclosures generally indicate the nature of the liabilities, maturity dates, interest rates, call provisions, conversion privileges, restrictions imposed by the borrower, and assets pledged as security; the fair value of the long-term debt is also disclosed. Non-current liabilities that mature within one year should be reported as a current liability unless retirement is to be accomplished with other than current assets.

Analysis of Non-Current Liabilities

30.   Long-term creditors and stockholders are interested in a company's long-run solvency and the ability to pay interest when it is due. Two ratios that provide information about debt-paying ability and long-run solvency are the **debt to total assets ratio** and the **times interest earned ratio**.

DEMONSTRATION PROBLEMS

1.   Buffet Company issued $250,000 of 10% bonds on January 1, 2012, due on January 1, 2022, with interest payable each July 1 and January 1. If investors desire to earn an effective interest rate of 12%, how much should they pay for the bonds?

<u>**Solution:**</u>

Maturity value of bonds		$250,000
Present value of $250,000 due in ten years		
at 12% interest payable semiannually		
(Table 6-2, 6% for 20 periods)		
.31180 × $250,000	$ 77,950	
Present value of $12,500 interest payable		
semiannually for 10 years at 12%		
(Table 6-4, 6% for 20 periods)		
11.46992 × $12,500	<u>143,374</u>	
Proceeds from sale of bonds		<u>221,324</u>
Discount on bonds		<u>$ 28,676</u>

(If investors pay $221,324 for this bond issue, the
effective interest rate on these 10% bonds would be 12%.)

2.   Using the facts in the problem above, prepare a schedule showing the amounts that would be used in recording the first two semiannual interest payments (July 1, 2012 and January 1, 2013).

<u>**Solution:**</u>

Date	Cash Credit	Interest Expense Debt	Bond Discount Credit	Carrying Value of Bonds
1/1/12				$221,324
7/1/12	$12,500 (a)	$13,279 (b)	$779 (c)	222,103 (d)
1/1/13	12,500 (e)	13,326 (f)	826 (g)	222,929 (h)

(a)	$250,000 × .10 × 6/12		(e)	same as (a)
(b)	$221,324 × .12 × 6/12		(f)	$221,103 × .12 × 6/12
(c)	$13,279 – $12,500		(g)	$13,326 – $12,500
(d)	$221,324 + $779		(h)	$222,103 + $826

GLOSSARY

Bearer (coupon) bonds.	Bonds not recorded in the name of the owner and may be transferred from one owner to another by mere delivery.
Callable bonds.	Bonds that give the issuer the right to call and retire the bonds prior to maturity.
Collateral trust bonds.	Bonds that are secured by stocks and bonds of other corporations.
Commodity-backed bonds (asset linked bonds)	Bonds that are redeemable in measures of a commodity, such as barrels of oil, tons of coal, or ounces of rare metal.
Convertible bonds.	Bonds that are convertible into other securities of the corporation for a specified time after issuance.
Debenture bonds.	Bonds that are unsecured.
Deep discount bonds (zero interest debenture bonds).	Bonds that are sold at a discount and do not bear an interest rate.
Effective rate (effective yield or market rate).	The rate of interest actually earned by the bondholders.
Face value (par value, principal amount, or maturity value).	Amount stated on the face of the bond that serves as the basis for periodic interest computations and represents the amount due at maturity.
Financial instruments.	Cash, an ownership interest in an entity, or a contractual right to receive or deliver cash or another financial instrument on potentially favorable or unfavorable terms.
Income bonds.	Bonds that pay no interest unless the issuing company is profitable.
Indenture.	Describes the contractual agreement between the corporation issuing the bonds and the bondholders.
Junk bonds.	Bonds that are unsecured and also very risky, and therefore pay a high interest rate.
Long-term notes payable.	Notes payable that are not expected to be paid within a year or the operating cycle, whichever is longer.
Mortgage bonds.	Bonds that are secured by a claim on real estate.
Non-current liabilities.	Probable future sacrifices of economic benefits arising from present obligations that are not payable within a year or the operating cycle of the business, whichever is longer.

Off-balance-sheet financing.	An attempt to borrow monies in such a way that the obligations are not recorded.
Premium.	When bonds sell for more than face value.
Registered bonds.	Bonds issued in the name of the owner and require surrender of the certificate and issuance of a new certificate to complete a sale.
Revenue bonds.	Bonds that pay interest from specified revenue sources, and are most frequently issued by airports, school districts, counties, toll-road authorities, and governmental bodies.
Secured bonds.	Bonds that are backed by a pledge of some sort of collateral.
Serial bonds.	Bond issues that mature in installments.
Stated rate (coupon rate or nominal rate).	The interest rate written in the terms of the bond indenture (and ordinarily printed on the bond certificate).
Term bonds.	Bond issues that mature on a single date.
Unsecured bonds.	Bonds that are not backed by collateral.

CHAPTER OUTLINE

Fill in the outline presented below.

(L.O. 2) Bonds Payable

Types of Bonds

(L.O. 4) Discount on Bonds—Effective Interest Method

Premium on Bonds—Effective Interest Method

Bonds Issued Between Interest Dates

Costs of Issuing Bonds

(L.O. 5) Long-Term Notes Payable

Special Notes Payable Situations

Notes exchanged for cash and other rights

Notes issued for property, goods and services

Imputed interest

Mortgage Notes Payable

(L.O. 6) Extinguishment of Debt

Reacquisition of Debt

Reporting Gains and Losses

Chapter Outline *(continued)*

(L.O. 7) Fair Value Option

(L.O. 8) Off-Balance-Sheet Financing

(L.O. 9) Reporting Non-Current Liabilities

Analysis of Non-current liabilities

REVIEW QUESTIONS AND EXERCISES

TRUE-FALSE

Indicate whether each of the following is true (T) or false (F) in the space provided.

_____ 1. (L.O. 1) Non-current liabilities are ordinarily used by an enterprise as a more or less permanent means of financing to increase the earnings available to stockholders.

_____ 2. (L.O. 1) Generally, non-current liabilities, in whatever form, are issued subject to various covenants or restrictions for the protection of corporate stockholders.

_____ 3. (L.O. 2) Commodity-backed bonds are redeemable in measures of a commodity such as barrels of oil, tons of coal, or ounces of a rare metal.

_____ 4. (L.O. 2) Revenue bonds are bonds whose interest rate is a function of the revenue earned by the company issuing the bonds.

_____ 5. (L.O. 2) Bonds issued by a corporation represent a means of borrowing funds from the general public or institutional investors on a long-term basis.

_____ 6. (L.O. 2) When bonds are issued by a corporation, the IASB requires that the issue be placed with an independent underwriter.

_____ 7. (L.O. 3) When bonds are issued between interest dates, the purchaser pays for interest accrued since the date the bonds were originally issued.

_____ 8. (L.O. 3) The stated rate of interest on bonds is the rate set by the party issuing the bonds.

_____ 9. (L.O. 4) If bonds are sold at a premium, the effective rate of interest is greater than the stated rate of interest.

_____ 10. (L.O. 4) The effective interest method amortizes bonds sold at a discount or premium in such a way as to result in a constant rate of interest being applied to the carrying amount of the debt at the beginning of each period.

_____ 11. (L.O. 4) The amortization of a bond discount increases the amount of bond interest expense recorded each period.

_____ 12. (L.O. 4) Under the effective interest method semiannual interest expense is computed by multiplying the effective interest rate times a constant carrying value of the bonds.

_____ 13. (L.O. 4) The expenses associated with the issuance of bonds (printing costs, legal fees, etc.), should be recorded as a reduction to the issue amount of the bond payable and then amortized into expense over the life of the bond.

_____ 14. (L.O. 6) Any excess of the net carrying amount over the reacquisition price is a loss from extinguishment.

_____ 15. (L.O. 5) When a zero-interest-bearing note is given in return for property, the present value of the note is measured by the fair value of the property or by an amount that reasonably approximates the fair value of the note.

_____ 16. (L.O. 5) An imputed interest rate used to determine the present value of a debt instrument may change during the life of the debt if a change occurs in the prevailing interest rate.

_____ 17. (L.O. 5) Mortgage "points" raise the effective interest rate above the rate specified in the note.

_____ 18. (L.O. 8) Off-balance-sheet financing is an attempt to borrow monies in such a way that the obligations are recorded in the retained earnings statement.

_____ 19. (L.O. 8) Two reasons often cited for off--balance-sheet financing are: (a) keeping debt off the statement of financial position enhances the quality of the statement of financial position and permits credit to be obtained more easily and (b) loan covenants often impose a limitation on the amount of debt a company may have.

_____ 20. (L.O. 8) In a project financing arrangement, a single company sets up a second company for the purpose of financing a specific project that has a maximum life of five years.

_____ 21. (L.O. 9) Non-current liabilities that mature within one year should be reported as a current liability, unless retirement is to be accomplished with other than current assets.

_____ 22. (L.O. 9) Disclosure is required of future payments for sinking fund requirements and maturity amounts of non-current liabilities during each of the next 5 years.

_____ 23. (L.O. 9) The times interest earned ratio indicates the company's ability to meet interest payments as they come due.

_____ 24. (L.O. 9) The debt to total assets ratio measures the percentage of total assets provided by creditors.

_____ 25. (L.O. 9) The numerator of the times interest earned ratio is income before income taxes and interest expense.

MULTIPLE CHOICE

Select the best answer for each of the following items and enter the corresponding letter in the space provided.

_____ 1. (L.O. 2) If a corporation issues a debenture bond, it means the bond:

      A.   is secured by stocks and bonds of other corporations.
      B.   matures in installments.
      C.   is unsecured.
      D.   may be converted into other securities of the corporation for a specified time after issuance.

_____ 2. (L.O. 2) Bonds that pay no interest unless the issuing company is profitable are called:

      A.   collateral trust bonds.
      B.   debenture bonds.
      C.   revenue bonds.
      D.   income bonds.

_____ 3. (L.O. 2) Bonds that are secured by stocks and bonds of other corporations are called:

      A.   collateral trust bonds.
      B.   registered bonds.
      C.   serial bonds.
      D.   treasury bonds.

_____ 4. (L.O. 2) The interest rate actually earned by a bondholder who buys the bond at a discount, as compared to the stated rate on the bond is:

	Higher	**Lower**
A.	Yes	No
B.	Yes	Yes
C.	No	Yes
D.	No	No

_____ 5. (L.O. 2) Bonds with par value of $500,000 carrying a stated interest rate of 6% payable semiannually on March 1 and September 1 were issued on July 1. The proceeds from the issue amounted to $510,000. The best explanation for the excess received over par value is:

    A.   the bonds were sold at a premium.
    B.   the bonds were sold at a higher effective interest rate.
    C.   the bonds were issued at par plus accrued interest
    D.   no explanation is possible without knowing the maturity date of the bond issue.

_____ 6. (L.O. 3) If bonds are issued initially at a premium and the effective interest method of amortization is used, interest expense:

    A.   decreases each year as the carrying value of the bond decreases.
    B.   increases as the carrying value of the bond increases.
    C.   is the same as the cash amount of the interest payments.
    D.   decreases each year as the carrying value of the bond increases.

_____ 7. (L.O. 4) King Cole Corporation markets a 10-year bond issue dated January 1, 2012. The bonds pay 9% interest semi-annually on January 1 and July 1. If these bonds are sold on September 1, 2012 how many months accrued interest must be paid by the purchaser and over how many months would any premium on the bonds be amortized?

	Months of Accrued Interest	**Amortization Period**
A.	8	120 months
B.	8	112 months
C.	2	120 months
D.	2	112 months

_____ 8. (L.O. 4) When a bond is issued at a premium

    A.   the market rate of interest is greater than the stated rate of interest.
    B.   the amount paid by the company at maturity is more than the issue amount.
    C.   amortization of the premium decreases bond interest expense.
    D.   All of the choices are correct.

The following information applies to both questions 9 and 10. On July 1, 2012 Sinatra Corporation issued 5%, 10-year bonds with a par value of $300,000 at 104, with an effective interest rate of 4%. Interest is paid on July 1 and January 1, with any premiums or discounts amortized using the effect interest method.

_____ 9. (L.O. 4) The entry to record the issuance of the bonds would include:

    A.   a credit of $7,500 to Accrued Interest Payable.
    B.   a credit of $312,000 to Bonds Payable.
    C.   a credit of $288,000 to Bonds Payable.
    D.   a debit of $312,000 to Bonds Payable.

_____ 10. (L.O. 4) The Bond Interest Expense reported on the December 31, 2012 income statement of Sinatra Corporation would be:

      A. $7,500

      B. $15,000

      C. $6,240

      D. $12,480

_____ 11. (L.O. 4) Which of the following statements correctly depicts the nature of discounts or premiums as applied to a bond issue?

      A.   When bonds are issued at a discount, the seller has an advantage in that interest payments are based upon an amount less than face value.

      B.   The terms "discount" and "premium" are the same as loss and gain, respectively, to both buyer and seller.

      C.   The difference between the effective rate of interest and the market rate of interest is the reason discounts and premiums arise.

      D.   The net cash outflow (ignoring bond issue costs) to the seller of bonds issued at a premium will be less than the maturity value of the bonds plus total interest payments.

_____ 12. (L.O. 4) Bond issue costs, such as printing fees, legal fees, commissions, etc. are most appropriately accounted for by:

      A.   charging them to an expense account in the year the bonds are actually sold so there is revenue to charge them against on the income statement.

      B.   debiting them to Unamortized Bond Issue Costs, setting them up as an asset on the statement of financial position, and amortizing them in a manner similar to bond discount over the life of the bond.

      C.   charging them to an expense account in the year the bonds are originally dated, whether or not they are sold in that year.

      D.   adding them to any discount on bonds or subtracting them from any premium on bonds when the bonds are sold.

_____ 13. (L.O. 4) If bonds are held to maturity any premium or discount:

      A.   should be written off directly to a bond retirement account as the bond will be redeemed.

      B.   are carried forward and written off in the same manner as that used prior to the maturity date.

      C.   will be fully amortized as their amortization period is designed to coincide with the life of the bond issue.

      D.   should be used to calculate the gain or loss resulting from the maturity of the bonds.

_____ 14. (L.O. 6) When debt is extinguished before its maturity date, any difference between the reacquisition price of outstanding debt and its net carrying amount per books should be:

      A.   amortized over the remaining original life of the extinguished issue.

      B.   amortized over the life of the any newly issued debt.

      C.   recognized currently in income as a loss or gain.

      D.   treated as a prior period adjustment.

_____ 15. (L.O. 5) When a zero-interest-bearing note is given for property, goods, or services, the present value of the note is best measured by:

    A.   the fair value of the property, goods, or services or by an amount that reasonably approximates the note.

    B.   the prime interest rate unless that rate is not applicable to the entities involved in the transaction.

    C.   the interest rate on similar notes being offered in the market place for similar property, goods, or services.

    D.   a negotiated interest rate between the issuer of the note and the owner of the property, goods, or services.

_____ 16. (L.O. 5) A debt instrument with no ready market is exchanged for property whose fair market value is currently indeterminable. When such a transaction takes place:

    A.   the present value of the debt instrument must be approximated using an imputed interest rate.

    B.   it should not be recorded on the books of either party until the fair market value of the property becomes evident.

    C.   the board of directors of the entity receiving the property should estimate a value for the property that will serve as a basis for the transaction.

    D.   the directors of both entities involved in the transaction should negotiate a value to be assigned to the property.

_____ 17. (L.O. 5) Hendrix Corporation exchanged land with a fair market value of $150,000 for Gray Company's $226,000, zero-interest-bearing, 4-year note. If the $150,000 amount represents the present value of the note at an appropriate rate of interest, Hendrix Corporation should record the difference ($76,000) as:

    A.   gain on the sale of land.

    B.   premium on the sale of land.

    C.   premium on notes receivable.

    D.   discount on notes receivable.

_____ 18. (L.O. 8) Which of the following is not a characteristic of a project financing arrangement?

    A.   Two or more entities form a new entity to construct an operating plant that will be used by both parties.

    B.   The project must be one that neither entity could enter into on its own.

    C.   The new entity borrows money to finance the project and repays the debt from the proceeds received from the project.

    D.   One of the companies that formed the new entity guarantees that it (or some outside party) will purchase all the products produced by the plant.

_____ 19. (L.O. 8) When a business enterprise enters into what is referred to as off-balance-sheet financing, the company:

    A.   is attempting to conceal the debt from shareholders by having no information about the debt included in the statement of financial position.

    B.   wishes to confine all information related to the debt to the income statement and the statement of cash flow.

    C.   can enhance the quality of its financial position and perhaps permit credit to be obtained more readily and at less cost.

    D.   is in violation of IFRS.

_____ 20. (L.O. 9) Ewell Corporation's 2012 Annual Report disclosed total liabilities of $5,400,000, total assets of $8,000,000, interest expense of $400,000, income taxes of $600,000, and net income of $1,000,000. What is Ewell's times interest earned ratio?

      A.   10
      B.   8
      C.   5
      D.   2.5

_____ 21. (L.O. 8) Types of off-balance-sheet financing include all of the following except:

      A.   non-consolidated subsidiaries.
      B.   special purpose entities.
      C.   collateral trust bonds.
      D.   operating leases.

_____ 22. (L.O. 6) Garcia Company recently has experienced declining profits, liquidity problems, and an unfavorable trend in its debt to equity relationship. The company completed its negotiations in 2012 for a creditor to accept 50,000 shares of Garcia common stock in settlement of a note payable for $300,000. Market value of the shares was $200,000. In accounting for this transaction, the appropriate treatment for Garcia is to:

      A.   reduce liabilities by $300,000, increase paid-in capital by $200,000, and increase retained earnings directly for $100,000.
      B.   reduce liabilities by $300,000 and create a separate paid-in capital section entitled "equity of former creditors-$300,000."
      C.   reduce liabilities by $300,000, increase paid-in capital by $200,000, and recognize a gain of $100,000.
      D.   reduce liabilities and increase paid-in capital by $300,000.

REVIEW EXERCISES

1.   (L.O. 3 and 4) Turner Corporation issued $800,000 of 6% bonds at 97.5 on January 1, 2012. The bonds were issued with an effective interest rate of 7%. The bonds are 9-year bonds January 1, 2012, and pay interest on July 1 and January 1, each year. The company's fiscal year coincides with the calendar year; the effective interest method is used.

Instructions:
Prepare the journal entries that Turner Corporation would make on January 1, 2012, July 1, 2012, December 31, 2012 (if any), and January 1, 2013.

General Journal			
			J1
Date	**Account Title**	**Debit**	**Credit**

2.   (L.O.4) The following information relates to a $200,000, 4-year, 6% bond issue by Garfunkel Co. The bonds, issued on 1-1-11, are due on 1-1-15 and pay interest on January 1 and July 1. The bonds are sold to yield 5%.

Instructions:

a.   Calculate the premium on bonds for Garfunkel Co. by filling in the missing amounts below.

Maturity value of bonds payable	$200,000
Present value of $200,000 due in 8 periods at 2 1/2%, semiannual interest (Table 6-2)	_____
Present value of $6,000 interest payable semiannually for 8 periods at 2 1/2% (Table 6-4)	_____
Proceeds from sale of bonds	_____
Premium on bonds	_____

b.   Prepare an amortization schedule for Garfunkel Co. using the effective interest method.

Schedule of Interest Expense and
Bond Premium Amortization
Effective Interest Method
6% Bonds Sold to Yield 5%

Date	Credit Cash	Debit Interest Expense	Debit Bond Premium	Carrying Value of Bonds
1-1-11				$207,171
7-1-11	$_____	$_____	$_____	_____
1-1-12	_____	_____	_____	_____
7-1-12	_____	_____	_____	_____
1-1-13	_____	_____	_____	_____
7-1-13	_____	_____	_____	_____
1-1-14	_____	_____	_____	_____
7-1-14	_____	_____	_____	_____
1-1-15	_____	_____	_____	_____
Totals	_____	_____	_____	_____

3.   (L.O. 3 and 4) On July 1, 2012, the Sting Company issued $200,000 of 6%, 10-year bonds with interest dates of March 1 and September 1.   The company received cash of $200,250, which included the interest accrued since the authorization date of March 1, 2012. .

Instructions:

Compute the following amounts:

    a.   The amount of accrued interest received by Sting Company from investors on July 1, 2012.

    b.   The amount of the discount or premium.

    c.   The amount of cash that will be paid to bondholders on September 1, 2012.

    d.   The amount of bond interest payable that would appear on the December 31, 2012 statement of financial position.

4.   (L.O.3 and 4) On October 1, 2012, Costello Company issued $600,000 par value 12%, 10-year bonds dated July 1, 2012, with interest payable semiannually on January 1, and July 1. The bonds are issued at $767,592 (to yield 8%) plus accrued interest. The effective interest method is used for amortization purposes.

Instructions:

a.   Prepare the journal entry on the date the bonds are issued.
b.   Prepare the year-end adjusting entry for bond interest as of December 31, 2012.
c.   Prepare the entry for the interest payment on January 1, 2013.

a.

General Journal			J1
Date	**Account Title**	**Debit**	**Credit**

b.

General Journal			J1
Date	**Account Title**	**Debit**	**Credit**

c.

	General Journal		
			J1
Date	**Account Title**	**Debit**	**Credit**

SOLUTIONS TO REVIEW QUESTIONS AND EXERCISES

TRUE-FALSE

1. (T)

2. (F) Non-current liabilities are subject to various covenants or restrictions. However, these covenants and restrictions are for the protection of the lenders and the borrowers.

3. (T)

4. (F) Revenue bonds are bonds whose interest is paid from specified revenue sources. Such bonds are usually issued by airports, school districts, counties, toll-road authorities, and other governmental bodies.

5. (T)

6. (F) Companies issuing bonds may choose to place privately a bond issue by selling bonds directly to a large institution, financial or otherwise, without the aid of an underwriter. The IASB has no rules about initial bond placements.

7. (F) When bonds are issued between interest dates, the purchaser pays for interest accrued from the last interest payment date to the date of the purchase. Thus, the maximum amount of accrued interest a purchaser can be required to pay is 6 months (assuming semiannual interest).

8. (T)

9. (F) If bonds sell for more than face value, they are said to have sold at a premium. Thus, the effective rate of interest is less than the stated rate of interest.

10. (T)

11. (T)

12. (F)   Under the effective interest method, the interest expense for each interest period is computed by multiplying the effective interest rate times the carrying amount of the bonds at the start of the period. The carrying amount of the bonds either increases (for bonds issued at a discount) or decreases (for bonds issued at a premium) each period by the amount of the amortized discount or premium.

13. (T)   .

14. (F)   Any excess of the net carrying amount over the reacquisition price is a gain from extinguishment.

15. (T)

16. (F)   An imputed interest rate is determined at the time a debt instrument is issued. Any subsequent changes in prevailing interest rates are ignored.

17. (T)

18. (F)   Off-balance-sheet financing is an attempt to borrow monies in such a way that the obligations are not recorded.

19. (T)

20. (F)   Project financing arrangements arise when a special purpose entity (SPE) is created to build a plant. The SPE finances and builds the plant, allowing a company to keep the asset and liability off its books.

21. (T)

22. (T)

23. (T)

24. (T)

25. (T)

MULTIPLE CHOICE

1. (C)   A debenture bond is an unsecured bond that is issued on the good name of the company. Alternative A describes a collateral trust bond. Alternative B refers to a serial bond, and alternative D describes a convertible bond.

2. (D)   Bonds that pay no interest unless the issuing company is profitable are called income bonds.

3. (A)   Bonds that are secured by stocks and bonds of other corporations are called collateral trust bonds.

4. (A)   When a bond is sold at a discount the effective rate of interest is higher than the stated rate on the bond. This is due to the fact that the amount paid for the bond is less than its face amount, yet the interest earned is the same as that earned if the bond had been sold at par.

5. (C) $500,000 × .06 = $30,000 annual interest
$30,000 ÷ 12 = $2,500 interest per month
March 1 to July 1 is 4 months accrued interest
4 × $2,500 = $10,000 accrued interest
$500,000 + $10,000 = $510,000 proceeds

6. (A)   Interest expense is based on the carrying value of the bonds (face value plus unamortized premium). Early in the life of the bond issue, interest expense is higher under the effective interest method because the carrying amount of the bonds includes the total premium. Each year, as premium is amortized and the carrying value of the bond decreases, interest expense also decreases.

7. (D)   The payment of accrued interest by the purchaser of the bonds is from the last interest payment date to the date of the purchase. The last interest payment date was July 1, so the accrued interest required is for July and August. The amortization of any premium or discount is over the period of time the bond issue will be outstanding. In the case of the bonds noted in the question, they will be outstanding for 9 years and 4 months (112 months).

8. (C)   When a bond is issued at a premium, the market rate of interest is less than the stated rate of interest, and a maturity the company pays less relative to the issue price. Amortization of a premium decreases bond interest expense.

9. (B)   Cash   312,000
     Bonds Payable   312,000
($300,000 × 1.04 = $312,000)

10. (C)   Annual Cash Interest: $300,000 × .05 = $15,000/year × ½ = $7,500
Interest Expense: $312,000 × 4% = $12,480 × ½ = $6,240

11. (D)   For a $100,000, 10%, 5-year bond issued at a $12,000 premium, the following cash flow applies:

Bond Proceeds		$112,000
Bond Interest (5 years at $10,000)	$ 50,000	
Maturity Value	100,000	150,000
Net Cash Outflow		$ 38,000

12. (D)   Bond issue costs should be recorded as reduction to the issue amount of the bond payable (added to the discount or subtracted from the premium).

13. (C)   At maturity date of the bonds any premium, discount, or issue costs will be fully amortized. As a result, the carrying amount will be equal to the maturity (face) value of the bond. As the maturity or face value is also equal to the bond's market value at that time, no gain or loss exists.

14.   (C)   Gains or losses from extinguishment of debt should be reported in the income statement.

15.   (A)   Present value is best measured in these circumstances by the fair value of the property, goods, or services involved in the transaction. The interest element is the difference between the face amount of the note and the fair value of the property, goods, or services.

16.   (A)   If the fair value of the property is not determinable and if the debt instrument has no ready market, the present value of the debt instrument must be estimated. The estimation involves approximating (imputing) an interest rate. The imputed interest rate is used to establish the present value of the debt instrument by discounting, at that rate, all future payments on the debt.

17.   (D)   The difference between the fair market value of the land and the face value of this zero-interest-bearing note is considered a discount on the notes. The discount should be amortized over the life of the note.

18.   (B)   A project financing arrangement has nothing to do with the ability of either entity involved to enter into the project on their own. The other three alternatives (A, C, and D) are relevant characteristics.

19.   (C)   Many companies enter into off-balance-sheet financing arrangements to enhance their statement of financial position and potentially allow future credit to be obtained more readily from potential lenders. There are many off-balance-sheet financing arrangements that companies enter into which are acceptable. However, these arrangements normally have to be disclosed in the footnotes to the financial statements so investors and creditors are not completely void of information on the kinds of arrangements an entity has entered into.

20.   (C)   The times interest earned ratio is:

$$\frac{\text{Income before income taxes and interest expense}}{\text{Interest expense}}$$

Ewell's times interest earned ratio is computed as follows:

$$\frac{\$1,000,000 \ + \ \$600,000 \ + \ \$400,000}{400,000} = 5$$

21.   (C)   Collateral trust bonds are secured by shares and bonds of other corporations. Non-consolidated entities, SPEs and operating leases are all forms of off-balance-sheet financing.

22.   (C)   When a transfer of noncash assets or the issuance of the debtor's stock are used to settle a debt obligation, the noncash assets or equity interest given should be accounted for at their fair market value. The excess of the carrying amount of the payable over the fair market value of the assets or equity interest transferred should be accounted for as a gain. When equity is issued by the debtor, it is recorded in the normal manner.

REVIEW EXERCISES

1. 1-1-12   Cash 780,000*
                    Bonds Payable...   780,000

      *($800,000 × .975) = $780,000

      07-1-12   Bond Interest Expense... 27,300**
                      Cash..   24,000***
                      Bonds Payable...   3,300

  **$780,000 × 7% × ½ = $27,300
  ***$800,000 × 6% × ½ = $24,000

      12-31-12   Bond Interest Expense... 27,416****
                        Interest Payable...   24,000
                        Bonds Payable...   416

  ****($780,000 + 3,300) × 7% × ½ = $27,416

      01-1-13   Interest Payable.. 24,000
                      Cash..   24,000

2. Maturity value of bonds payable... $200,000
    Present value of $200,000 due in 4 years at 5% semiannual
        interest (Table 6-2) ($200,000 × .82075) $164,150
    Present value of $6,000 interest payable semiannually for
        4 years at 5% (Table 6-4) ($6,000 × 7.17014)........................   43,021
    Proceeds from sale of bonds...   207,171
    Premium on bonds .... $ 7,171

Schedule of Interest Expense and
Bond Premium Amortization
Effective Interest Method
6% Bonds Sold to Yield 5%

Date	Credit Cash	Debit Interest Expense	Debit Bond Premium	Carrying Value of Bonds
1-1-11				$207,171
7-1-11	$6,000(a)	$5,179(b)	$821(c)	206,350(d)
1-1-12	6,000	5,159	841	205,509
7-1-12	6,000	5,138	862	204,647
1-1-13	6,000	5,116	884	203,763
7-1-13	6,000	5,094	906	202,857
1-1-14	6,000	5,071	929	201,928
7-1-14	6,000	5,048	952	200,976
1-1-15	6,000	5,024	976	200,000
Totals	$48,000	$40,829	$7,171	

(a) $6,000 = $200,000 × .06 × 6/12
(b) $5,179 = $207,171 × .05 × 6/12
(c) $ 821 = $6,000 – $5,179
(d) $206,350 = $207,171 – $821

3.   a. $4,000: ($6,000 × 4/6).
     b. $3,750: discount [($200,000 + $4,000) - $200,250].
     c. $6,000: amount of semiannual interest payment.
     d. $4,000: accrual of 4 months' interest, Sept. 1 - Dec. 31.

4. a.   Cash   785,592
              Bond Interest Payable   18,000   (1)
              Bonds Payable   767,592

     (1) $600,000 × .12 = $72,000 × 1/4 = $18,000

     b.

Date	Credit Payable	Debit Interest Expense	Premium Amortized	Carrying Amount of Bonds
10/1/12				$767,592
12/31/12	$18,000	$15,352	$2,648	764,944

          Bond Interest Expense   15,352
          Bonds Payable   2,648
              Bond Interest Payable   18,000

     c. Bond Interest Payable   36,000
             Cash   36,000

NOTES

NOTES

NOTES

NOTES

NOTES

NOTES